Innovative
Aging
Programs
Abroad

Innovative Aging Programs Abroad

Implications for the United States

CHARLOTTE NUSBERG
with Mary Jo Gibson and Sheila Peace

Prepared under the Auspices of the
International Federation on Ageing

Contributions to the Study of Aging, Number 2

GREENWOOD PRESS
Westport, Connecticut · London, England

Library of Congress Cataloging in Publication Data

Nusberg, Charlotte.
  Innovative aging programs abroad.

  (Contributions to the study of aging, ISSN 0732-
085X ; no. 2)
  Bibliography: p.
  Includes index.
    1. Aged—Government policy.   2. Aged—Government
policy—United States.   I. Gibson, Mary Jo Storey.
II. Peace, Sheila M.   III. International Federation on
Ageing.   IV. Title.   V. Series.   [DNLM: 1. Aging—
Congresses.   2. Cross-cultural comparison—Congresses.
3. Geriatrics—Congresses.   4. International coopera-
tion—Congresses.   W1 C0778W no. 2]
HQ1061.N93   1984   362.6   83-10811
ISBN 0-313-23684-4 (lib. bdg.)

Library of Congress Catalog Card Number: 83-10811
ISBN: 0-313-23684-4
ISSN: 0732-085X

First published in 1984

Greenwood Press
A division of Congressional Information Service, Inc.
88 Post Road West
Westport, Connecticut 06881

Printed in the United States of America

10 9 8 7 6 5 4 3 2 1

To the founding members of the International Federation on Ageing, especially the American Association of Retired Persons, who shared a common belief in the value of international information exchange

Contents

Tables

Foreword

In this book, the International Federation on Ageing has made a major contribution to the growing literature in the field of aging. Based on background papers prepared for the White House Conference on Aging held in Washington, D.C., in December 1981, the book explores in highly readable fashion what other industrialized countries are doing for their elderly citizens and what lessons their experiences suggest for the United States. Such a compilation is long overdue and hopefully will stimulate increased interest in learning about and evaluating broad-based experience elsewhere in meeting the needs of older adults in the United States. Faced with a larger proportion of older persons than the relatively "younger" United States, a number of other industrialized countries already have well-tested programs, the counterparts of which are only slowly getting under way in the United States. We can learn from both the successes and the problems encountered.

The subject areas are distinct, yet complementary in providing insights into comprehensive programming country by country. To collect and then integrate the material from the various countries by program was a major task in itself. The subjects cover health care and mental health, housing, income, employment, flexible retirement, support for families, community services, educational opportunities and formalized participation in decision making. Some programs are familiar; some are only in the early stages of consideration in the United States; others have not been dealt with at all. The references are helpful as they reflect the scope of the inquiry for each paper. With the exception of two chapters by Mary Jo Gibson and one by Sheila Peace, all are the work of Charlotte Nusberg, the editor of the quarterly *Ageing International*.

To attempt to comment on the papers individually in any detail is beyond the scope of this preface. Rather, it seems important to look at selected special questions raised for the United States under each topic, based on current developments in this country.

Our health care system is largely dominated by for-profit programs, even when payments are made from public funds. Furthermore, income tests remain the rule for low-income persons in need of health care. This is not the case in many other industrialized countries, where health services are universally available at token or no direct out-of-pocket cost to the patient being treated. Emphasis on geriatric medicine and a strong team approach between health services and social services are practices that appear to provide successful models. The same issues arise in mental health but with even greater emphasis on coordination of medical and community resources in the countries surveyed.

One of the continuing debates in the United States, related closely to health maintenance, centers on housing for the elderly. A plethora of suggestions for housing arrangements and choices tends to delay development of clear trends or widely accepted social policy. Even where there are well-tested solutions, the lack of both public and private funding for construction results in continued deplorable housing for large numbers of the elderly in the United States. On the other hand, the variety of imaginative and often both cost-effective and interaction-oriented housing developments in some other countries has provided increased accessibility and options to older people, to their proved benefit. Not all of the aged are served due to fiscal constraints, but the directions are clear.

Since one cannot get very far in assessing how to meet the health, housing and other needs of older adults without considering income, the extent of poverty among older adults must be dealt with.

With the recent debate on Social Security in the United States, it is timely to study with care the longer-established systems in Western Europe for providing financial security in old age. Payments are sometimes more generous relative to former earnings; the taxes to support the systems are higher; and a number of the persistent inequities in the United States system have been reduced or eliminated. Of special significance are the relationships between public and private pension systems in some countries; these deserve special study. While change will not be easy at best, tested experience in similar economies should not be ignored in a period of intensive study of necessary adjustments to the United States system.

Closely related to the concern with basic income is the chapter on employment. Other countries are also grappling with methods of retaining older workers in the work force after they become eligible for pensions and looking for ways of doing this in the most productive manner. Whether on an experimental basis with individual employers or on a larger scale, the experiences of other industrialized nations offer specific illustrations of how to deal with what is becoming an increasing demand from older workers themselves. Certainly with increased longevity and the continued good health of older workers, early retirement followed by one, two or even three decades of unproductive leisure will raise more and more questions.

Continued employment often requires continued education at older ages. All industrialized nations have programs for job training and retraining. The issues center on the availability of such education in all areas of the United States and to all age groups, the extent to which older persons take advantage of the opportunities, and the meshing of training and available jobs.

In the still new area of pre-retirement planning, the United States has the longest tradition among industrialized countries. Even so, the current programs meet only a small percentage of the potential demand. Actually the United States has the opportunity for greatly expanded efforts in this important area and for evaluating the relative success of differing approaches to planning for retirement under both public and private initiatives.

In any survey of the elderly, there is no more important topic than family relationships, relationships that are importantly affected by all of the areas suggested above and also by increasing longevity and hence changing intergenerational patterns. Despite social and economic change, in every country the family provides the major support and care to its older members. Issues that are becoming more and more pressing in the United States include community services for the elderly themselves, support programs for family caregivers and the extent to which the costs and responsibilities of caring for the aged should be shared among families, community-based agencies, and government. Generally the United States has lagged behind other Western nations in the provision of community services, but after all, the other nations faced an aging population earlier than the United States. When helping to maintain the elderly in their own homes, where most want at all costs to remain, the needs for social care are basically the same in industrialized countries. Home help assistance (called homemaker home health aide service in the United States) is the core service, combining both home management and personal care. In Sweden and Denmark over 20 percent of the elderly use part-time home help services, yet the programs fail to meet total demand. While in-home services are increasing in the United States, problems of funding and the continued bias toward institutional care, unavailability of services in many communities, and lack of emphasis on quality of care result in major lags behind some European countries. Current data suggest that available aides in the United States, trained and untrained, amount to no more than 55 per 100,000 population despite recent substantial increases. A guideline developed in the United Kingdom suggests a ratio of 12 aides per 1,000 persons 65 and older, probably a reasonable, though obviously far from met, guideline for the United States as well. Lack of a carefully developed, generally accepted, national long-term care policy adds to the difficulties in providing services in the United States.

Other U.S. needs include accessibility to existing services, a continuum of health and social services so that varied and changing types of needs can be met, multiple points of entry into the system, and more focus on public and private non-profit services. Non-profit organizations are the only auspices generally considered appropriate for social care in other industrialized countries.

How fast and how well all of the issues discussed in this volume are addressed in the United States may depend largely on the degree of organized participation by older persons themselves in decision making that affects their lives. Again developments in the United States have been spotty, but through legislation or substantial demands, more and more groups representing the elderly are being heard from. The political power of older voters is already evident. Whatever the organized groups are called in the various countries, or however they function, there is no doubt that their number will increase, and organized efforts will become ever more visible and effective in policies that affect older citizens.

Obviously a short preface can only touch upon a few points in relation to such an information-filled volume. Moreover, it inevitably reflects some of the special interests of the author. Hopefully, however, stress has successfully been placed on the importance for U.S. policy-makers and program planners at all governmental levels to familiarize themselves with the growing body of policy positions and tested experience in other industrialized countries. Dissemination of "best practice" in meeting the needs of older adults should not be limited to a single state or to the United States, as is often the case today. Only a sharing of successful experience in many countries will lead to wide development of those programs essential to contented, comfortable lives for elderly persons wherever they live.

The overwhelming impression from this review of programs in industrialized countries is that there must be a well-developed national policy with respect to the changing circumstances identified with the older years. Without a well-defined, generally accepted framework, programs will continue to be fragmented and services uncoordinated and under-financed. So far the decennial White House Conferences on Aging have moved the United States only partially toward the objective of a clear, comprehensive, non-partisan national policy on the elderly. This volume offers valuable suggestions on achieving such a desirable goal.

Ellen Winston
Chairman, U.S. Committee/The International Conference on Social Welfare and the U.S. Committee on World Aging

Preface

The genesis of this book lies in a series of papers prepared for the 1981 White House Conference on Aging by the International Federation on Ageing (IFA). A number of discussion papers were prepared on subjects still surrounded by controversy in the United States. These included, amongst others, the role of Social Security in providing retirement income, health care, community services or ''social care,'' support for carers of older persons, and the like. These papers have now been expanded and updated to form this volume.

Those of us working at IFA welcomed the opportunity given by the White House Conference planners to provide background materials on foreign developments in aging relevant to the United States. We believe that information about what other industrialized countries are doing for their elderly population could enhance the dialogue about creative policy alternatives open to Americans in dealing with their own elders. A number of other countries already have a considerably larger proportion of older persons than does the United States— our future may, in many ways, be reflected in their present. Some of the policy alternatives that have been discussed or only tested in the United States on a demonstration basis have already been systematically applied for some time elsewhere. The experiences of others thus potentially hold important lessons for the United States.

There are difficulties involved in trying to apply the experience of other countries to the United States. Such attempts are inevitably fraught with risk. Nevertheless, an underlying assumption behind the establishment of the IFA was the belief that such attempts are both worthwhile and necessary. Despite the many differences among industrialized countries, the problems facing the elderly and the solutions that have been tried share striking similarities—enough, we believe, to serve as a rough yardstick on which to base some generalizations of relevance to the United States. Examples of cross-national learning in the field of aging already abound—from the institution of social security, a concept first developed in Germany, to the adoption of the United States "Foster Grandparents" program by other countries.

How did we obtain our information? There are relatively few cross-national studies available. Comparative gerontology is still at a stage where it must largely rely upon information drawn from country-specific sources. Our information was derived through the regular contributions of IFA member organizations around the world (eighty-three organizations in forty-three countries), a network of international correspondents, systematic scanning of other countries' publications and periodicals in gerontology and social welfare matters, participation in key international and regional conferences on aging, and selected site visits. Some of the source material appeared over the years in IFA's own publications, especially its quarterly, *Ageing International*. This book is an attempt to synthesize the knowledge we have gained for the benefit of Americans.

Charlotte Nusberg

Innovative Aging Programs Abroad

1

Provision of Retirement Income

Charlotte Nusberg

PUBLICLY SUPPORTED PENSIONS

Structure of Foreign Pension Systems

Many other industrialized nations resemble the United States in having old age pension systems which are related to past earnings or work history and which pay benefits when the individual reaches retirement or a certain chronological age, after having met a requisite number of years of contributions. (The terms *pension* and *old age pension* are used synonymously in this book to refer to publicly supported benefits paid upon retirement or upon reaching a certain chronological age. The term *private pension* is used when discussing employer/employee negotiated systems.) Almost all are "pay-as-you-go" systems. However, there are important variations with differing implications for eligibility and financing.

The Scandinavian countries, Canada, and the United Kingdom, in addition, provide a universal pension, or demogrant, that is payable to all residents simply upon reaching a certain chronological age.[1] No prior work history is required, nor is a means test imposed. Demogrants are funded through general revenues and provide the same benefit amounts to everyone. The earnings-related pension in these countries provides, in effect, a second tier of protection. This tier resembles the U.S. Social Security benefit except that it is usually partially funded through general revenues.

Most other industrialized nations also consider private pensions as an additional tier of income support in retirement. In several countries, private pension coverage is broader and more secure than it is in the United States. Countries such as France and Sweden, in fact, have integrated their private pension systems closely with the publicly supported ones. (The subject of private pensions will be discussed in greater detail in the second half of this chapter.)

Despite these several tiers, no country has been able to dispense with welfare payments—the equivalent of the U.S. Supplemental Security Income (SSI)—to older people who, for some reason, do not qualify for a pension or receive such a low level of benefits that their income remains below an acceptable level. Welfare payments typically are means tested, and despite the desire in other countries to minimize the use of means tests in public benefits, so far no adequate alternatives have been devised.

Regardless of whether a country relies primarily on demogrants, or an earnings-related retirement benefit, or some combination of both, income adequacy can be assured under any of these systems. In practice the provision of demogrants tends to give some advantage to women, since a work history is not required in order to receive a benefit. Under a strict earnings-related system, as in the United States, there is always a group of people not eligible for a Social Security benefit because of a variety of life circumstances, and who may not have heard of or be willing to apply for the means-tested SSI.

Coverage

Demogrants by definition are provided to all residents who have reached a certain chronological age—usually 65. Earnings-related benefits, however, are not always based on a strict definition of earnings. The Federal Republic of Germany, for example, provides individuals with pension credits for periods of study or training, military duty, extended illness or maternity leave.[2] The United Kingdom similarly credits individuals with hypothetical contributions for periods of sickness or unemployment.[3] France provides mothers with two years pension credits for each child they have raised a certain number of years, regardless of the mother's status in the labor force.[4] Switzerland credits all housewives, divorced women and widows with contributions for years spent at home, whether or not they had children.[5] And the United Kingdom provides pension credits to men and women who have stopped working in order to take care of a child or a dependent relative for a period of up to twenty years.[6]

In addition, some countries allow individuals to purchase pension coverage voluntarily, either to supplement their earnings-related benefits or to establish coverage if they are not part of the regular labor force.[7] In Austria, France and Italy, workers who cease or interrupt their employment can continue their coverage by paying both the employer's and employee's shares. The same countries, as well as Japan, also allow workers to purchase additional pension credits so that their retirement income will be higher. And the Federal Republic of Germany, the United Kingdom and Japan allow individuals who have never joined the labor force to establish pension coverage through voluntary contributions. Japan, in fact, has a second national retirement plan entirely based on voluntary contributions.[8]

In Japan, the proportion of voluntary contributions from housewives, who are the most likely to take advantage of the opportunity, rose from 13.5 percent in 1962 to 22.6 percent in 1976, showing rising awareness of the adverse financial consequences of possible divorce.[9] In Germany, voluntary contributions have not proven as popular because of the financial burden placed on housewives, who must contribute both the employer's and employee's share.[10] The result is that only minimum amounts are contributed. The system works best in cases where only short periods of contributions are required to obtain pension entitlement.

Special Protection for Women

In the case of women, the trend in other industrialized countries seems to be in the direction of providing them with pension coverage in their own right, rather than through the traditional dependent relationship as a wife, through a combination of credits for work and raising a family, and through voluntary contributions.[11] The European Economic Community, in fact, has requested member countries to equalize benefits between the sexes by 1984.[12]

Among the interesting measures that have been taken to better protect women's retirement income are:

1) The splitting of pension credits accumulated during a marriage at the time of divorce (in the Federal Republic of Germany and Canada).[13] This also applies to private pensions in Germany; in New Zealand, it is limited to private pensions.

2) Using a deceased or ex-husband's earnings record (up to the termination of the marriage) in calculating one's retirement benefits if it results in a higher payment (in the United Kingdom and Switzerland).[14] In the United Kingdom, a man can also use a deceased wife's earnings record for this purpose.

3) Permitting the earnings record of a wife who does not qualify for a pension in her own right to be combined with the earnings record of her husband (in Switzerland).[15]

4) Permitting divorced women to drop the years of their marriage in calculating average annual earnings if this results in a higher benefit.[16] On the other hand, they can also count the years of their marriage if this allows them to qualify for a full rather than a partial pension (in Switzerland). Switzerland, in fact, has made a deliberate policy choice of favoring displaced homemakers over single working women or married women. Displaced homemakers receive a higher old age benefit than the other two groups of women when they have comparable work histories.

5) Permitting widows who have no dependents and who are between ages 40 and 50 to receive a portion of the survivors' benefits (in the United Kingdom and the Federal Republic of Germany).[17]

Adequacy of Retirement Income

Economists in industrialized countries are in general agreement that a 60–80 percent replacement rate of former earnings should provide most individuals with the ability to maintain their pre-retirement living standards.[18] What there is less agreement about is the extent to which publicly supported benefits, private pensions and, to a lesser extent, savings should be counted on to make up this vital proportion. There is no doubt, however, that publicly supported pensions constitute the chief source of retirement income practically everywhere in the industrialized world.[19] And savings everywhere constitute a very small source of retirement income. Thus, for most persons, retirement income must be primarily based on a combination of publicly supported and private pension benefits.

While the replacement rate for Social Security retirement benefits for Americans has been steadily increasing over the last decade and is beginning to compare favorably—at least for the retired couple—with those in some European countries (see Table 1.1), there are large numbers of retirees who continue to live in poverty or near poverty. This is especially true of the single older person, a disproportionate number of whom are widows receiving a replacement income of 44 percent or even less through Social Security—in contrast to replacement rates of 66 percent, 68 percent and 69 percent for single persons in France, Sweden and Italy respectively. Typically, such persons have no private pension or savings with which to supplement their social security income, nor the range of health and social services available in many European countries, which serve to decrease out-of-pocket expenses. In 1978, 12 percent of American couples and 20 percent of single persons aged 65 or older were dependent on Social Security as their only source of income, and in 1980, Social Security pensions accounted for 80 percent of the total income for recipients whose in-

TABLE 1.1.
Replacement Rates For Social Security Old Age
Pensions for Workers with Average Wages in Manufacturing and
for Couples, Selected Countries, 1980

COUNTRY	PENSION AS PERCENTAGE OF EARNINGS IN YEAR BEFORE RETIREMENT	
	Single Worker	Aged Couple
Austria	68	68
Canada	34	49
Denmark	29	52
France	66	75
Federal Republic of Germany	49	49
Italy	69	69
Japan	54	61
Netherlands	44	63
Sweden	68	83
Switzerland	37	55
United Kingdom	31	47
United States	44	66

Source: Jonathan Aldrich, "Earnings Replacement Rate of Old-Age
          Benefits in 12 Countries, 1969-80," Social Security Bulletin
          (November 1982):5.

come fell below $5,000.[20] According to economist James Schulz, ". . . very few are projected to achieve replacement rates of 65 percent or more. Over all, the projections paint a rather dismal picture of pension income adequacy for those totally dependent on Social Security."[21]

As of 1980, couples in the United States (on the basis of men's average earnings in manufacturing) obtained about a 66 percent replacement rate through Social Security. While this is not as high as in some European countries (Italy, 69 percent; France, 75 percent; Sweden, 83 percent), it is quite respectable, especially if it can be supplemented with a private pension or savings. However, only 28 percent of retirees in 1978 received a private pension, and less than half of the labor force remains covered by a private pension plan.[22] More important, when one spouse dies, the survivor falls back to receiving the lower single person's replacement rate.

The net result is that almost 16 percent of Americans lived in poverty in 1980— a number that has been increasing in recent years despite improvements in the replacement rate. Nor has poverty among the elderly been eliminated in all the countries listed in Table 1.1 which offer relatively high replacement rates.[23] Some systems simply have not matured yet, and individuals may not meet the length in service requirements to receive full benefits upon retirement. Poverty everywhere tends to be concentrated among older women, many of whom have had either no or incomplete work histories or are mainly dependent on survivors' benefits.

Inflation

One of the major reasons pensions have been slow to provide adequate income replacement levels for retirees is widespread inflation in many of the industrialized countries, a phenomenon that has appeared simultaneously with increasing unemployment. The economic drain posed by unemployment, as well as other adverse economic conditions, has limited the resources available to adjust pensioners' income for inflation.

Nevertheless, practically all industrialized countries have some built-in mechanisms to adjust publicly supported pensions for inflation. These can range from eliminating low-income years from the calculation of a worker's retirement benefits to indexing benefits to a wage or price index. Many countries do both or use yet other mechanisms to compensate the retiree for inflationary effects. However, relatively few countries provide for practically automatic adjustment of pension benefits each time some movement occurs in the index used (usually price or wage or some combination thereof). Sweden is the only country that has a fully automatic process whereby "the amount of benefit increase reflects the exact movement in the index without review."[24]

Other countries have introduced a review process triggered by a movement in the wage and/or price index.[25] Unlike the U.S. mechanism for adjusting to inflation, such reviews can take place several times a year and may each time result in a benefit increase, although the amount and timing of such increases are subject to debate. Even where benefit increases equal the index change, if they are not available until a year after the index change, the pensioner has not been able to keep up with the rate of inflation. And in recent years, because of the economic recession, the amount of the cost-of-living increase has often been less than that called for by the index or benefit formula.[26] Belgium, for example, has temporarily introduced a flat-rate cost-of-living increase which works in favor of low-income retirees.[27]

Countries also differ in whether they use a wage or price index by which to calculate changes in pension benefits. If the index used is moving at a slower rate than another index, the pensioner may lose out. In the early 1970s, wage indexes increased more rapidly than price indexes. In the second half of the decade, this situation was reversed.[28] Some countries have reduced their budget deficits by changing the nature of the index used.[29]

Financing

How are some of these more generous provisions financed? In most industrialized countries, employers, employees and government together finance old age pensions, although the mix varies from country to country. Practically no nation, with the exception of the Netherlands, relies solely on employer/employee contributions, as does the United States, and even the Netherlands exempts low-income workers from paying payroll taxes—these are paid for by the government.[30] On the average, about two-thirds to three-fourths of earnings-related pensions are paid for through employer/employee contributions, according to the findings of a ten-nation study of countries belonging to the Organisation for Economic Co-Operation and Development (OECD).[31] Exceptions are Canada and Sweden, where less than half of the pension is financed in this manner. Both of these countries also provide demogrants as a first tier of protection, which is entirely financed through general revenues. General revenues can also be used to make annual subsidies to the pension system, make up deficits, or fund specific programs.

Thus, other industrialized countries experience far fewer inhibitions about utilizing general revenues and other forms of taxation, such as the "value-added" tax (VAT), to supplement employer/employee contributions. The fear, expressed by some in the United States, that funding from general revenues makes Social Security more vulnerable to shifts political in support, has not materialized in other industrialized countries, where the "social contract" remains strong.

Table 1.2 indicates the extent of government support, which varies from approximately 4 percent in the Netherlands to 61 percent in Canada.

The VAT, a tax of 13–21 percent on a wide range of consumer items (usually in the luxury range), is an especially important source of funding for enriching general revenue coffers. (See Table 1.3.) It is also a popular tax with governments because it is more hidden than direct forms of taxation and thus less vulnerable to political opposition.[32] It is a tax that also comes under heavy criticism because its hidden nature may lead to distortions in the economy.

TABLE 1.2
Government Contributions to Pension Programs by Percentage of Total Receipts 1974

COUNTRY	CENTRAL GOVERNMENT CONTRIBUTION	COMBINED CENTRAL AND LOCAL GOVERNMENT CONTRIBUTION
Canada	60.7	60.7
Sweden	30.7	35.4
Austria	30.4	30.4
Italy	21.7	21.7
Germany (Federal Republic)	19.2	19.2
Belgium	18.9	18.9
Switzerland	17.3	24.2
Japan	14.5	14.6
France	13.5	13.5
Netherlands	3.5	3.6

Source: *Social Security in a Changing World* (Washington, D.C.: U.S. Department of Health, Education and Welfare, Social Security Administration, September 1979).

In addition, some countries have special taxes that are earmarked for funding the social insurance system, for example, alcohol and tobacco taxes. These, however, have proven unreliable over time to provide the increases in revenues needed to pay for inflationary adjustments in pensions.[33] In Canada, where for twenty years, until the mid–1960's, a percentage of the income tax was ear-

TABLE 1.3
Value-Added Tax (Standard Rates) in Selected Countries, as of June 1979

COUNTRY	PERCENTAGE
Austria	18.0
Belgium	16.0
Denmark	20.2
France	17.6
Germany (Federal Republic)	13.0
Ireland	20.0
Italy	14.0
Luxembourg	10.0
Netherlands	18.0
Norway	20.0
Sweden	17.1
United Kingdom	15.0

Source: U.S., Department of the Treasury, Office of Tax Analysis. Reproduced in *Social Security in a Changing World*.

TABLE 1.4
Payroll Tax Rates for Social Security Programs, 1981
(As percentage of payroll)

COUNTRY	ALL PROGRAMS			(OASDI)		
	Employers	Employees	Total	Employers	Employees	Total
Austria	27.80	15.90	43.70	11.35	9.75	21.10
Belgium	27.77	10.10	37.87	8.86	6.25	15.11(a)
Canada	4.49(b)	3.95	8.44	1.80	1.80	3.60
France	37.41	10.14	47.55	8.20	4.80	13.00(c)
Germany (Federal Republic)	17.95	16.45	34.40	9.25	9.25	18.50
Italy	47.57	7.45	55.02	17.31	7.15	24.46
Japan	12.22	9.85	22.07	5.30	5.30	10.60
Netherlands	29.58	28.05	57.65	12.90	22.00	34.90(d)
Sweden	35.05	.15	35.20	21.15	--	21.15
Switzerland	8.24	9.48	17.72	4.70	4.70	9.40
United Kingdom	13.70	7.75	21.45	(e)	(e)	(e)
United States	11.35	6.65	18.00	5.35	5.35	10.70

(a.) Disability benefits financed through sickness insurance.
(b.) Excludes work injury insurance.
(c.) Disability and survivors' benefits financed through sickness insurance.
(d.) Disability insurance also includes worker's compensation.
(e.) Not available.

Source: Comparative Studies Staff, Office of International Policy, Office of Policy, Social Security Administration. Reproduced in U.S., Senate, Special Committee on Aging, Social Security in Europe: The Impact of an Aging Population, December 1981.

marked for old age pensions, deficits in the fund still had to be made up through general revenues. And when surpluses occurred, pressure built up to increase benefits. Canada has since abandoned earmarked taxes for general revenue financing.[34]

While government financing of pension funds adds to their solvency and the level of pensions permitted, so do the higher rates of employer/employee contributions paid in most industrialized countries.(See Table 1.4.)

One item to note in Table 1.4 is the higher contributions paid by employers in some countries. (During recessions, some employers have been given payroll tax exemptions in order to encourage employment, for example France. Finland also taxes capital-intensive firms at a higher rate than labor-intensive firms, presumably in order to discourage shifts from labor- to capital-intensive operations.[35]) Also, bear in mind that many other countries supplement the employer/employee contribution through public financing from general revenues and other taxes. The United States, in fact, has among the lowest rates of taxation for Social Security of any developed country.(See Table 1.5.)

The rate of taxation in other industrialized countries may seem a little less

Table 1.5
Expenditures on Benefits for Old Age, Survivors', and Disability Insurance as a Percentage of Gross National Product, Selected Countries, 1957-77(a)

COUNTRY	1957	1960	1963	1966	1971	1974	1977
Austria	4.0	5.0	5.3	6.0	7.0	7.0	8.0
Belgium(b)	3.0	3.1	4.0	4.0	4.2	5.1	6.0
France(b)	3.0	2.2	3.0	3.2	(c)	5.1	6.2
Germany (Federal Republic)	6.0	6.0	6.0	6.2	6.4	7.4	9.0
Netherlands	3.0	4.0	5.0	6.3	7.4	8.3	10.2
Sweden	3.4	3.3	4.0	5.0	6.0	7.1	9.2
Switzerland	2.0	2.2	2.3	3.0	4.0	5.3	7.1
United Kingdom(d)	4.0	3.2	4.0	4.0	4.0	5.0	6.0
United States(d)	1.5	2.2	2.6	3.4	3.4	4.0	4.3

(a.) Based on data provided by the International Labour Office, adjusted to include cash OASDI benefits. Gross national product figures of the International Monetary Fund were used.
(b.) Disability insurance is administered together with sickness insurance and is not included.
(c.) Not available.
(d.) Adjusted to fiscal year.

Source: Comparative Studies Staff, Office of International Policy, Office of Policy, Social Security Administration. Reproduced in U.S., Senate, Special Committee on Aging, Social Security in Europe: The Impact of an Aging Population, December 1981.

Table 1.6
Federal, State and Local Tax Revenues for Selected Countries as a Percentage of Gross Domestic Product, by Type of Tax, 1975. (Figures in parentheses indicate country rankings.)

COUNTRY	TOTAL	INDIRECT TAXES, SALES, AND EXCISE(a)	DIRECT TAXES TOTAL(b)	SOCIAL SECURITY(c) TOTAL	SOCIAL SECURITY(c) EMPLOYER	SOCIAL SECURITY(c) EMPLOYEE AND SELF-EMPLOYED	CORPORATE INCOME	NONCORPORATE INCOME(d)	PROPERTY(e)	OTHER(f)
Belgium	41.43(5)	10.87(6)	30.56(4)	13.14(5)	8.44(4)	4.70(5)	3.07(6)	13.24(4)	1.01(12)	0.10(8)
Canada	33.98(9)	19.94(4)	23.04(11)	3.22(12)	(g)	(g)	4.67(2)	11.32(7)	3.13(3)	.70(4)
Denmark	43.05(4)	11.71(1)	28.34(5)	.48(13)	.31(12)	.17(12)	1.37(13)	23.86(1)	2.57(4)	.06(10)
France	36.90(6)	12.44(2)	24.16(9)	14.72(3)	10.61(2)	4.11(6)	2.00(9)	4.58(13)	1.46(9)	1.70(2)
Germany (Federal Republic)	35.22(8)	9.37(8)	25.85(7)	12.03(6)	6.60(7)	5.43(4)	1.56(12)	10.60(8)	1.09(11)	.57(6)
Italy	32.34(10)	9.34(10)	23.00(12)	14.83(2)	11.92(1)	2.91(9)	2.04(8)	4.95(12)	1.17(10)	--
Japan	20.23(13)	3.67(13)	16.56(13)	5.09(11)	2.63(11)	2.46(10)	3.43(4)	5.07(11)	1.94(7)	1.03(3)
Luxembourg	46.74(2)	9.72(7)	37.02(1)	14.05(4)	7.80(6)	6.25(2)	3.61(3)	12.78(5)	2.34(5)	.63(5)
Netherlands	46.90(1)	10.91(5)	35.99(2)	17.99(1)	8.40(5)	9.59(1)	3.61(1)	12.66(6)	1.48(8)	.25(7)
Sweden	45.96(3)	11.48(3)	34.48(3)	8.89(7)	8.47(3)	.42(11)	1.99(10)	21.17(2)	.51(13)	1.92(1)
Switzerland	29.49(12)	5.90(11)	23.59(10)	8.49(8)	3.05(10)	5.44(3)	2.46(7)	10.51(9)	2.13(6)	--
United Kingdom	36.77(7)	9.24(10)	27.53(6)	6.71(10)	3.75(9)	2.96(8)	1.92(11)	14.29(3)	4.54(1)	.07(9)
United States	30.31(11)	5.49(12)	24.82(8)	7.42(9)	4.18(8)	3.24(7)	3.29(5)	9.98(10)	4.13(2)	--

(a.) Includes general sales, value added, and specific excise taxes.

(b.) Computed by subtracting sales and excise taxes from total.

(c.) Includes employer, employee, and self-employed contributions. Broadly defined to include all tax payments to institutions of general government providing social welfare benefits, provided they are levied as a function of pay or as a fixed amount per person. For the United States, includes contributions to the railroad retirement fund, unemployment insurance fund, workmen's compensation fund, and civil service retirement program in addition to the more familiar payments for social security made pursuant to the Federal Insurance Contributions Act.

(d.) Includes income taxes on individual and unincorporated enterprises, such as proprietorships and partnerships.

(e.) Includes taxes on net wealth, immovable property, estates, and gifts.

(f.) Includes taxes on employers based on payroll or manpower and miscellaneous taxes that cannot be classified within a specific direct tax category.

(g.) Data not available.

Source: Derived by U.S. Department of the Treasury, Office of Tax Analysis, from revenue statistics of OECD member countries, 1965-75. Reproduced in Social Security in a Changing World.

onerous if one remembers that low-income workers in Canada, the Federal Republic of Germany, the Netherlands and Japan may be partially or totally exempted from payroll contributions. Compensation for them is made by governmental funding through the more progressively structured general taxation system or through additional contributions from the remainder of the labor force.

Another important offset to the high costs of funding old age pensions is the fact that publicly supported pensions are taxable in practically all other industrialized countries when total income exceeds specified levels. If the principle of progressive taxation is preserved, such a policy need not unduly affect the low-income persons who can afford such taxation least.

Countries with relatively new systems, such as Canada, Japan and Sweden, have built up reserve funds which they hope will carry them "over the hump" when the proportion of the older population reaches its peak.[36] Yields from invested reserves are used for a variety of public purposes, and in Sweden the reserve fund is the chief source of investment capital.[37]

It should be noted, too, that generous levels of retirement income and high taxes in other industrialized countries have not led to a low rate of savings by individuals for investment purposes[38]—a link that is assumed to exist by some American economists.[39] (Nor, in fact, have steady increases in payroll taxes over time in the United States significantly affected individual savings rates.[40])

Taxation for pensions alone, of course, does not give the total picture of the incidence of tax burdens in different countries. But here, too, if one looks at the level of taxation by all levels of government, the United States still ranks at the lower end of the scale. (See Table 1.6.)

There is little question, however, but that all the industrialized countries are worried about the future financing of their pension systems. Payroll taxes seem to be brushing up against the maximum acceptable rate. On the whole, countries are avoiding adding new benefits with costly tax implications and postponing some benefits already in place.

At the same time, public support for the high rate of benefits currently provided seems firm. Some countries are, in fact, purposely reinforcing strong feelings of solidarity between generations, something that has not been evident in the United States.[41] What's more, policy-makers seem confident that if programs for the elderly require higher taxes in the future, public support will be forthcoming.[42]

Some Implications for the United States

An examination of the old age pension systems of other countries provides one with a smorgasbord of tantalizing options with which the equity and financial soundness of our own system could be improved—given the political will and appropriate statesmanship. While other systems may be brushing up against the limit in terms of their own taxation policies, the United States has a long way to go before it reaches the same level of taxation. The United States has one of the lowest Social Security contribution rates of all of the industrialized countries, both for employers and employees, and for many years the U.S. projected dependency ratio will not be as great as it already is in many of the European countries. Worries about the regressivity of the Social Security tax can easily be met through measures such as exempting low-paid workers from contributions or other means.

In addition, the United States remains anomalous in its reluctance to fund any aspect of its Social Security system from general revenues, a funding tool that is widely used elsewhere. The use of special taxes, such as the VAT, from which to draw revenues for Social Security or the taxation of Social Security benefits if total income exceeds certain levels, has also not been widely explored here.

While American taxpayers may be reluctant to raise taxes generally, as far as Social Security is concerned, polls have shown that the general public would prefer higher taxes to lowered benefits.[43] Ironically, while continuing political debate and sensationalist reporting in the media has led more than half of those polled to believe that Social Security will not be around when they are old enough to retire, two-thirds opposed dropping the Social Security system and an even larger majority opposed abandoning the system for any other alternative.

A second important lesson that can be learned from the experience of other developed countries is the desirability of maintaining strong feelings of solidarity between generations and of keeping discussion regarding pension systems separate from the political fray surrounding debates about other taxation policies. While there is no question that pension policies have a major effect on a country's economy, recent efforts in the United States to treat Social Security taxes as simply another tool of fiscal policy risk undermining the wide social support and intergenerational solidarity that have built up around the funds—if anything, these should be promoted during the coming years.

Changes in old age pension systems are difficult to achieve everywhere, and the pace of adding new benefits abroad has certainly slowed down in recent years. Nevertheless, innovative changes to increase equity in pension coverage, such as splitting pension credits earned during a marriage upon divorce, permitting voluntary contributions by non-participants in the labor force and providing pension credits for the care of young or old dependents, have still taken place. Many of these measures have been proposed in the United States as well. Evaluating the effectiveness and impact of these reforms could provide important lessons for the United States.

Finally, at a time of increasing economic austerity, some other industrialized countries have moved towards a closer integration of the publicly and privately supported pension systems—a direction in which the United States also may be headed. These developments are discussed below.

PRIVATE PENSIONS

A number of European countries, such as Sweden and France, are ahead of the United States in providing greater income security in retirement through private pensions because of more universal coverage, more liberal vesting and portability requirements, greater integration with the publicly supported system, and more flexible financing mechanisms. In Sweden, some 90 percent of blue and white collar workers in the private sector are covered; in the Netherlands, 80 percent; and in Switzerland, 66 percent, compared to approximately 50 percent in the United States.[44]

Sweden and France have a long history of labor and management agreements governing fringe benefits, which often cover a larger proportion of the compensation package than do collective bargaining agreements in the United States. The institution of practically universal private pension coverage through nationally negotiated agreements was a natural evolutionary step.[45] In other countries this history of labor/management cooperation does not exist, and in the case of Switzerland, a constitutional amendment had to be enacted in order to mandate universal private pension coverage.[46] The Netherlands, similarly, has reached general agreement on a mandatory private pension system. Difficult economic circumstances, however, have postponed the implementation of mandatory private pension systems in both Switzerland and the Netherlands.[47]

Moves to mandate or "quasi-mandate" private pension coverage are thought necessary for several reasons.[48] First, inflation and rising expectations regarding the adequacy of retirement income have resulted in a recognition that publicly supported pensions can not carry the load alone. (Interestingly, Italy, which is the only capitalist industrialized country to have relied overwhelmingly on publicly supported benefits, has begun exploring the institution of widespread private pension coverage.) Second, there has been a desire to increase equity in retirement income between retirees receiving private pensions and the many who do not. Third, it has been recognized that mandatory private pensions with liberal vesting and portability requirements might facilitate the mobility of labor from unproductive to more productive areas of the economy. Fourth, unlike most social security funds, private pensions provide a source of funds for capital investment.

Many European countries have set specific goals regarding the percentage of final pre-retirement earnings that retirement income from publicly and privately supported pensions should replace. This varies from 50 percent in the United Kingdom to 60 percent in Switzerland to 70 percent in the Netherlands.[49] The intent is for retirees to be able to preserve their former lifestyles, at least from a financial point of view. Public and private pensions together are seen to provide this replacement income—a minimum role is relegated to savings, which, as in the United States, have never proven themselves to be a significant source of retirement income.

Sometimes the public and private systems are so integrated that the two benefits become inversely correlated to each other in order to maintain a constant replacement rate; as payments under one system go up, the others come down.[50] Typically, lower-wage earners receive most, if not all, of their retirement income through public benefits; higher-salaried employees receive a larger proportion through private benefits. But the replacement rate received by both groups remains the same. The weighting benefit formula of the U.S. Social Security system in favor of low-income persons is not a common feature of other industrialized countries.[51]

In Switzerland, the United Kingdom and Sweden, vesting typically occurs during one's mid to late 20s, either immediately or after several years of employment.[52] Full vesting is usually immediate, and pensions are fully portable. A few countries, such as France and Sweden, do limit the portability of pensions beyond the confines of industry-wide agreements.

Despite these many generous features, not all persons will receive adequate private pension benefits. The pension plan in the United Kingdom, for example, is quite new, and it will be many years before it fully matures and workers have accumulated the requisite number of years of credit to gain full benefits. The same problem will be faced by Dutch and Swiss workers if the proposed mandated private pension systems take effect. In the interim, retirees will continue to obtain less than the ideal replacement rate.

In addition, many workers, especially women, casual workers and the self-employed, will be unable to meet the twenty- to forty-years length-of-service requirements necessary to obtain full benefits. The categories of workers not fully protected by private pension coverage vary from country to country, but for such groups, some sort of supplementary income, much like SSI in the U.S., will continue to be required over and above the basic old age pension to which they may be entitled.

Finally, if private pensions are not indexed for inflation, over time the value of their benefits diminishes.

Financing

Most private pension plans in other industrialized countries have been established on a funded basis through employer and employee contributions. Important exceptions are Sweden, which does not require employee contributions, and France, where private pension plans are financed on a "pay-as-you-go" basis. Typically, that part of the wage or salary which is already covered by the publicly supported old age pension is excluded from private pension coverage.

To assure adequate financing of private pensions which are indexed for inflation, several different policies have been adopted or proposed.[53] The first is to establish "equalization funds" or a pooling of funds either on an industry-wide or a general basis, in order to spread out the risks incurred by small employers and industries in weak financial positions. In effect, strong industries subsidize the weak. France has chosen this option, and it has also been proposed under the Dutch and Swiss systems.

In the United Kingdom, the indexing of all earnings-related pensions, whether public or "contracted out" (that is, private), against post-retirement price increases, is the responsibility of government. In Sweden the employer is only required to make adjustments in the private pension if he has a budget surplus.

Similar limitations on the employers' liability for indexing pensions to their full current value have been recommended in the proposed Dutch system. In the Netherlands, in the case of employees who have long since changed jobs, an employer would only be responsible for indexing the pension on the basis of 70 percent of the wage increases experienced during the period the employee was on his payroll.[54] And while the proposed Dutch and Swiss mandatory private pension plans would be funded essentially by employers and employees, all readjustments would be financed on a pay-as-you-go basis—either through public taxation or through industry-wide contributions.[55]

Finally, countries with practically universal private pension coverage have closely integrated the plans with their publicly-supported systems.[56] This can be done, for example, by offsetting increases or decreases in the old age pension by similar amounts in private pensions so that the replacement rate remains stable. A disadvantage of "offsetting," as this process is called, is that, historically, old age pensions have tended to increase and private pensions to disappear under such arrangements.[57] Another method is to exclude from private pension coverage that part of the wage or salary that is subject to taxation for the old age pension.

The United Kingdom has recently introduced a unique mechanism to integrate public and private pension coverage.[58] It permits employers to "contract out" from the public earnings-related benefit, which is paid in addition to a flat rate universal pension, rather than come under the government plan. This means that employers choosing this option must substitute an occupational pension that pays at least the equivalent of the flat rate pension.

Some Implications for the United States

The United States does not have the long history of collective bargaining that countries such as Sweden and France have had. American unions have not had much experience working with management cooperatively in the pursuit of common interests, nor do they cover as large a proportion of the labor force as unions do elsewhere. It is therefore highly unlikely that agreements in the United States will evolve into anything approaching universal private pension coverage, as they have in some other countries.

It is conceivable for the United States to enact legislation, much the way Switzerland has amended its constitution, mandating almost universal private pension coverage. Years of debate preceded this innovative step on the part of Switzerland, the labor/management relations of which are more comparable than most to the United States experience, but the necessary public support was eventually obtained. On the other hand, perhaps a sweetener to employers in the form of "contracting out" all or part of the earnings-related component of Social Security—after the British example—might prove more palatable to Americans.

There is no question but that extending private pension coverage to cover most of the labor force is a very expensive policy, and both Switzerland and the Netherlands have delayed acting on their proposals because of adverse economic circumstances and an unwillingness to burden business with any more financial demands. On the other hand, it might be possible to at least put a nationwide system into place in the United States even if the income replacement rate generated by the combination of private pensions and Social Security remains at less than an optimal level. Adjustments in the replacement rate could then be made as more favorable economic circumstances permitted or other financing mechanisms suggested themselves.

NOTES

1. Frank B. McArdle, "Sources of Revenue of Social Security Systems in Ten Industrialized Countries," in *Social Security in a Changing World*, pp. 30–31.

2. James H. Schulz et al., *Providing Adequate Retirement Income*, p. 106.

3. Elizabeth Kirkpatrick, "Social Security Benefits for Women in the Federal Republic of Germany, Switzerland, and the United Kingdom," in *Social Security in a Changing World*, p. 133.

4. Organisation for Economic Co-Operation and Development (OECD), *Old Age Pension Schemes* (Paris, 1977), p. 76.

5. Kirkpatrick, "Social Security Benefits for Women," p. 114.

6. Ibid.

7. McArdle, "Sources of Revenue of Social Security," pp. 47–49.

8. Karen C. Holden, "Coverage of Non-Working Wives by Public Pension Programs in the U.S. and Japan: The Policy Choice and Equity Questions" (paper presented at the International Congress of Gerontology, Tokyo, 1978), p. 1.

9. Tomio Higuchi, "Pensions in the Japanese Rural Sector," *International Labour Review* (November-December, 1977), p. 320 (quoted in McArdle, "Sources of Revenue of Social Security," p. 48).

10. Kirkpatrick, "Social Security Benefits for Women," p. 114.

11. Stanford G. Ross, "Social Security: A Worldwide Issue," p. 8.

12. Ibid.

13. Joseph G. Simanis, "Worldwide Trends in Social Security, 1979," *Social Security Bulletin* (August 1980):9.

14. Ibid., p. 114.

15. Ibid.

16. Ibid., p. 119.

17. Dalmer Hoskins and Lenore H. Bixby, *Women and Social Security: Law and Policy in Five Countries*, p. 26; and U.K. Department of Health and Social Security, *Pensions: Britain's Great Step Forward* (August 1975), p. 12.

18. James H. Schulz, "Pension Policy at a Crossroads: What Should Be the Pension Mix?" p. 49.

19. OECD, *Old Age Pension Schemes*, p. 139; and OECD, *Socio-Economic Policies for the Elderly* (Paris, 1979), p. 155.

20. President's Commission on Pension Policy, *Coming of Age: Toward a National Retirement Income Policy* (Washington, D.C., February 26, 1981), p. 21; and M. Levy, *The Tax Treatment of Social Security* (quoted in Schulz, "Pension Policy at a Crossroads," p. 50).

21. Schulz, "Pension Policy at a Crossroads," p. 50.

22. *Coming of Age: Toward a National Retirement Income Policy*, p. 21; *Pension Facts, 1981* (Washington, D.C.: American Council of Life Insurance, 1981); and U.S., Bureau of the Census, *Current Population Reports*, Series p–23, No. 110, 1980.

23. U.S., Bureau of the Census, *Current Population Reports*, Series p–60, No. 127, 1980.

24. Martin Tracy, "Maintaining Value of Social Security Benefits During Inflation: The Foreign Experience," *Social Security Bulletin* (November 1976):38.

25. Ibid., p. 36.

26. U.S., Senate, Special Committee on Aging, *Social Security in Europe: The Impact of an Aging Population*, p. 31.

27. Ibid.

28. Ibid., p. 21.

29. Ibid., p. 32.

30. Max Horlick and Alfred M. Skolnick, *Mandating Private Pensions: A Study of European Experience*, p. 16.

31. McArdle, "Sources of Revenue of Social Security," p. 42.

32. Ross, "Social Security in a Changing World," p. 16.

33. McArdle, "Sources of Revenue of Social Security," p. 42.

34. John Osborne, "General Report," in *Methods of Financing Social Security* (Geneva: International Social Security Association, Studies and Research Report No. 15, 1979), p. 88.

35. U.S., Senate, *Social Security in Europe*, p. 25.

36. McArdle, "Sources of Revenue of Social Security," p. 59.

37. U.S., Senate, *Social Security in Europe*, pp. 9, 30.

38. See, for example, Schulz et al., *Providing Adequate Retirement Income*, p. 116.

39. Martin Feldstein, "Social Security Induced Retirement and Aggregate Capital Accumulation," *Journal of Political Economy* 82, No. 5 (September/October 1974):905–926.

40. James H. Schulz, in a presentation made before the American Association of Retired Persons, "Ageconomics: Do Economic Theories Determine Aging Public Policy," June 24, 1982.

41. Ross, "Social Security: A Worldwide Issue," pp. 5, 7.

42. Sara Rix and Paul Fisher, *Retirement Age Policy: An International Perspective* (Elmsford, N.Y.: Pergamon Press, 1982).

43. *Older American Reports*, July 4, 1980.

44. Horlick and Skolnick, *Mandating Private Pensions*, p. 34.

45. Ibid., p. 23.

46. Ibid., p. 18.

47. Ibid., p. 10.

48. Ibid., pp. 28–29.

49. Ibid., pp. 52–53; and Kirkpatrick, "Social Security Benefits for Women," p. 132.

50. Horlick and Skolnick, *Mandating Private Pensions*, p. 31.

51. Ibid., p. 52.

52. Ibid., p. 44.

53. Ibid., pp. 38–40.

54. Ibid., p. 50.
55. Ibid., p. 38.
56. Ibid., pp. 30–31.
57. Ibid., p. 31.
58. Ibid., pp. 8–9.

2

Employment of Older Persons

Charlotte Nusberg

The employment situation of older persons is remarkably similar in most of the western industrialized countries. Labor force participation by older people has dropped dramatically in the past few decades, to the point where no more than an average of about 23 percent of persons of pensionable age continue to work beyond retirement for any period of time.[1] Many countries have had a 50 percent or more reduction in older worker participation in the past 30 years.[2] The average labor force participation rate for men 65 or older in developed countries was 23 percent in 1975 compared to 53 percent for men in developing countries; for women, it was only 8 percent, compared to 17 percent for women in developing countries.[3] By the year 2000, the International Labour Organisation (ILO) projects that these rates will decrease even further, to 17 percent and 6 percent for men and women respectively in the developed countries.[4] (For figures compiled by the OECD, tracing this trend from 1965 to 1985, see Table 2.1.)

These figures translate into even smaller percentages when the proportion of the labor force constituted by those 65 and older is considered. (See Table 2.2.) The reasons for such low labor force participation are multiple, but certainly among the major ones are expanded and improved retirement benefits, which permit older people to choose retirement over work, and the changing nature of the economy—away from labor-intensive agricultural work, permitting many kinds of work participation, to the more highly skilled industrial and service sectors which, generally, have shown a preference for younger and better educated workers.

These changes in the economy have also adversely affected workers approaching retirement age, and sometimes starting as early as middle age. Although many studies have shown that older workers' capabilities remain com-

Table 2.1
Activity Rate of the Population Aged 65 Years and Upwards (as Percentage of the Total Population in This Age Group)

COUNTRY	1965	1975	1985 (Projected)
United States	17.0	14.0	13.0
Japan	34.0	30.7	25.7
Belgium	6.4	6.3	6.2
United Kingdom	12.4	10.6	10.2
Sweden	18.1	12.5	7.3
France	13.1	7.1	3.8
Germany (Federal Republic)	14.0	9.9	4.7
Netherlands	9.3	6.7	4.7
Italy	10.8	7.0	5.3
Denmark	22.8	20.0	15.4
Finland	9.9	8.9	7.3

Source: Organisation for Economic Co-Operation and Development (OECD), Demographic Trends 1970-1985, Paris, 1974. Reproduced in Socio-Economic Policies for the Elderly (Paris: OECD), 1979.

petitive with those of younger workers—except in certain physically arduous occupations and those requiring rapid reflex responses—once unemployed, older workers, on the average, remain unemployed for longer periods of time, and many are forced to take early retirements for lack of alternatives.[5] If they do find work, it is often at lower status and lower earnings than before. Although older workers are disproportionately employed in declining industries, they are under-represented in training and retraining programs.[6] Those programs that do include older workers have often not thought through the best instruction techniques and course contents for reaching their students. And on the whole, official job placement services have not had great success in locating employment for older workers.[7]

To these factors must be added the effects of age discrimination; mandatory retirement practices, which are still widespread in other countries; inflexibility with regard to work hours; unhealthy working conditions; retirement tests; and so on—all of which serve to discourage continued participation in the labor force by older workers. When these factors are combined with the relatively generous unemployment or retirement benefits provided in many nations, the rapid decline in labor force participation by older people becomes less surprising.

Nevertheless, many older people do continue to work and many wish they could. In Norway, about 38 percent of men continue to work beyond age 67—the official pensionable age—and usually full time, and more than a fifth work up to age 74.[8] In Japan, 41 percent of men 65 and older continued to work in

Table 2.2
Older Workers as a Proportion of All Workers,
1975 (percentage)

MAJOR REGION	TOTAL 45 +	45-54	55-64	65+
World	26.9	15.5	8.2	3.2
More developed regions	32.4	19.7	9.6	3.1
Less developed regions	24.4	13.6	7.5	3.3
Africa	22.3	12.3	7.0	3.0
Latin America	23.0	13.0	7.0	3.0
South Asia	23.1	13.2	7.0	2.9
U.S.S.R.	27.6	21.7	4.9	1.1
East Asia	27.9	15.2	8.8	3.9
Oceania	28.0	16.7	9.9	2.4
Europe	34.1	19.6	10.8	3.7
North America	34.7	18.6	12.6	3.5

Source: International Labour Office (ILO), Labour
Force Estimates and Projections 1950-2000, 2nd
ed., Vol. 5, World Summary, Geneva, 1977.
Reproduced in Older Workers: Work and
Retirement (Geneva: ILO, 1979.)

1980.[9] And in the German Democratic Republic, about 10 percent of the country's labor force is over the pensionable age (65 for men; 60 for women).[10] The chief of the Danish employment service expressed the belief that in Denmark thousands more pensioners would work if part-time jobs were available, but because of high unemployment among the young, the government has done nothing to facilitate work opportunities for older persons.[11]

Given the many obstacles to employment of the elderly, who then is likely to work? In all developed countries, it is mainly the workers in two categories who are likely to continue to work beyond the normal retirement age—those who are most in control of their work environments (and thus less susceptible to discriminatory practices), such as farmers and the self-employed; and highly educated and skilled workers, such as professionals and senior management, who obtain great psychological satisfactions from their jobs. For example, in Japan, which has an unusually large number of small family businesses, the proportion of older people continuing to work remains somewhat higher than in most western industrialized countries.[12] Many of these businesses are started following retirement, which until very recently was set at the unusually low age of 55 by most private employers.

The desire of many older persons to work runs counter to policies in a number of western countries to reduce unemployment among the young, in part at the expense of the old. Thus, while not going as far as imposing a mandatory earlier retirement, countries such as the United Kingdom and Belgium offer older workers an early retirement at almost full pension if they vacate their jobs and do not look for other employment—and provided their employers hire unemployed persons to fill the resulting vacancies. (In France the eligibility age for receipt of such early pensions was recently reduced to 55.) In all these cases the workers still remain eligible to draw a full pension at the normal retirement age! China, too, has persuaded exceptionally large numbers of older workers in urban areas to retire early by offering them the opportunity to give their jobs to unemployed offspring.[13]

Despite such encouragement of early labor force withdrawal by older workers, policy-makers, by and large, are resisting pressures for universal earlier retirement ages in recognition of both the costs that would be involved to their nations' pension systems and the fact that it would be too sweeping a response to a situation that requires more finely tuned solutions. (France is an exception, however. Starting in April 1983, the retirement age was lowered to 60 from 64.[14]) In fact, voters in Switzerland in 1978 rejected a referendum to lower the retirement age in order to free jobs for the younger unemployed.[15]

Nevertheless, controversy about retirement ages continues. Only in the U.S. and Japan, among the industrialized countries, have steps been taken to raise the retirement age in the face of rising pension costs and adverse demographic ratios.[16] Japan is committed to raising its retirement age to 60 by 1985 and to a yet greater age thereafter.[17] Other countries are still experiencing pressures for reducing the retirement age yet further, and nations which have a differential in the retirement age between men and women (usually five years) have experienced political resistance to equalizing the ages.

Thus far, only the United States, Chile and Uruguay have been successful in officially raising the retirement age. Japan, however, has achieved some success through non-legislative means.[18] Since the early 1970's the Japanese government has been bringing steady pressure to bear on industry to extend the retirement age. Most unions and industries have now accepted this goal and are in various stages of implementing contractual agreements providing for a gradual increase in the retirement age. The general consensus is that workers should be assured of full-time employment until age 60. Following that, a range of options should be provided, including full retirement, full-time employment, and part-time employment.[19]

SAFEGUARDS FOR OLDER WORKERS

In light of older workers' competitive disadvantage with the rest of the labor force, many of the industrialized countries have adopted some measures to provide older workers with a modicum of protection. No country has enacted anything comparable to the U.S. Age Discrimination in Employment Act (1967, 1972, 1979), but many incorporate language in national labor codes extending safeguards to older workers. It should be noted, though, that some serious policy disagreements exist about whether special safeguards for older workers serve to further segregate rather than integrate them in the labor force. Even where safeguards do exist, on the whole they only extend to workers below the pensionable age. Sweden, for example, permits the dismissal of employees who have reached retirement age, and the United Kingdom similarly does not protect persons over pensionable age against unfair dismissal.[20]

An exception to this is the socialist countries of Eastern Europe, where employment is guaranteed to those who wish it.[21] In the Soviet Union, this is guaranteed by the constitution. Additional regulations prohibit the dismissal of an employee because he or she has reached pensionable age. A retired person, similarly, may not be refused employment because he or she has been inactive and receiving a pension. Evidence on how strictly such safeguards are enforced is sketchy.

Among the legislative safeguards that have been enacted on behalf of older workers are Sweden's Employment Security Act (1974), which requires longer notice periods before workers 45 years or older are dismissed, and the Act on the Promotion of Employment of Older Workers in the Free Market (1974), which establishes "adjustment groups" composed of employee/ employer/employment bureau representatives in all firms with more than fifty employees.[22] The task of the adjustment groups is to promote the hiring of older and handicapped individuals and facilitate their integration in the work force. In extreme cases of age discrimination, firms can also be ordered to hire only older workers.

Since the early 1970's, more than 5,000 "adjustment groups" involving some 30,000 people have come into being to facilitate the employment of older and handicapped persons.[23] While many of these groups have not accomplished much, a number have been quite successful, particularly in adjusting work conditions so that older and handicapped employees could be kept on the job. They have been less successful in bringing into their firms many more older and handicapped persons off the unemployment rolls.

The work of adjustment groups is difficult, and most have not yet lived up to expectations. Among the major problems are the difficulties involved in changing negative public attitudes about older worker employment and the constant need to train the shifting membership of the groups. A shortage of personnel and resources has also hampered the groups' work. While policy-makers in Sweden now realize that more time than originally anticipated will be required to obtain fully effective adjustment groups, they remain confident that this is the approach for Sweden to take in order to overcome barriers to employment for the disadvantaged groups.[24] In fact, the Netherlands is now considering following the Swedish example of setting up adjustment groups in its large firms.

In times of recession and potentially high unemployment among the most vulnerable groups in society, such as the elderly and the handicapped, the Swedish government also takes special measures to protect workers threatened with lay-offs because of business fluctuations. To maintain employment, firms are en-

couraged to increase their inventories during recessions and draw on the investment reserves they have accumulated during previous "boom" periods. A
frequently used policy during such periods is to subsidize in-service training for
underutilized employees on the condition that any notices of dismissal that had
been given would be withdrawn during the training period. The hope is that
when industrial demand picks up again, firms will then be in a better position
to respond because of the availability of a more productive staff. As business
turns up again, these training subsidies are reduced and replaced by "recruitment" subsidies to facilitate the employment of the newly hired. The subsidies
can also be combined with grants for semi-sheltered employment to hire the
"occupationally disadvantaged." As a result of such programs, the number of
persons in semi-sheltered employment actually increased during Sweden's
recession in the mid–1970's.[25]

In the Federal Republic of Germany, the Work Constitution Act (*Betriebver-
fassungsgesetz*) makes the employer and work council in each firm directly responsible for preventing any discrimination against older workers.[26] In France,
the Labor Code (*Code du Travail*) prohibits the setting of upper age limits to
prevent worker access to jobs.[27] And in Japan, the Older Workers' Employment Promotion Law urges firms to keep the proportion of workers 55 years or
older above 6 percent of their labor force.[28]

By and large, the impact of such legislative safeguards has been slight. The
monies and personnel have simply not been available to enforce the legislation
effectively. In Japan, where the majority of firms do now have slightly more
than 6 percent of their labor force composed of workers 55 and older, the variations among companies remain wide.[29]

An unofficial admission of this failure is the enactment of special provisions
providing more generous compensation to older workers who become unemployed than to younger ones, by, for example, extending the period over which
unemployment benefits are paid and, in some cases, permitting the conversion
of the unemployment benefit to an early retirement. Thus, much unemployment
remains hidden because of early withdrawals from the labor force. Some of the
unanticipated consequences of such generous compensation policies are less reluctance on the part of an employer to dismiss older workers and less motivation on the part of the older unemployed worker to seek work aggressively.

With regard to older workers' safety and health, Norway's Workers' Protection and Working Environment Act allows older workers to be excused from
overtime for health or family reasons and recommends that older workers requesting it be excused from night work.[30] Outside the realm of legislation, many
collective bargaining agreements provide special protection for older workers.
In France, to permit older workers to stay on their jobs, national agreements
call for the creation of special working conditions such as shorter work weeks,
protection against irregular or night shifts, extended annual leave, and wage
guarantees in case of demotion to lower-paying jobs.[31] Similarly, in the Federal
Republic of Germany, many collective bargaining agreements guarantee that if

they have worked for a firm a minimum of 10 to 15 years, workers over 45 cannot be dismissed in the ordinary way or, if transferred to lower-paying jobs for health or other reasons, are guaranteed the same wages.[32] And in the Soviet Union, firms have a right to grant working pensioners up to two months of unpaid leave each year, in addition to paid annual leave, in order to permit a long rest during the summer period.[33]

INCENTIVES TO HIRE OLDER WORKERS

Policy-makers have not relied solely on the "stick" approach to discourage age discrimination in employment, but are also experimenting with positive incentives to employers—mainly in the form of grants and wage subsidies—in order to encourage the hiring of older workers. In Norway, for example, firms which employ persons 60 years or older are granted a supplement equal to 50 percent of the worker's wages for six months, followed by a 40 percent supplement for the second six months.[34] (The Committee for Older Workers in Norway has recommended that the age limit for this benefit be reduced to 50 and that the supplement be made available for an additional six months.) Firms hiring persons 50 or older who have been unemployed more than three months receive a grant equal to one-third of their wages plus social security benefits for a six-month period.[35]

In the Federal Republic of Germany, firms hiring unemployed persons 45 years of age or older are eligible for grants equivalent to 80 percent of the new employees' wage costs for up to two years, and firms which specifically recruit older workers to fill positions over and above their normal work force may receive grants for up to 50 percent of the wage costs of their new hires.[36]

Japan also provides wage subsidies to enterprises hiring older individuals if the new jobs remove them from the unemployment rolls. For every middle-aged person hired (age 45–55), the government will subsidize three-fifths (four-fifths for small businesses) of their wages for six months and one-half (two-thirds for small businesses) of their wages for the next six months.[37] For unemployed individuals over the age of 55, employers are subsidized three-fifths (four-fifths for small business) of their wages for one year and one-half (two-thirds for small businesses) of their wages for the next six months. In 1979, an average of 6,445 unemployed individuals were hired each month as a result of such incentives.[38] Funding for such subsidies is made possible through employer contributions to the Employment Stabilization Fund which was created to preserve employment through the vicissitudes of business cycles.

Probably because Japan is the only industrialized nation committed to raising its retirement age from the unrealistically low age of 55, it provides the greatest variety of incentives to retain or hire older employees. For example, employers who extend an older worker's employment for at least one year beyond the normal retirement age of 55 are entitled to an "extension of age limit benefit"— usually $1,125 (270,000 yen) per worker for large enterprises and $1,500

(360,000 yen) for small and medium enterprises.[39] Many firms, especially smaller ones, are taking advantage of this benefit. Larger firms have preferred to "reemploy" selected older workers, usually at lower status and pay.

A "benefit for continuous employment" is given to employers who continue to employ an individual beyond the age of 60 for at least one year. To receive the benefit, the enterprise must rehire an employee within seven days after his retirement. Large enterprises receive $295 (68,000 yen); medium and small enterprises $391 (90,000 yen) per year for each worker so extended. Following their formal "retirement," 17,231 older workers were rehired in 1978.[40]

Japan also provides grants to firms raising their retirement age; these grants are related to the number of jobs thus extended. Finally, on-the-job training for older workers is encouraged through governmental grants to employers approximating about $56 each month for up to six months. Some 20,000 older workers or handicapped persons profited from this opportunity each month in the late 1970's.[41]

While Japan has been unsuccessful in legislating a higher retirement age, government pressures are making themselves felt in the collective bargaining agreements that are being struck. A number of enterprises have already raised the retirement age by a few years, and in what may become a major precedent, a recent industry-wide agreement raised the retirement age from 58 to 60, provided that individuals who continue to work beyond 58 take a 20 percent cut in pay even though they continue to perform the same duties. Because of the rigid correlation between pay and seniority in Japan, it was felt that the only way older employees could be extended was through their acceptance of lower pay. This agreement actually fell somewhat into line with the recommendations of a recent government "white paper," which proposed that employers provide little or no pay increases to workers age 45 or older, in exchange for raising the retirement age to 60.[42] In turn, the government would ease the financial squeeze on older workers by providing more adequate pensions, lowering the cost of educational loans for children, and making various concessions to homeowners.

Other Japanese firms are offering varying retirement ages for their managerial categories with the option of reemployment at a reduced salary. Thus, one enterprise offers certain managers the opportunity to retire at age 50 rather than 55 with the possibility of reemployment as a "non-managerial specialist" at a 20 percent reduction in pay until age 60.[43]

While keeping older workers on at a reduction in pay is seen as a good compromise by some in Japan, such "downward mobility" has not been equally welcomed by trade unions elsewhere. Collective bargaining agreements in countries such as France and the Federal Republic of Germany specifically call for the preservation of wage and salary levels if job transfers of older workers to lower-paying jobs occur. Such restrictions may be necessary in countries where the size of retirement benefits is related to earnings level in the last few years of employment.

INCENTIVES TO OLDER PEOPLE TO REMAIN IN THE LABOR FORCE

A variety of policies have been experimented with, designed to induce older people to remain in the labor force by either not taking an early retirement or postponing retirement following normal pensionable age. (Financial incentives built into nations' pension systems will be discussed in the next chapter, on flexible retirement.)

Job Redesign and Realignment

Job redesign—that is, the restructuring of a job or the work environment so that it maximizes the capabilities of the worker—permits older workers suffering from particular handicaps or declining abilities to continue on in the same jobs without major discomforts or declines in productivity. Such adaptations can do much to permit older workers to perform their jobs more easily and "maintain the same level of efficiency as younger workers."[44] The International Labour Organisation (ILO), in norms adopted in 1980, has called on nations to remove work conditions which accelerate the process of aging and adapt jobs and work hours, if necessary, to permit older employees to continue working under satisfactory conditions.[45] According to the ILO, "There is more to be gained from both the human and the economic standpoint by changing the content of the job and the conditions in which it is performed . . . than by moving them to another job."[46]

While the desirability of such adaptations has been generally recognized and knowledge about redesigning jobs is certainly available, implementation of the adaptations on behalf of older workers remains minimal everywhere.[47] One explanation proposed for the reluctance of employers to engage in job redesign is their fear that, given the still sizable trend towards early retirement, the costs of job redesign may never be justified.

Some signs of progress can be seen, however. For example, in Sweden, a number of the adjustment groups described above have been quite successful in having work adapted to the needs of older and handicapped people. Two plants of the Volvo Company, Sweden's largest automobile manufacturer, have as much as 20–25 percent of their labor force in the "occupationally handicapped" category, thanks in part to jobs redesigned in response to promptings from adjustment committees.[48]

Job redesign may be particularly important if the policy objective is to persuade relatively large numbers of older persons—particularly those past the normal retirement age—to remain in the labor force. The U.S.S.R., for example, has found that no more than 28 percent of the persons of pensionable age can be persuaded to continue working through the removal of financial disincentives, such as retirement tests, and that additional measures, such as improving work conditions and more flexible work hours, may have to be introduced if larger numbers of older people are to remain employed.[49]

Job "realignment," as the Japanese call it, or job transfer, is a much more common manpower tool for keeping older workers employed when they can no longer perform their regular jobs well or when the costs of keeping older workers on in the same job become too high. Job transfers are more likely to occur when older workers are required to perform heavy physical labor or have rapid responses to the demands of machinery. Usually, the older workers are transferred to lower-paying and less demanding jobs, although as we have seen in a number of European countries, their wages may be protected for a certain number of years if they have achieved some seniority. On the Israeli kibbutz, where work must be provided for every member regardless of age, a shift in occupation often takes place in later years, with women moving from teaching to services and men from agriculture to industry.[50]

One Japanese study suggests that while job aptitudes for certain tasks, such as casting, decrease after age 60, aptitude actually increases for other functions, such as machine operation and assembly work.[51] One firm has taken advantage of these findings to shift older employees to computer operations and the assembly and inspection of integrated circuits—work that was previously performed by young men and women. Although most of the older workers came to their jobs with no special experience in these areas, they proved eager to learn and mastered the skills required. According to the firm, job morale is high and employment satisfactory.[52] Another Japanese study found "that with greater maturity and interpersonal skills, older workers are better suited to jobs requiring extensive social contact than are younger employees."[53]

Implicit in both job redesign and job realignment are the "identification of detailed performance standards for each job to accurately fit the task with the worker," a procedure that has been recommended by industrial gerontologists in a number of different countries.[54]

Part-Time Work

Despite what seems to be an overwhelming preference for part-time work by persons of pensionable age who would consider continuing in employment, part-time jobs remain scarce practically everywhere and are relatively menial and of low status where they do exist. (An interesting exception to this is found on the Israeli kibbutz, where part-time work *must* be found for members 65 or older wishing it.[55]) Part-time jobs are more common in the service sector than in the industrial sector; typical part-time jobs are those of porter, janitor, cleaner, and clerk.

Employers generally resist experimenting with alternative work forms unless there are severe labor shortages or they are persuaded that innovations, such as job sharing, are worth trying. For example, during periods of recession, employers may be tempted to try part-time work, although primarily as a means of labor force attrition.

Some of the more aggressive volunteer placement bureaus have been successful in convincing employers to hire elderly persons on a job-sharing basis on the grounds that they will gain highly motivated and reliable employees whose productivity may well exceed that of fewer people filling the positions full-time. A few agencies, as a further incentive, have assumed the additional administrative work that is involved in processing more than one employee for a job. On a national level, the Soviet Union is trying to increase the number of part-time jobs available for pensioners in recognition of the fact that the productivity of pensioners working part-time is higher than that of their peers working full-time.[56]

(A discussion of phased or gradual retirement, permitting older persons to work part-time to ease the transition to full retirement, will be found in Chapter 3. Training opportunities will be discussed in Chapter 9.)

JOB CREATION

The availability of jobs, and desirable jobs, probably is as powerful an incentive as any in persuading individuals to work. What is available to older persons?

Self-Employment

Both Sweden and Japan provide low-interest loans to older people wishing to set up their own businesses. In Japan, this can be a particularly effective manpower tool because small family businesses have played an important part in that country's modernization. The relatively large numbers of older persons who continue to work beyond the pensionable age in Japan is undoubtedly made possible by the fact that some 70 percent of those who do so are self-employed or working in family businesses.[57] In fact, the proportion of the Japanese labor force that is self-employed rises quite dramatically with increasing age. While the greatest number of family enterprises and opportunities for self-employment are in the primary industries (agriculture, fishing, mining), a considerable number also exist in the secondary (industrial production) and tertiary (service) sectors.

Expansion of Existing Companies

Under the Federal Republic of Germany's Promotion of Employment Act, loans and grants covering up to 50 percent of the total cost of the operation may be given to employers wishing to create or enlarge an enterprise for the purpose of employing older workers.[58] Grants are limited to non-profit employers or firms planning to employ a majority of unemployed older workers. Not many companies have availed themselves of these opportunities.

In Japan, some firms, on an individual basis, are establishing affiliated companies manned almost entirely by older employees nearing retirement age. The "living service" companies, as one electronics firm calls the branches it has set up in several major Japanese cities, manage welfare services and adjunct activities provided by the parent corporation for all its employees; some also handle quality control, repair and maintenance, and general administration.[59] The Teijin Co., for example, a manufacturer of synthetic fibers, established a subsidiary to provide employment for its older workers who would otherwise be subject to retirement at the relatively young ages of 55–60.[60] The 170 workers in the Teijin Mihara Kosan Company are responsible for managing the welfare programs for employees of the larger Teijin concern. Efforts are continuously being made to expand the older workers' responsibilities and the number of jobs they can take on. All its employees work forty-hour weeks and are allowed to work until age 65. This company for seniors was created through the cooperative effort of labor and management, which undertook joint responsibility for its planning.

In Israel, an experimental factory for retirees has become a regular part of the Ligat clothing manufacturing firm.[61] The factory, which employs about sixty persons between the ages of 65 and 80, was set up through the joint efforts of the Ligat concern and the national and municipal governments. The only criterion for employment was previous experience in a factory setting. Training in sewing was given as needed, and its employees started producing a clothing line that was not competitive with Ligat's main enterprise. The older employees all work five-hour shifts, five days a week, and are paid according to the regular work scale.

During the first two years of the factory's operation, the program was heavily subsidized by government. This subsidy has now been sharply reduced, although some funding from the Ministry of Labor and Welfare continues. The experiment is generally considered a success. Employee turnover is practically non-existent, and there is a very low level of absenteeism. It has become an important source of income for retirees, as well as performing some of the functions of a social club.

Work at Home

City officials in Leningrad, who were trying to motivate pensioners to take up some work, found that a number would be willing to do so provided they could work at home. As a result, they persuaded a manufacturer of optical equipment to farm out some of its work to pensioners in their own homes. Among the interesting findings was that twenty pensioners working part-time at home could release an average of eight full-time younger workers, who could then perform more physically demanding work.[62] With this kind of evidence in hand, city officials have since convinced other employers to reapportion their work along similar lines, thereby easing labor shortages.

Home work arrangements of this kind now exist in a number of republics of the Soviet Union. Many produce goods designed for domestic consumption. Home workers are entitled to many of the same benefits as regular workers, including annual leave and disability pay.[63]

Age-Segregated Enterprises

While age-segregated enterprises remain rare, interest in them continues. An innovative model that has attracted the attention of many is the "Strength Through

Work'' (Sterk door Werk) company formed in Eindhoven, the Netherlands, in 1959.[64] The company employs several hundred "retired" workers, who work an average of three hours a day, five days a week. The average age of the company's employees is 68, an average that has increased over time, suggesting that work has been helpful in assisting older persons to retain their vitality.

Strength Through Work was founded at the initiative of the Philips Corporation for its own retired employees. Although the original goal was to find some meaningful activity for older people to engage in, rather than make a profit, the company soon became economically self-sustaining through the manufacture of a wide range of miniature machines and electronic equipment which could be used as teaching aids in vocational schools. A product line was purposely chosen which would not be competitive with goods produced by younger workers. At the same time, the choice of these particular products permitted employees to develop close working relationships with vocational students from local schools, who were taught the use of the products and apprenticed to the company for short periods of time.

Strength Through Work has become quite independent of the Philips Corporation, employing retirees from other industries as well. It has paid back its loans with interest and been able to declare dividends for its members. (The company is organized as a cooperative.)

All the positions—from management to unskilled labor—are filled by retirees. Absenteeism is rare and averages no more than three hours a month. Time off for vacations, domestic duties, family visits, or simply inclement weather can be easily arranged, however. By and large, the employees continue to perform tasks similar to the ones they engaged in prior to their retirement, but the pace has been changed to take into account the changing work rhythms of older persons and their desire for greater personal freedom. The employees have also found it highly desirable to work with their age peers, and the work has stimulated friendships which have continued outside the work place.

On a governmental level, the Soviet Union has encouraged the establishment of special enterprises and workshops in both the industrial and service sectors, designed for the employment of pensioners and disabled persons.[65] These establishments provide more flexible work hours, easier work conditions, longer rest periods and stricter monitoring of health and safety standards. The level of state subsidies to such enterprises is larger than for ordinary production units, permitting greater investment in upgrading the work environment and quality of life for workers.

In Israel, the *kibbutzim* (agricultural collectives), where a strong work ethic has always prevailed, were faced with a dilemma when their own founding members became too old to do physically demanding agricultural work, yet were unwilling to retire. The solution in some kibbutzim was to create light industry to occupy older workers. Some of these industries, such as light plastics, have been so successful that younger people have been added to the payrolls in order to meet production schedules.

Since 1968, several hundred retired men in Dortmund, Federal Republic of Germany, have provided their time and mechanical and crafts skills on a voluntary basis to charitable organizations throughout Germany and neighboring countries in return for room and board and a small daily allowance.[66]

Using the men's own vehicles and tools, this Goodwill Company (Kompanie des guten Willens) helps repair or renovate institutional homes for young and old and other welfare facilities which have small budgets for such contingencies. Recent activities have included renovating a parish community house in Birmingham, England, and a vacation facility for families in Bad Gastein, Austria, and, with local workers, rebuilding a hospital for children in Dortmund.

The body of the Goodwill Company is formed of 200 retired men, and 500 more are on a waiting list. The appeal of the company to the volunteers is that it provides them with meaningful work which is always gratefully received by the employers and a welcome change in their routine and surroundings.

Another interesting idea comes from Caritas in Munich, which has opened a workshop to help pensioners retain their occupational skills, with an emphasis on those skills which cannot be practiced at home because of the noise levels involved or the lack of appropriate equipment.[67] The elders participating in the workshop make small repairs for their peers at no charge. Caritas hopes to extend its facilities to unemployed youths as well, so they may learn some useful skills and have an opportunity to interact with older persons.

In Berlin and several other German cities, where the isolation of special workshops for the elderly made it difficult to obtain work materials and managerial staff, a solution was found by placing the workshops in the middle of a factory, where participants work alongside the regular labor force. The employer contributes the space and pays for the work done. Each participant is paid an hourly wage and is free to come and go as he chooses.

Another interesting experiment was the creation in Germany of separate organizations heavily funded by the public sector to absorb hard-core older unemployed workers. These societies, or Gesellschäfte zur Verbesserung der Beschäftigungsstruktur (Societies for the Improvement of Occupational Structure), sought to enhance the employability of older workers by improving their manual dexterity through labor intensive production schedules. Available evidence indicates, however, that for reasons that are not clear, only a minority of their employees were successfully transferred to the private sector.[68]

Sheltered Workshops

Examples of sheltered workshops for the elderly can be found in most countries. These provide older people who, because of health reasons or extreme old age, can no longer find work in the marketplace, with an opportunity to earn some extra money while working at a pace adapted to their rhythms. Often some social services, such as meals and transportation, are also provided.

In Sweden, some 55,000 persons (of all ages) are working in sheltered or semi-sheltered employment. [69] Some 15,000 are engaged in administrative "archive'' work with government or other public organizations; most of their wages are completely subsidized by the national government. Private employers and local governments arranging semi-sheltered employment obtain subsidies equal to 75 percent of the total wage costs for the first year, 50 percent for the second year, and 25 percent for the third and fourth years. In addition, subsidies equal to 25 percent of wage costs are payable for employees who must be transferred to semi-sheltered employment.

Sweden's Commission on Long-Term Employment Policy recommended in 1978 that the system of employment with wage subsidies for the ''occupationally disadvantaged'' be expanded by 25 percent a year for a five-year period so that the number of jobs available to this vulnerable group would be raised to 75,000.[70] The commission also came out strongly in favor of linking sheltered employment as closely as possible to regular employment so that the occupationally disadvantaged could enjoy the same benefits as other employees and increase their chances of someday transferring to unsheltered employment.

In the United Kingdom, the Employment Fellowship has been instrumental in starting about 100 sheltered workshops throughout the country by providing organizers with easily replicable models.[71] All but twenty are operated by voluntary organizations, and generally there are many more applicants than places available. The primary motive is not to provide participants with additional income, although this is an important secondary objective, but to help maintain their morale, health and self-confidence.

One of the most unique sheltered workshops can be found in Jerusalem, where more than 200 elderly persons, with an average age in the high seventies, work every morning five days a week producing high-quality crafts that have won several major awards. [72] Lifeline for the Old employs professional designers, who design products they think the public will purchase. They are assisted by part-time teachers, many of whom are volunteers, who teach both the elderly attending the workshop and homebound older persons the necessary skills. Although the quality of work is not uniform among all the workshop participants, all are paid at the same rate, and only products meeting certain standards are sold in Lifeline's shops. The founder of Lifeline for the Old has purposely turned down the repetitive assembly-line work usually farmed out to sheltered workshops in favor of this more creative work, which she feels is commensurate with older persons' dignity.

Lifeline for the Old has also for many years won the bookbinding contract with the Jerusalem city schools. Not only does the task of binding old textbooks earn the workshop the money it needs to add on to its crafts workshops, but it has permitted valuable intergenerational relationships to develop between the older participants and schoolchildren who come to pick up their books. Lifeline for the Old operates on a small budget of about $120,000 a year; half of its revenues are derived from its sales; the remainder is contributed by government or private charity.

Since individuals are chosen to participate in sheltered workshops on the ba-

sis of need rather than productivity, few workshops have ever become economically self-sustaining. Cooperation among the voluntary, public and private sectors remains crucial. Volunteers generally provide management services; local
government and the private sector usually provide subsidies and/or work contracts.

It has been the experience of workshop organizers, such as the Employment
Fellowship, that it is very important to have the voluntary sector run such ven-
tures.[73] Not only can it better provide the kind of individual attention and flexibility that participants need, but firms are often more willing to deal with the
voluntary sector than with local government.

The key to the success of a sheltered workshop usually lies with the manager, who is responsible for strategically locating the workshop so that it is easily accessible both to elderly participants and client firms. He or she must know
the capacities of the workers and be able to break complex tasks down into
simpler ones. The flow of work is completely dependent on the organizer's tal-
ent for attracting business and for convincing firms that the work will be done
well, that delivery dates will be adhered to and that normal rates will be charged.
Often, trade unions need to be consulted in advance to allay suspicions about
undercutting or exploitation.

Some British experts believe that economically self-sustaining workshops for
unskilled and semi-skilled older persons could be created which could perform
many useful tasks for industry that would not compete with the younger work
force.[74] These would include jobs not susceptible to a regular work rhythm,
such as mending tools and materials, salvaging and conserving materials, and
transmitting skills to the young. Such activities would complement regular labor force operations. Several industries acting together could assure some variety and continuity in the work provided to the workshop.

Placement Services

A number of countries have developed separate placement or employment
services for the elderly, sometimes under the auspices of government, sometimes under those of the voluntary sector, to facilitate the employment of older
workers, who are presumed to need special advocacy and attention. Other
countries have refused to treat older workers as a separate category for fear of
segregating them further from the labor force.

According to one study of employment service staff in nine European countries, most are opposed to separate bodies or campaigns on behalf of older
workers, although at the same time most admit that without such special efforts, older workers are probably more difficult to place.[75]

The experience of special placement services for the elderly has been a mixed
one. Canada's ''special consultation services'' for workers 45 and older have
had good results. According to one study, about two-thirds of the individuals
who sought assistance from this government service found jobs, and a follow-

up study showed that 90 percent of these placements were still in their jobs eighteen months later.[76]

On the other hand, Japan, which has some 188 vocational counseling offices in city and town halls throughout the country, reports less success. A study of one employment service found that older people were being placed in low-paid, menial jobs with wages that were insufficient to meet their financial needs.[77]

Another type of employment agency promoted by governments in urban areas is run by the elderly themselves. A typical example is the "work corporations" established in a number of districts in Tokyo.[78] Membership is open only to persons 60 years of age or older, and the members elect their own board of directors, which hires necessary staff.

The corporations accept any jobs suitable for older workers. All the money paid to the corporations is divided among the workers according to the number of hours worked, minus a 5–10 percent deduction for expenses. All members are covered by workmen's compensation and are given annual health checkups. By dividing their members geographically into blocks and designating a leader for each group of about twenty persons, the corporations also facilitate social contacts.

The work corporations have, however, experienced difficulties in finding enough work for the members. According to one study, the types of jobs in which members were placed did not utilize their abilities well and wages sometimes fell below the minimum rates.[79]

In the United Kingdom, where the most extensive network of voluntary placement services can be found outside the United States, the rationale for their existence is that the nature of the work available to the elderly differs substantially from that which appeals to people who are younger. Generally, the types of job openings available to the elderly either demand great reliability and accuracy or are thought to have "no future" by the young—jobs such as porters, security guards, clerks, and so on. These are also the kinds of placements that for-profit employment agencies are reluctant to handle because they are time-consuming and hard to fill. As a result, the voluntary placement bureaus feel they are meeting a real need. Their success seems related more to the drive and enthusiasm of the bureaus' directors than to factors such as the general unemployment rate, which is sometimes thought to affect heavily the possibilities for older worker employment.

POLICY IMPLICATIONS FOR THE UNITED STATES

In the United States the issue of older worker employment should continue to increase in significance in coming years, both because of policy-maker concerns about rising Social Security and pension costs resulting from a larger retired population, and because of an increased desire on the part of the current labor force to continue in some kind of work beyond today's popular retirement ages. According to a 1978 Harris poll, most U.S. workers wish to work either full- or part-time at the same or another less demanding job beyond the normal retirement age.[80] A more recent Harris survey (1981) reinforced this finding by revealing that almost 80 percent of persons in the key pre-retirement ages of 55–64 would prefer part-time employment to total retirement.[81]

The United States has never seriously pushed the issue of older worker employment. It is no coincidence that Social Security and its liberalization to permit earlier retirement were introduced at times of high unemployment; they had the desired effect of stimulating labor force withdrawal by older workers. And the lifting of the mandatory retirement age ceiling has been mainly a symbolic measure thus far—it has not opened up a significant number of jobs for older people, although it has certainly removed a significant barrier to their working.[82] What impact the gradual raising of the retirement age after the year 2009 will have on older worker employment remains to be seen.

Pressures to increase older worker employment prior to 2009 are already apparent and are likely to increase if present demographic trends persist. Declining numbers of young people entering the labor force should naturally create a demand for more and longer older worker employment. To the extent this scenario unfolds and the United States approaches full employment, employers can probably be relied on to remove barriers to older worker employment which prevent the employers from meeting their production goals, such as the lack of flexible work hours and part-time jobs. In periods of labor shortages, many more imaginative labor market practices come to the fore. At most, government might facilitate the situation by providing information about older worker capabilities and ways of redesigning work to maximize those capabilities.

For example, in Eastern Europe, where there has been a concerted effort to encourage older worker employment beyond the normal retirement age, it has been found that while industrial workers up to 65 are largely capable of bearing a full-time work load and being practically as productive as younger workers, this is generally not true with those over 65, who need lighter work and fewer hours of work.[83] It also became evident that it was much easier to persuade older workers to remain in employment beyond the normal pensionable age than to lure them back into the labor force once they had retired.

While the U.S. experience is not comparable to that of a country like the U.S.S.R., there are probably some lessons which should be seriously considered in any effort to promote older worker employment. The United States might also consider removing present disincentives to work, such as the retirement test, and perhaps increasing the amount of the Social Security supplement for each year that retirement is postponed.

In periods of relatively high unemployment, which has been the U.S. pattern for many years, older worker employment becomes more difficult to achieve because of the competing interests of other vulnerable groups, such as racial and ethnic minorities. If grants and wage subsidies to stimulate the employment of older workers, which have served as useful incentives in more homogeneous countries such as Japan, were instituted in the United States, the government would probably come under considerable political pressure to extend the same policy to other groups. On the other hand, an age-neutral policy of stimulating paid leave for educational and training purposes to workers of all ages might both be politically feasible and remove the stigma of skills-obsolescence from many older workers.

The "carrot" rather than the "stick" approach seems to be more effective in encouraging older worker employment. Sanctions against age discrimination may be a necessary back-up policy, but no country has been able to muster the funds and personnel necessary to enforce such provisions effectively. The establishment of quota systems has also not been very effective, even in countries like Japan, where there is much closer collaboration between government and business than there is in the United States.

A manpower tool that deserves closer examination is Sweden's "adjustment group," which brings together all interested parties—the employer, the employees, and the government employment service—at the actual job level to work together in a cooperative fashion in order to stimulate older worker employment and job adaptations. While a small army of people is involved in Sweden's adjustment groups, they are truly grassroots-based and operate on an on-going basis. They hold the potential for being much more effective than an army of equal size of impersonal enforcers coming in from the outside on an ad hoc basis.

Another Swedish policy worthy of closer study is the practice of encouraging firms to stockpile their products during periods of recession and providing in-service training to prevent lay-offs of underemployed workers, on the presumption that such investments will ease the strains accompanying the starts of business upturns. Through utilizing such incentives, Sweden was able to keep its unemployment rate down to 2 percent during its last recession.[84]

At the same time, the United States could do more to stimulate job creation among older people in the form of self-employment and special workshops. Such workshops might perform tasks to complement those of existing industries or might even develop new product lines, in the manner of the Strength Through Work company in the Netherlands.

These many suggestions reinforce the need to develop a variety of policies to encourage older worker employment. No single policy or program can reach more than a minority of people or can be effective without the reinforcement of other measures. Abolishing the retirement test, for example, would probably mainly serve as an incentive to low-income older persons. Attractive working conditions, whether in the form of interesting work or shorter work hours, might prove influential with more affluent older people. If a variety of measures like these were adopted, enough people might remain in the labor force to ease the financial burdens on the Social Security system. However, even when the eligibility age for receiving Social Security retirement benefits is raised, some of these same measures will have to be considered if many older people, if for health reasons only, are to remain productive members of the labor force.

NOTES

1. International Labour Organisation, *Older Workers: Work and Retirement* (Geneva; 1979), p. 8.

2. Ibid.

3. Ibid., pp. 8–9.

4. Ibid.

5. Ibid., pp. 11, 15; S. Smirnov, "The Employment of Old-Age Pensioners in the U.S.S.R.," *International Labour Review* (July/August 1977):90; "Socio-Economic Policies for the Elderly: Questionnaire and Analytical Synthesis Report" (unpublished report of the Organisation for Economic Co-Operation and Development [OECD], Paris, May 19, 1980), pp. 10, 90, 93.

6. *Older Workers: Work and Retirement*, p. 56; "Socio-Economic Policies for the Elderly: Questionnaire," pp. 28, 31.

7. "Socio-Economic Policies for the Elderly: Questionnaire," p. 20.

8. *Elderly Norwegians* (Oslo: Norwegian Institute of Gerontology, November 1979).

9. Kenuchi Furuya and Linda G. Martin, "Employment and Retirement of Older Workers in Japan" (Tokyo: Nihon University, Population Research Institute, December 1981), p. 3.

10. Ervin Kisfaludi, "Work After Retirement," *Implications for Social Security of Research on Aging and Retirement* (Geneva: International Social Security Association, 1977), p. 57.

11. Aage Valbak, "The Responsibility of the Labor Market Towards the Elderly," *OS-Information*, No. 2 (1979).

12. OECD, *Socio-Economic Policies for the Elderly* (Paris, 1979), p. 20.

13. *Washington Post*, July 16, 1979.

14. International Benefits Information Service, April 22, 1982, p. 7.

15. *Wall Street Journal*, February 27, 1978.

16. "Socio-Economic Policies for the Elderly: Questionnaire," p. 49.

17. Shiro Sekiguchi, "The Problems Faced in the Japanese Industrial Workplace" (paper presented at a seminar, sponsored by the Japan Society, on The Aging Labor Force: Implications for Japan and the U.S., New York, June 6, 1980).

18. Ibid.

19. Ibid.

20. *Older Workers: Work and Retirement*, p. 53.

21. A. G. Soloviev, "The Employment of Pensioners in the National Economy of the U.S.S.R.," *International Social Security Review*, No. 2 (1980):157.

22. *Socio-Economic Policies for the Elderly*, p. 42.

23. *Adjustment Groups* (Stockholm: AMS National Labour Market Board, May 1978), p. 5.

24. Ibid., p. 11; *Employment for Handicapped Persons* (Stockholm: Ministry of Labor, 1978), p. 44.

25. I. Eliasson, "How to Provide Work for the Disabled During a Recession" (paper

presented at the ILO European Symposium on Work for the Disabled, Stockholm, 1980), p. 123.

26. *Socio-Economic Policies for the Elderly*, p. 42.

27. Ibid., p. 39.

28. "Socio-Economic Policies for the Elderly: Questionnaire," p. 34.

29. Yasuyuki Nodera, "Japanese Employment Policies for Older Workers," *Aging and Work* (Spring 1981):104.

30. "Socio-Economic Policies for the Elderly: Questionnaire," p. 31.

31. *Socio-Economic Policies for the Elderly*, p. 53.

32. Ibid., pp. 38–39.

33. Soloviev, "Employment of Pensioners," p. 158.

34. "Socio-Economic Policies for the Elderly: Questionnaire," p. 31.

35. Ibid.

36. *Socio-Economic Policies for the Elderly*, p. 53.

37. *Nihon Keizai Shimbun* (November 26, 1979).

38. Ibid.

39. Ibid.

40. Ibid.

41. Ibid.

42. *Japan Report*, September 16, 1979.

43. Shiro Sekiguchi, "How Japanese Business Treats Its Older Workers," *Management Review* (October 1980):17.

44. *Older Workers: Work and Retirement*, p. 60.

45. *Infor Senior* (December 1980).

46. United Nations, "Problems of Employment and Occupation of Older Workers," Report of the International Labour Organisation for the World Assembly on Aging (A/Conf. 113/15, February 17, 1982, p. 21.

47. See, for example, Stephen Griew, *Job Re-Design* (Paris: OECD, 1964); G. Marbach, *Job Redesign for Older Workers* (Paris; OECD, 1968).

48. *Employment for Handicapped Persons*, p. 34.

49. Dmitri F. Chebotarev and Nina N. Sachuk, "A Social Policy Directed Toward the Health and Welfare of the Aged in the Soviet Union," *Journal of the American Geriatrics Society 27*, No. 2 (Febuary 1979):55; Soloviev, "Employment of Pensioners," p. 156.

50. David Atar, "Aging in Kibbutz Society," *Gerontology* (June-August 1975).

51. Sekiguchi, "How Japanese Business Treats Its Older Workers," p. 17.

52. Ibid.

53. Masako Osako, "How Japanese Firms Are Coping with the Effects of an Aging Labor Force on Industrial Productivity," *Aging and Work* 5, No. 1 (1982):24.

54. Ibid.; Leon F. Koyl, *Employing the Older Worker* (Washington, D.C.: National Council on Aging, 1974).

55. Uri Leviatan, "To Whom to Be Grateful, Whom to Bless: Work and Labor," *And You Reached Old Age* (1977).

56. Soloviev, "Employment of Pensioners," pp. 159–160.

57. Toshi Kii, "Status Changes of the Elderly in Japan's Legal, Family and Economic Institutions," in Charlotte Nusberg and Masako Osako (eds.), *The Situation of the Asian-Pacific Elderly* (Washington, D.C.: International Federation on Ageing, 1981), pp. 78–81.

58. *Socio-Economic Policies for the Elderly*, p. 53.

59. Sekiguchi, "How Japanese Business Treats Its Older Workers," p. 17.

60. Courtesy of the Teijin Mihara Kosan Company, Mihara, Japan 1981.

61. Courtesy of Yehudit King, Authority for Pensioners and the Aged, Jerusalem, 1981.

62. *Soviet Life* (September 1978).

63. Soloviev, "Employment of Pensioners," p. 160.

64. "Work Beyond Retirement: Two Experiences in Britain and Holland," *Ageing International* 4, No. 4 (Winter 1977):15–17.

65. Soloviev, "Employment of Pensioners," pp. 158–159.

66. *Senior* (May 1979).

67. *Presse-und Informationsdienst des KDA* (October/November 1979):10–12.

68. Engelen-Kefer, "Managing the Older Worker Out of the Labor Market," p. 48.

69. *Employment for Handicapped Persons*, p. 15.

70. Ibid., p. 18.

71. T. H. Oakman, "Work Centres for the Elderly," *Elderly Mind* (reprinted in *Opus*, Summer 1974).

72. "To Be Is To Do," *Ageing International*, 5, No. 4 (Winter 1978):15–17.

73. "The Voluntary System in the Administration of Work Centres" (London: Employment Fellowship, undated).

74. Robert Gordon, H. B. Wright and F. Le Gros Clark, "Workshops for Retired Men and Women" (preliminary report, undated).

75. G. Boglietti, "Discrimination Against Older Workers and the Promotion of Equality of Opportunity," *International Labour Review* (October 1974):362.

76. *Older Workers: Work and Retirement*, p. 54.

77. Shingo Honma, "The Social Utilization of the Abilities of the Aged and the Free Employment Agency for the Aged," *Japanese Journal of Gerontology* (October 1978).

78. Saeko Murayama, "Programs and Services for the Japanese Elderly" (paper presented at the annual meeting of the Western Gerontological Society, San Diego, Calif., March 1976).

79. Yutaka Shimizu, "The Social Utilization of the Abilities of the Aged and the Senior Citizens Labor Corporation," *Japanese Journal of Gerontology* (October 1978).

80. *1979 Study of American Attitudes Toward Pensions and Retirement* (Harris Survey for Johnson & Higgins, New York).

81. *Aging in the Eighties: America in Transition* (Washington, D.C.: Harris Survey for National Council on the Aging, 1981).

82. U.S., Department of Labor, *Interim Report to Congress on Age Discrimination in Employment Act Studies* (Washington, D.C., 1981).

83. Smirnov, "Employment of Old Age Pensioners," p. 90.

84. Eliasson, "How to Provide Work to the Disabled During a Recession," p. 124.

3

Flexible Retirement

Charlotte Nusberg

Since the early 1970's many European countries have enacted legislation or included in their patterns of collective bargaining measures to expand workers' choice of age of retirement and ability to phase in the retirement period. These measures might also be considered part of a larger societal effort to break down the barriers between education, work, training, leisure and retirement, so that individuals throughout their lives are empowered to seek the solutions best adapted to their needs. Measures to increase the flexibility of the retirement age have not, however, always been brought about solely for such altruistic reasons. The hope that these measures might expand or contract the size of the labor force at particularly critical times in nations' economies has also been a factor.

There are a number of complementary approaches through which flexibility of retirement age is currently being enhanced. For example, individuals may be allowed to continue to work beyond the normal pensionable age (the age at which one usually becomes entitled to full pension benefits) because of personal preferences or in order to obtain the necessary credits to become eligible for a full old age pension. At the other end of the age scale, individuals may be permitted early retirement with actuarially reduced pension benefits, or even at full benefit levels, if they meet certain eligibility criteria. Finally, in order to alleviate the traumas sometimes associated with the sudden transition to full retirement, workers may also progressively reduce the number of hours worked over several years prior to the retirement age.

RETIREMENT AGES

The normal retirement age in industrialized countries, at which most first become eligible to draw full government-funded pension benefits, varies from a high of 67 in Norway, Denmark and Iceland to a low of 55 (for women) in Italy, Japan and many of the socialist countries of eastern Europe. Age 65 remains the most common pensionable age, however, even though in a number of countries, such as the United States and the Federal Republic of Germany, the majority of persons now retire before the normal pensionable age.[1] (See Table 3.1.)

The lower retirement age for women in many cases was chosen in recognition of the dual role many women play as both housewife and employee, and in the desire to permit both spouses to retire at about the same time. (It is assumed that men tend to marry women about five years younger than they are.)

Except in the United States and Japan, where steps have been taken to raise the retirement age, pressures for reducing the retirement age even further continue in industrialized countries, especially on the part of labor unions. To some extent policy-makers have been sympathetic to this demand among the young, but most governments are resisting these pressures because of mounting social security costs and increasingly adverse dependency ratios. Switzerland, in fact, had a nationwide referendum in which voters rejected a lowering of the retirement age.

An exception is France, which since April 1983 has permitted workers to retire starting at age 60 with the ability to draw the same size pension they formerly could only receive at age 65 (assuming they have met all the eligibility criteria).[2] A stringent retirement test is being imposed at the same time, and older persons will no longer have an opportunity to increase the size of their pensions if they defer their pensions and continue to work. This, in effect, decreases the flexibility of the retirement age by penalizing older persons who wish to remain employed.

Rather than lower the retirement age, most other governments have preferred to expand options available within their retirement packages to permit both earlier and later retirement. These options are described below.

POSSIBILITIES FOR EARLY RETIREMENT

Most industrialized countries do permit retirement three to five years before the normal retirement age with a 5–6 percent annual reduction in benefits.[3] However, in addition, some twenty countries (including a number in the developing world) also permit individuals to draw a full old age pension several years prior to the normal retirement age if contributions have been paid over a certain number of years (ranging from thirty-five to forty years in the industrialized countries).[4] In the Federal Republic of Germany, for example, one can retire at 63 with full benefits instead of the normal 65 if one has thirty-five years of contributions or insurance credits.[5]

Early retirement at full pension is also permitted in some forty countries, including Belgium, France and Japan, for workers who have been employed in arduous or hazardous occupations, such as mining or the maritime industry.[6]

Table 3.1
Normal Pensionable Ages in Selected Countries, by Sex, 1979

COUNTRY AND YEAR SYSTEM ENACTED	1979 Men	Women
Argentina (1944)	60(a)	55(a)
Australia (1908)	65	60
Austria (1906)	65	60
Belgium (1924)	65	60
Canada (1927)	65	65
Czechoslovakia (1906)	60	57
Denmark (1891)	67	62(b)
Finland (1937)	65	65
France (1910)	60	60
Germany (Democratic Republic) (1889)	65	60
Germany (Federal Republic) (1889)	65	65
Greece (1934)	65	60
Hungary (1929)	60	55
Iceland (1936)	67	67
Ireland (1908)	66	66
Italy (1919)	60(c)	55(c)
Japan (1941)	60	55
Luxembourg (1911)	65	60
Netherlands (1913)	65	65
New Zealand (1898)	60	60
Norway (1936)	67	67
Poland (1927)	65	60
Spain (1919)	65	65
Sweden (1913)	65	65
Switzerland (1946)	65	62
Union of Soviet Socialist Republics (1922)	60	55
United Kingdom (1909)	65	60
United States (1935)	65	65

(a.) Age 65 for self-employed men and 60 for self-employed
women.
(b.) For single women.
(c.) Pension payable at any age after 35 years of
contribution.

Source: Adapted from Thomas G. Staples, The Pensionable Age
          in Selected Industrialized Countries, HEW SSA Research
          and Statistics Note No. 15, August 26, 1977.

The number of years that one can retire early in the industrialized countries ranges from five in France and Japan to one in Belgium.[7] A minimum number of years of contributions is usually required.

Early retirement at full pension is also provided in countries such as Austria, France, Sweden, the Federal Republic of Germany and Denmark (and twenty-five others) for partial disability, whether or not it is work related.[8] Germany chose this policy option over early retirement for persons who had worked in arduous occupations because of the difficulties involved in identifying such occupations.[9] Early retirement because of "unfitness" to work avoids the prob-

lem of determining whether or not this unfitness was related to a particular occupation and proving the nature of past jobs held.

Because of heavy unemployment, several countries, such as France, Belgium
and the United Kingdom, are permitting workers to retire as early as age 60
and, in France, even at age 55, at about 70 percent of former gross wages if,
besides surrendering their jobs, they do not take on any other kind of work.[10]
The hope is to open up jobs for the young unemployed. In the case of France,
these benefits are indexed twice a year for inflation and provide income almost
equivalent to the net wages forgone. At the normal retirement age of 65, these
early retirees are still eligible for a full pension which in some cases is actually
less than what they have been receiving through their "guarantee of resources."[11] (In the case of France, this "guarantee of resources" policy expired in 1983, when what is equivalent to a reduced retirement age came into
effect.) France, Belgium and the United Kingdom also require employers to fill
the vacancy from the ranks of the younger unemployed. (The new hiree need
not perform the same job.)[12] Not as many individuals as expected have taken
advantage of these retirement opportunities, because of the financial penalty they
impose in some cases and because of fears among older workers about escalating inflation.[13]

Several countries also permit older workers, who are commonly within one
to five years of retirement and have been unemployed for long periods of time—
usually a year or more—to convert their unemployment benefits to an old age
pension.[14] Sometimes the amount is equal to a full pension, and sometimes it
is higher than the unemployment benefit but lower than the full pension, to which
they are still entitled when they reach the normal pensionable age (usually 65).
These pensions, too, are paid on condition that no other employment is taken.

Finland and France have set the age of entitlement for early retirement in
case of unemployment as early as 55—usually on condition of accepting no
other employment. In Denmark, persons aged 55 or older who are deemed to
be excluded from the labor market for special social or occupational reasons
may also choose early retirement; these pensions are means-tested and subject
to review every two years until age 60.

In Denmark, the interim payment between the time unemployment benefits
have expired and the full pension becomes payable (at age 67) is called the
"after-wage" (*efterløon*) and can be drawn at the same rate as the unemployment benefit for a period of two years.[15] (The unemployment benefit corre-
sponds to 70–90 percent of the former salary.) Thereafter, the amount is scaled
down gradually until the pensionable age is reached. A condition of receiving
the "after-wage" is that the recipient not work more than 200 hours a year.
One of the reasons for the introduction of this payment was a desire to provide
an option for early retirement which provided a greater income than would be
obtained by simply awarding the pension at an earlier age at actuarially reduced
levels.

While as many as 30 percent of eligible older workers in France have taken advantage of these early retirement schemes—either through voluntary surrender of their jobs or because of unemployment, the evidence to date suggests minimal impact on unemployment rates for younger people, not only in France but in other countries as well.[16] In the Netherlands, only 25 percent of the vacated jobs have been filled by persons from the unemployment rolls.[17] Employers have, in effect, used these schemes as a form of job attrition during a time of recession. In many cases, the vacated positions have simply been abolished.

POSSIBILITIES FOR POSTPONING RETIREMENT

During the 1960's, when the economies of most industrialized countries were prospering and even suffering from labor shortages, many countries enacted provisions to encourage older workers to postpone their retirement by offering them supplements to their pensions for each year they deferred drawing them. The supplements now range from a low 3 percent (United States) to a high 12.5 percent (Finland) annual increase in the benefits otherwise payable at the normal pensionable age.[18] (The U.S. supplement will be gradually increased to 8 percent between the years 1990 and 2010.) Usually, pensions can only be deferred for a certain number of years.

However, in the first comparative study done on the effectiveness of such retirement deferral credits, researcher Martin Tracy suggests they have not been notably successful in encouraging workers to remain in the labor force.[19] In countries where pensions provide adequate replacement income, those who remain in the labor force tend to do so for non-economic reasons. And in countries other than the United States a major disincentive to the less affluent to continue in work despite generous retirement deferral credits is the mandatory retirement practices still in effect in many private firms. This affects both eligibility criteria for the receipt of a private pension and the availability of jobs. This is not to suggest that retirement deferral credits are useless as a policy tool, but that other factors influencing the decision to work must also be examined and perhaps changed at the same time if the goal is to encourage more people to postpone their retirement.

The more mature the retirement system, also the less likely a country is to impose a retirement test to determine eligibility for obtaining pension benefits after the normal pensionable age is reached.[20] The trend over time, in fact, has been to relax such work restrictions. The more old age pensions come to be looked on as a right rather than as insurance against loss of earnings, the less likely there are to be any retirement tests. Examples of countries with no retirement tests following the normal pensionable age include the Federal Republic of Germany, New Zealand, the Netherlands, and Canada. However, the private pensions systems in some of these countries do impose a retirement test—in effect serving as a disincentive for continuing in work even though publicly supported benefits are not jeopardized. Again, as with supplements awarded for deferring retirement, the absence of retirement tests is not by itself a sufficient incentive to encourage large numbers of older persons to continue to work—at least not in countries where pensions are relatively generous. The more generous the retirement benefits, the more likely individuals will have to be motivated to remain in the labor force by the psychological pleasures derived from work.

The experience of eastern Europe has been somewhat different. Here nations have intentionally and with some success manipulated retirement tests as a tool of national manpower policy in order to encourage pensioners to remain in the labor force. Many of the eastern European countries suffer severe labor shortages and pay rather meager pensions. Since the mid–1960's countries like the U.S.S.R. have gradually expanded the number of occupations that are either completely or largely free of retirement tests.[21] In some cases, all workers in certain geographical regions, such as Siberia, are exempted from retirement tests. This means that pensioners can work full-time and draw full retirement benefits at the same time. Hungary has even gone one step further and waived the payment of taxes on earnings of pensioners in certain jobs.[22]

The result in the U.S.S.R. has been to increase labor force participation by persons of pensionable age from about 10 percent in the mid 1960's to 24 percent in 1975.[23] (This compares to a labor force participation rate of 16.2 percent for persons 65 or older in the United States in 1975).[24] However, Russian gerontologists believe they have reached the limit in the numbers that can be persuaded to remain in the labor force through financial incentives of this sort.[25] If more older people are to be encouraged to remain in the labor force, it is believed greater emphasis must be placed on measures such as job redesign and flexible work hours. It is mainly low-paid workers who are induced to stay on in the labor force through eliminating the retirement test; others must be appealed to by attractive working conditions and earnings. And, in any case, most incentives are not successful in inducing pensioners to return to the labor force once retired.

Finally, Japan is developing some unique solutions to its unusual situation of having the mandatory retirement age set by most firms precede the age of entitlement to publicly supported pension benefits by several years. (Until relatively recently, the common mandatory retirement age in private companies was 55, while the pensionable age was 60!) For example, a collective bargaining agreement was recently reached in Japan's steel industry permitting workers to continue in their jobs beyond age 58 (the normal retirement age for that industry); however, their earnings cannot exceed 80 percent of the pay received prior to age 58, even when they continue in the same job with the same responsibilities. This was considered a good compromise between the desirability of maintaining older workers in the labor force and the need of employers to reduce the high costs associated with older workers who have accumulated enough seniority to project them into the highest earnings groups.

OPPORTUNITIES FOR A GRADUAL RETIREMENT

Collective Bargaining

The shock that sudden and complete retirement from work can impose on older people is everywhere recognized as a risk with possibly very adverse consequences for the retirees' health. Increasingly, efforts are being made to provide opportunities to older workers to progressively reduce the number of hours worked in the hope that they will use their leisure time to develop activities that can be continued into retirement.

Most of these efforts are being arranged by individual firms through collective bargaining agreements, which usually provide for a reduction in work hours on a weekly, monthly or annual basis at less than a proportional reduction in pay—if a reduction takes place at all. The pattern varies with individual firms. For example, E. R. Squibb, in the United Kingdom, allows workers to shorten their work week by four hours during the first six months of the last year preceding retirement, and by one day a week during the second six-month period.[26] In addition, no worker is allowed overtime employment during the two years preceding retirement. A different kind of phased retirement was for many years offered by Gillette France.[27] At age 60, workers were allowed two additional weeks of vacation; at age 61, this was raised to four weeks; at age 62 to six weeks; at age 63 to twelve weeks; and at age 64 to twenty weeks.

In the Federal Republic of Germany, the pattern tends to be one of longer paid holidays for older workers, and in Norway, legislation was enacted several years ago entitling older workers, starting at age 60, to take an additional week of paid holidays a year.[28] This extra week is paid for by the National Social Security Institute, rather than by the employer, who must shoulder the burden in the above-mentioned examples from other countries.

In the first cross-national study of phased retirement opportunities provided in four European countries, the National Council for Alternative Work Patterns, which is based in the United States, found among the ten corporations it studied in 1981 that eligibility for such programs started anywhere from five years to one year before retirement.[29] Phased retirement was usually offered as a voluntary option to employees at little or no reduction in pay or benefits. And part-time workers remained eligible for full retirement benefits at the normal pensionable age. With the exception of some categories of workers, such as managers and senior level personnel, part-time workers largely stayed on in their same jobs. Not surprisingly, the large majority of eligible workers opted to take advantage of phased retirement opportunities. And they were using their leisure time not to find additional employment but in avocational pursuits, such as hobbies and travel. According to the anecdotal evidence, the impact on participants was positive. (No firms have conducted research on the cost/benefits of phased retirement.)

Employers, too, view phased retirement as a successful initiative. It has not resulted in severe scheduling or coverage problems; rather, it forces firms to plan ahead, which management considers to the good. Some firms are using phased retirement as a training mechanism by which they can pair older workers with their eventual replacements. The financial costs to firms so far have been low because older workers do not yet constitute a large part of most companies' labor forces. Many of the companies studied, in fact, had not even bothered to calculate the costs.

Phased retirement has so far not served to reduce unemployment (through new hiring for the hours reduced), nor has it resulted in the extension of employment for older workers beyond the normal retirement age. Phased retirement opportunities end at the pensionable age. What is not clear is whether the availability of phased retirement has permitted some older workers to continue in work when they would otherwise have been forced to take an early retirement.

Phased retirement programs in the private sector do not function in a vacuum vis-à-vis government policies. Efforts by government to stem unemployment, for example through financial incentives to older workers to retire early, have reduced participation in some phased retirement plans, which usually do not become available as early as these public "early-out" benefits. This has been particularly evident in France. And what is tantamount to reducing the retirement age in France to 60 starting in 1983 will make most French industries' phased retirement plans as presently structured obsolete, since the majority permit eligibility only at age 60 or older. Gillette France, one of the European pioneers in phased retirement, has already cancelled its program.[30]

Public Initiatives

The advantage, of course, of providing the opportunity for a gradual retirement through public rather than private initiatives is that the costs can be generalized over the whole economy, and firms which are not in a strong financial position can also offer this benefit to their workers, since they continue to pay for only the number of hours actually worked. Thus, more workers enjoy flexibility regarding their retirement age where phased retirement forms part of a national system. On the other hand, employers may experience less flexibility if they have to pay additional payroll taxes. This can have a differential impact on firms, however; employers with a large proportion of older workers will benefit more from a national system than firms with a younger work force, especially when, as in the case of Sweden discussed below, the system is financed through a tax on total payroll. This is because partial pensions are paid through public funds rather than by the employer. The cost of supporting a partial pension scheme may also be less than that of paying full disability benefits to older workers. Both Sweden and Norway have chosen this course by enacting legislation permitting the drawing of a partial pension by older workers choosing to work part-time. In the case of Sweden, the partial pension is payable up to five years before the normal retirement age, which is 65; in Norway, it is payable for up to three years after the pensionable age, which is age 67.

As the plan works in Sweden, all persons between the ages of 60 and 64 who are insured under the social security program and meet certain other criteria—they must also have been gainfully employed for at least five of the preceding twelve months and have been wage earners for at least ten years after the age of 45—are eligible to reduce their work hours up to seventeen hours a week and receive a partial pension equal to 50 percent of the gross earnings lost as a result of the transition to part-time employment.[31] (Partial pensioners still net upwards of 80 percent of their take-home pay.) Part-time employment must be organized in such a manner that the individual works at least one month out of two. Because individuals continue to make payroll contributions during their part-time employment, they remain eligible to draw a full pension if they choose to retire at the normal pensionable age of 65. The scheme is financed by a .5 percent tax on payroll, financed solely by employer contributions.

In Norway, workers, starting at age 67, can reduce their work to three-quarters, one-half or one-quarter time and draw a one-quarter, one-half or three-quarters partial pension respectively until age 70, provided this combined income does not exceed 80 percent of pre-retirement earnings.[32] In addition, individuals who postpone their retirement beyond age 67 are entitled to a 9 percent supplement to their pensions for any portion of the pension that is not taken out up to age 70. According to the legislation, an employer is obliged to provide part-time employment for eligible employees requesting it, if such employment is thought feasible by management.

Relatively few people have taken advantage of the partial pension scheme in Norway, probably for the following reasons: (1) not many part-time jobs have opened up; (2) some employers have actually lowered the mandatory retirement age from 70 to 67; (3) there are pressures from the workers' unions and colleagues to conform by taking advantage of early retirement benefits; and (4) there are pressures on the workers from labor and management to leave the labor force in order to open up jobs for the young. According to researcher Svein Olav Daatland, "Flexible retirement requires a formal and social right to work beyond the pensionable age. However, access to an old-age pension seems to weaken the moral claim to work and creates an obligation to retire, especially when unemployment is high."[33]

The Swedish experiment, on the other hand, has proven much more successful, perhaps pointing to the advisability of starting partial pension schemes prior, rather than subsequent, to the normal retirement age. Almost one-third of eligible workers have taken advantage of the partial pension option since its inception in 1976, mostly by reducing their work hours by half.[34] This is a larger number than was originally anticipated and has necessitated both an increase in employers' contributions and a reduction in the percentage of former earnings replaced.

Part-time jobs have opened up, and workers generally are performing the same kinds of work for the same employers as when they worked full-time—with the exception of those who were in supervisory functions.[35] Most choose to work alternate weeks. Many more managerial personnel are also now taking advantage of partial pensions than was first thought possible. The system has proven to be very adaptable.

The majority of part-time jobs have developed in the manufacturing sector, and especially in firms having a large proportion of older employees.[36] About half the employers did not make up for the number of hours lost by workers converting to part-time work; the evidence, in fact, suggests that partial pensions provided a convenient opportunity for employers to reduce their work force during a time of recession.

Most of the employers contacted about their expectations regarding the partial pension plan did not think their productivity would be adversely affected by the shift to part-time employment, although personnel planning would certainly be more difficult.[37] In fact, a number of employers thought productivity would improve because part-time workers, they believed, produced more per working hour.

Most important, "partial pensioners" seem to have a higher quality of life than their age peers not choosing this option.[38] The slight reduction in income has not produced any noticeable changes in household expenditures.[39] Partial pensioners also report greater life satisfaction and less anxiety about the transition to retirement. Finally, the health of partial pensioners may be declining more slowly than among age peers continuing to work full-time or disabled pensioners.[40] In fact, no serious negative consequences have resulted as a consequence of the introduction of the partial pension scheme.

Difficulties have been experienced, however, in implementing the partial pension legislation.[41] For example, how does one keep track of the time worked by the self-employed or calculate the hours worked for those paid on a piece-rate basis? Small firms may also have a more difficult time than large firms in opening up part-time job opportunities. And the availability of part-time jobs beyond the normal pensionable age of 65 is not great for those who wish to continue working. Despite such difficulties, Sweden considers the program highly successful and plans to expand it to workers not included in the original legislation.

Finally, France has recently introduced measures permitting certain public and private employers to offer half-time work to older workers, starting at age 55.[42] They can continue in such part-time work until age 65, although, starting in 1983, they will also become eligible for normal retirement benefits at age 60. These partial pensioners will be reimbursed 30 percent of gross wages through public funds, which, combined with their part-time salary gives them the equivalent of 80 percent of their former take-home pay.[43] However, these measures were introduced, in part, as an effort to reduce unemployment among the young, and employers are obliged to hire new workers to make up for the lost hours.

Phased retirement here is clearly being used as a tool of manpower policy. Elsewhere—for example in Norway and Sweden—partial pension options seem to have been implemented more as a social welfare measure to enhance the lives of older persons and provide more flexibility.

SOME POLICY IMPLICATIONS FOR THE UNITED STATES

The trend towards liberalizing opportunities for a flexible retirement has been accelerating in most industrialized countries and is likely to continue to do so in the future. Public opinion surveys in both the United States and Europe show that older workers are increasingly going to want flexibility at both ends of the retirement age scale, including possibilities for early retirement and postponing retirement.[44] Some express preferences for remaining in the same work, but at reduced hours; others would like opportunities to "recareer."

In light of these trends, the Committee of Ministers of the Council of Europe adopted a resolution in 1976 urging each member nation to guarantee its citizens freedom of choice regarding the setting of their retirement age; to provide citizens the possibility of choosing between retirement and work following the normal pensionable age; and to remove punitive measures affecting work beyond the pensionable age.[45] Such policies, it is believed, would be in the best interests of both the individual and society.

More recently, delegates at the 1979 and 1980 annual conferences of the International Labour Organisation approved the following principles relating to flexible retirement:[46]

- The transition from active life to retirement should be arranged so as to have no damaging or lasting effects.

- The decision to retire should be made a voluntary one, and the pensionable age more flexible.

- Provisions for mandatory retirement should be reexamined in light of the above.

- A special benefit should be paid in compensation for any reductions in work as a result of measures such as "phased retirement."

- An income should be guaranteed in the event of prolonged unemployment.

- Early retirement pensions should be granted under various circumstances, such as employment in arduous and unhealthy occupations.

- Older workers should be allowed to defer their claim to an old age pension.

Finally, the Commission of the European Economic Community (the Common Market) in 1980 urged member nations to set a minimum and a maximum age for separation from the labor force under such conditions that "choice is not unduly influenced by significant differences in the amounts of pensions."[47] It also recommended increased opportunities for phased retirement in order to increase freedom of choice.

The commission recognized, however, the possible need for countries to modify these guidelines depending on economic circumstances. Thus, in times of high unemployment, financial inducements could be offered to encourage earlier retirement; in times of full employment, the emphasis could be shifted to facilitating phased or gradual retirement. It was thought that such shifts in emphasis would be more easily reversible under a policy of flexible retirement than is presently the case under more rigid policies, where some nations must consider a shift in the "normal" retirement age in order to achieve economic goals. The commission's recommendations must now be considered by the Community's Council of Ministers.

The measures that have already been adopted by some countries to increase the flexibility of retirement are not without their problems. Provisions permitting earlier retirement under a variety of circumstances tend to create a new retirement norm and pressures on older workers from both colleagues and employers to take advantage of the earlier retirement possibilities. This, in turn, has its effect on middle-aged workers, who may begin to experience greater difficulties in finding employment or being promoted. Sweden has experienced some of these pressures in the aftermath of its partial pension scheme.[48] In the United States such a downward drift in labor force participation by men 45 and over has also been seen, resulting in part from the early retirement incentives now available.

Attempts to provide older workers with opportunities to progressively reduce their work hours, whether through a national scheme like Sweden's or through collective bargaining agreements, as in France, have been largely considered successful. However, a number of questions remain unanswered. For example, little is known about the kind of person that takes advantage of these opportunities. Someone whose leisure time is already well-filled is not really in as much need of assistance in dealing with the transition to retirement that reduced work hours were intended to provide as another might be. It is also not clear whether part-time work or progressively reduced work hours serve as a means of easing workers out of the labor force or permits them to remain in it longer.

The question also remains open—at least in the case of Sweden—whether enough part-time jobs can also be found under different economic circumstances to accommodate all those wishing to take advantage of partial pensions. So far, employers have been happy to provide part-time jobs because they allow work force reductions during periods of recession. Contrary to the Swedish experience, Norway has not been notably successful in finding part-time jobs for its retirees. This may, however, reflect the fact that Norway's partial pension is an entitlement available only after the normal pensionable age of 67 is reached at which time individuals may have to take lower-paying and lower status jobs in order to take advantage of the flexible retirement opportunity. In Sweden, on the other hand, older workers largely stay in their same jobs and simply reduce the number of hours worked—they are not yet considered pensioners.

Other unanswered questions surrounding reductions in work hours include ignorance about the most effective approaches for preparing for retirement. Are extensions in annual vacations starting at age 60 (provided in Norway) more effective than gradually reduced work hours on a daily, weekly or monthly basis? Of the latter options, which are the most effective? And at what age must one start introducing such options for the desired results to occur?

Finally, how do phased retirement opportunities become integrated with pre-retirement training? Can they, to some extent, serve as a substitute for such training?

Despite such unanswered questions, partial pensions and opportunities for progressive reductions in work hours remain some of the most innovative programs currently being undertaken to increase options for a flexible retirement. Encouraging opportunities for part-time work may also be a more desirable and cost-effective policy than broadening options for yet earlier retirement, which for many represents a form of disguised unemployment. Individuals who work part-time continue to pay taxes and make other payroll contributions and are less likely to experience the traumas sometimes associated with full retirement. However, more research on the impact of part-time work on both the employer and employee are needed if such programs are ever to be taken out of the experimental stage and become institutionalized in more countries.

If the majority of workers in the United States are ever to enjoy such opportunities as Swedish workers do through the partial pension option or such as many French workers have experienced through progressively reduced work hours at relatively little loss in pay, national legislation will probably be required. Too little of the labor force is unionized for progressive retirement options to become widely available through national collective bargaining agreements. And firms in a weaker financial position, in any case, would not be able to subsidize such opportunities for their workers. In order to develop an equitable flexible retirement program, such costs would have to be generalized over the entire economy.

For any partial pension scheme to be acceptable to most potential applicants, however, it is important that Social Security benefits not factor-in part-time earnings during the last few years preceding full retirement. If this were the case, working part-time during this crucial period could spell economic suicide for many pensioners. In the various European phased retirement plans, part-time workers retain the right to eligibility for a full pension at the normal retirement age even though their take-home pay has been reduced for a few years preceding retirement.

While in the United States the pensionable age will be raised to 67 by the year 2027, older worker employment can in the meantime be encouraged through more finely tuned measures and, at the same time, create improved opportunities for flexible retirement. For example, measures such as abolition of the retirement test or increases in the supplement to Social Security benefits (earlier than 1990) for each year that retirement is deferred might persuade some older workers to remain in the labor force. In countries where pensions are inadequate and mandatory retirement non-existent, eliminating the retirement test has been credited with persuading significant numbers of low-income workers to postpone their retirement.

Similarly, while the size of the supplement paid for deferring an old age pension seems to have had little influence in encouraging workers of pensionable age to remain in the labor force in other countries, this may be explained in part by the existence of mandatory retirement practices and retirement tests in private industry, which serve as significant disincentives to labor force participation—no matter how generous the supplement. The United States is unique among western industrialized nations in having postponed the possibility of mandatory retirement for most workers until age 70. Because of the lack of countervailing disincentives on the part of private industry in the United States higher pension deferral credits here might serve as a useful incentive to older persons to postpone their retirement.

The experience of eastern Europe, and particularly the U.S.S.R., however, has been that there is just so far that one can go in encouraging individuals of pensionable age to remain in the labor force through financial incentives such as abolishing the retirement test. In the U.S.S.R. the ceiling seems to be about 28 percent of the population eligible for retirement benefits. Russian gerontologists attribute this to the fact that it is primarily the low-income elderly who will be attracted to the labor force through financial incentives; those who are financially more secure are attracted by other factors, such as the nature of the job, the working conditions and the opportunity for flexible hours. Thus, if the policy goal is to keep larger proportions of older workers in the labor force, efforts should probably also be directed to measures which increase the attractiveness of jobs for persons who cannot be reached by economic incentives alone.

Just as the United States has not been notably innovative in pursuing measures which might prolong older worker participation in the labor force—with the exception of raising the mandatory retirement and pensionable ages—it provides few options for early retirement short of accepting actuarially reduced benefits. Measures such as providing full pensions earlier than the normal retirement age for those who have worked in arduous occupations or contributed over a requisite number of years to the social security system are quite common in other countries. There is no question that such measures are costly, but these costs are justified on the grounds of humanitarianism. And to some extent, there is a trade-off between granting such early pensions and having to provide means-tested welfare benefits, which may carry a stigma for potential recipients, or more costly disability and medical benefits.

Similarly, in several countries an older worker who has been unemployed for a year or more can convert the unemployed benefits to an old age pension. In a few countries, older workers are even encouraged to surrender their jobs to the young unemployed in exchange for early pensions. While providing the unemployed older worker with a pension to replace expired unemployment benefits is certainly a humanitarian measure, it also serves as an excuse to stop aggressive job searches by older workers. Nonetheless, this solution provides a more generous alternative than neither providing any kind of benefits nor helping the older worker find a job, which is often the case in the United States.

While pension policy has major long-range consequences on labor force participation rates, the use of pension policy as a short-range manpower tool should be regarded as very risky. In itself, pension policy is not a very flexible manpower instrument. Because of its political sensitivity, it cannot be changed easily, to respond rapidly and selectively to labor shortages or surpluses. It is also a relatively blunt economic instrument. While changes in pension policy usually do have some effect on employment rates, these are highly unpredictable and do not necessarily bring about the results desired. In the meantime, a country may have saddled itself with a very expensive policy that becomes politically difficult to reverse. While pension policy can indeed serve as a crude manpower tool, this use should usually be subordinated to its primary goal of providing income security in old age and, increasingly, flexibility as to retirement age.

Over the years, the United States certainly has taken steps to provide older workers with expanded options for setting their own retirement ages, and in the case of mandatory retirement it has been a leader in easing the constraints imposed by such a policy. Nevertheless, the United States has not been as adventurous as some other industrialized countries in exploring the other options implied in a truly flexible retirement policy, raising the question of whether flexible retirement is, in fact, a major U.S. policy goal. If it is, the United States should investigate and learn from the experiences of other countries, some of which are experimenting with novel alternatives.

NOTES

1. Martin Tracy, *Retirement Age Practices in Ten Industrialized Countries, 1960–1976*, p. 77.

2. "International Benefits Information Service" (newsletter) April 22, 1982, p. 7.

3. *Older Workers: Work and Retirement* (Geneva: ILO, 1979), p. 69.

4. Martin Tracy, "World Developments and Trends in Social Security," *Social Security Bulletin* (April 1976):18; and Martin Tracy, "Flexible Retirement Features Abroad," *Social Security Bulletin* (May 1978):23.

5. Tracy, "Flexible Retirement Features Abroad," p. 27.

6. United Nations, *Income Maintenance and Social Protection of the Older Person: Income Security for the Elderly*, report of the International Labour Organisation for the World Assembly on Aging (A/Conf. 113/17, March 3, 1982), p. 6.

7. Tracy, "Flexible Retirement Features Abroad," p. 23.

8. *Older Workers: Work and Retirement*, p. 67.

9. Ibid., p. 66.

10. International Benefits Information Service, December 17, 1981, p. 3.

11. Constance Swank, *Phased Retirement: The European Experience*.

12. Lois S. Copeland, "New Retirement-Age Features in Belgium," *Social Security Bulletin* (July 1977):1; and Tracy, "Flexible Retirement Features Abroad," pp. 26, 35.

13. *New York Times*, December 5, 1977; and Age Concern England, *Information Circular* (January and April 1978).

14. Tracy, "Flexible Retirement Features Abroad," p. 25.

15. Henning Friis, "Social Programmes for the Aged in Denmark," *EURAG Newsletter* (June 1980):4–5.

16. Swank, *Phased Retirement*.

17. *Leeftijd* (July/August 1981):25.

18. U.S., Department of Health and Human Services, Social Security Administration, *Social Security Programs Throughout the World, 1979*, Research Report No. 54 (Washington, D.C.: Government Printing Office, 1980), p. 97.

19. Tracy, *Retirement Age Practices*, p. 97.

20. Elizabeth Kirkpatrick, "The Retirement Test: An International Study," *Social Security Bulletin* (July 1974):3–5.

21. Stephen Sternheimer, "Retirement and Aging in the Soviet Union: Who Works, Who Doesn't and What Can Be Done About It" (paper presented at the American Association for the Advancement of Slavic Studies, New Haven, Conn., October 11, 1979), p. 27.

22. Ervin Kisfaludi, "Work After Retirement," *Implications for Social Security of Research on Aging and Retirement* (Geneva: International Social Security Association, 1977), p. 53.

23. Murray Feshbach, "Structure and Composition of the Soviet Industrial Labor Force," *USSR in the 1980s* (Brussels: NATO, 1978), p. 59, cited in Sternheimer, "Retirement and Aging in the Soviet Union," p. 7.

24. *Yearbook of Labor Statistics, 1975* (Geneva: ILO, 1981), p. 27.

25. Sternheimer, "Retirement and Aging in the Soviet Union," pp. 27–28.

26. Council of Europe, *Preparation for Retirement* (Soc. 76, 4–E, Strasbourg, France, 1977), p. 10.

27. Ibid.

28. Ibid., p. 9.

29. Swank, *Phased Retirement*.

30. Communication from R. Pinard of Gillette France (Annecy, Switzerland) to the National Council for Alternative Work Patterns, May 17, 1982.

31. Göran Crona, "Experience of the Swedish Partial Retirement Scheme," October 1980, pp. 2–3, 5.

32. Svein Olav Daatland, "Ideals and Realities Concerning Gradual Retirement" (paper presented at a symposium on Society, Stress and Disease: Aging and Old Age, Stockholm, June 1976), p. 5.

33. Svein Olav Daatland, "Flexible Retirement in Industrial Companies," *Aging and Work* (Summer 1980):181.

34. Göran Crona, "Partial Retirement in Sweden" (paper presented at the 12th International Congress of Gerontology, Hamburg, West Germany, July 1981), p. 10.

35. Göran Crona, "Partial Retirement in Sweden—Developments and Experiences" (paper presented at the 9th World Congress of Sociology, Uppsala, Sweden, August 1978), p. 16.

36. Crona, "Experience of the Swedish Partial Retirement Scheme," p. 7.

37. "Evolution of the Partial Retirement Scheme," *International Social Security Review* No. 2, (1979):204.

38. Crona, "Partial Retirement in Sweden," pp. 14–20.

39. Crona, "Experience of the Swedish Partial Retirement Scheme," p. 7.

40. Ibid., p. 6.

41. Lars-Ake Ästrom, *Gradual Transition from Full-Time Work to Retirement with Income Deriving in Part from Reduced Pensions*, (Geneva: International Social Security Association, IVS/X/2, October 7, 1977) pp. 9–10.

42. "Nouvelle Possibilité de Pré-Retraite," *La Voix du Retraité* (April 1981):8.

43. "Contrats de Solidarité: 3ème Contrat: Aide au départ progressif à 55 ans," *B.H. No. 14* (April 8, 1982.)

44. *1979 Study of American Attitudes Toward Pensions and Retirement* (commissioned by Johnson & Higgins); and *The Attitude of the Working Population to Retirement* (Brussels: Commission of the European Community, May 1978).

45. Social Security Measures to Be Taken in Favour of Pensioners and Persons Remaining in Activity After Pensionable Age, Resolution (76)32, adopted by the Committee of Ministers, Council of Europe, Strasbourg, France, May 21, 1976.

46. "The 65th Session of the International Labour Conference, June, 1979," *International Labour Review* 118, No. 6 (November/December 1979):667; and "The 66th Session of International Labour Conference, June, 1980," *International Labour Review* 119, No. 6 (November/December 1980):668.

47. "Community Guidelines on Flexible Retirement" (Brussels: Commission of the European Communities, July 14, 1980).

48. Crona, "Experience of the Swedish Partial Retirement Scheme," p. 7.

4

Health Care

Charlotte Nusberg

The industrialized countries of the world share remarkably similar profiles with regard to the health and health care needs of their older populations. Despite popular stereotypes to the contrary, the large majority of the elderly are reasonably healthy and lead independent lives. They do tend, however, to suffer from chronic conditions of various kinds. In Australia and Finland, for example, 78 percent of the non-institutionalized elderly report one or more chronic conditions.[1] The presence of several chronic conditions simultaneously often makes accurate diagnosis and treatment difficult. In addition, older people often suffer from both "underdiagnosis" and "overdiagnosis."[2] This refers to a propensity of some older people not to seek treatment for particular conditions in the belief that these conditions are somehow part of the normal aging process and, conversely, the tendency of some doctors to overtreat older patients in the belief that symptoms of normal aging are pathological in nature. Factors such as these are increasingly making medical treatment of the elderly a special concern among health care professionals.

While the large majority of older people are in good or reasonably good health, a significant minority requires intensive care. Approximately 3–5 percent of the population 65 and older are in some form of skilled nursing facility in most western industrialized countries.[3] A similar, if not greater, proportion of older persons experiencing comparable levels of disability can be found still living in the community, largely through the assistance of their families. A cross-national study involving Denmark, Britain, Israel, Poland, Yugoslavia and the United States found that 2–4 percent of the non-institutionalized elderly are bedfast and 12–24 percent are housebound and ambulate with difficulty.[4] Of this number, perhaps 4–8 percent require a great deal of personal assistance.[5] The remainder—approximately 70–80 percent of the older population—are ambulatory and need minimal assistance.[6]

In large part it is this minority of older persons with intensive health care needs that accounts for the large proportion of national health budgets devoted to the elderly. In Norway and Finland, for example, one-half of health care resources are spent on older people.[7] In Denmark, New Zealand, Norway and the United Kingdom, at any one time, approximately one-half of the hospital beds will be occupied by older people.[8] In Sweden, this proportion rises to two-thirds.[9] The experience of Eastern European countries is that the need for hospital care among persons 60 and older is three times higher than that for the entire population, and their need for medical care is 50 percent higher than that for middle-aged persons.[10] In Denmark older people consume physician services at a 25–35 percent higher rate than younger people, and in almost all countries, older people account for the majority of the clientele of home nursing services.[11]

TYPES OF HEALTH CARE FINANCING SYSTEMS AND COVERAGE

Unlike the United States, most countries provide health care to their older people through the same system which serves all age groups, whether it be a national health service, a national insurance program, private insurance programs, voluntary sick funds or a public welfare program. National health services or insurance programs predominate in the large majority of industrialized countries. National insurance programs, financed largely through employer/employee contributions, exist in twenty-three of the market economies, while national health services, funded through general revenues, prevail in fourteen other industrialized countries, mainly the socialist nations, but also the United Kingdom and Italy.[12] Integrating the elderly into national systems is thought both to be more efficient and to entail less risk of segregating the elderly from the general welfare of the nation. Such policies are pursued even though health care contributions by the elderly, if required at all, fall well below the costs of their protection.[13] The philosophy underlying such national health care financing systems can be summarized in a statement made about the Swedish national insurance program: "The basic principle of health services in Sweden is the egalitarian principle—to give care to everybody whenever necessary in a system where the need for medical care is the entrance ticket to the system."[14]

However, the fact that a country has a generally good national health service or insurance program does not necessarily guarantee adequacy of services, knowledge by the consumer of benefits available, equitable distribution of services or comprehensive coverage of health care needs. Several—if not all—of these issues remain unresolved in most of the developed countries. Shortages in health care facilities and in trained personnel, especially with regard to the needs of the aged, exist practically everywhere.

Each form of health care coverage has its particular advantages and disadvantages. National health services and insurance programs do seem to provide more adequate coverage to their populations, however, than do private insurance programs. It was the inability or unwillingness of private insurance companies in the United States to provide good coverage for the elderly that led to the adoption of Medicare. And in Israel until 1975, the voluntary "sick funds" tended to reject applicants who might place a heavy financial burden on the system; this, of course, worked most against the elderly.

Many countries have a combination of health care financing systems, although one tends to predominate. Health care—at least under national insurance schemes—is often delivered by a combination of public and private resources.

While older people in other countries are usually covered by the same health care financing system as everyone else, recognition of their low-income status and unusually high need for medical services has led some countries to adopt special provisions applicable only to pensioners. For example, in the United Kingdom and Poland, pensioners can obtain medications at no charge.[15] Ireland enacted legislation in 1982 entitling pensioners to a full range of health services at no out-of-pocket expense, including a general practitioner of their choice, medications, appliances, and hospital, dental, ophthalmic, aural, and other specialist services.[16] In addition, many of the countries with national health insurance systems have exempted pensioners from further contributions upon retirement. This practice is beginning to change, however, under the pressure of rising costs. The Federal Republic of Germany, for example, since 1983 has required pensioners to bear part of their health insurance costs.[17]

Special measures directed towards the elderly also arise from a recognition of the more demanding nature of health problems among the aged. Thus the United Kingdom pays its general practitioners a higher fee for treating patients over age 65, on the assumption that they require more of the doctors' time and attention.[18] The fee is increased yet further for patients over age 75. This practice is thought to result in improved patient care for older people. Similarly, hospitals in New Zealand are provided with a higher daily benefit for geriatric long-term care patients in recognition of the heavier nursing load required.[19]

Table 4.1 summarizes some of the major provisions of medical coverage for the aged in selected industrialized countries. (A number of the provisions also apply to the population at large.)

The fact that patients must pay a fee for ambulatory services in countries such as the United States, France and some provinces of Canada, even though they may be partially or fully reimbursed later on, probably reduces access to health services for low-income older persons. And several countries, such as France, are beginning to raise the proportion of the fee paid by the patient as a cost-saving measure, despite research evidence suggesting that substantial increases in cost sharing reduce demand for health care disproportionately among the economically disadvantaged, who tend to be in poorer health to begin with.[20] In the long run such policies may lead to increased use of hospitals to treat

Table 4.1
**Patterns of Provision of Medical Care to the Aged in Various Countries,
by Payment at Point of Delivery**

COUNTRY	AMBULATORY CARE	HOSPITAL CARE	PRESCRIPTION DRUGS	DENTAL CARE	MEDICAL APPLIANCES
United Kingdom	No payment	No payment	No payment	Contribution at the rate of 50% of costs, up to a ceiling	Loaned by voluntary organizations or at a low price; spectacles without payment, up to a ceiling
Germany	No payment	No payments for 78 weeks every 3 years for the same disease, in a class C hospital	No payment	Contribution at the rate of 1/3 of the costs	Various rates of contribution in different sick funds
France	Full payment	First month 20%; over 30 days or expensive care-- no payment.	Full payment and reimbursement of 70% of the price, or 90% of the price of expensive drugs.		
Poland	No payment	No payment	No payment	No payment	No payment
Yugoslavia	No payment	No payment	Contribution at different rates in the various republics; no payment in Serbia	Contribution at different rates in the various republics; no payment in Serbia	Contribution at different rates in the various republics

Canada	No payment or payment with reimbursement of 85-90% at standard rates	No payment or nominal payment ($1 per day for hospitalization in British Columbia)	No payment in only two provinces	No payment in only one province; full payment in others	Varies among provinces
United States a) Medicare	No payment, or reimbursement at standard rates	Nominal payment for 60 days hospitalization for any disease; a smaller payment for 30 additional days. Partial coverage of physician's fees	Full payment only if hospitalized	Partial reimbursement	Full or partial coverage depending on circumstances
b) Medicaid	No payment	No payment	No payment	Varies from state to state	Varies from state to state
Israel	No payment; partial payment for house calls	No payment	Nominal payment of I£ 1 for each drug prescribed	Full payment	Full payment

Source: Adapted from Abraham Doron, Social Services for the Aged in Eight Countries (Jerusalem: Brookdale Institute of Gerontology and Adult Human Development, 1979).

diseases that might better have been treated at an earlier stage. Undesirable consequences of this sort are considered especially likely among low-income older people, who are more prone to use expensive hospital services which are available to them at no out-of-pocket expense, than the more appropriate primary care services, for which they must pay a fee.[21]

Partly from a desire to avert consequences of this sort, a number of countries, such as the United Kingdom and Poland, require no payment by patients at the point of health care delivery, whether for ambulatory or hospital services. The increasing costs of health care, however, are creating pressures in some countries to introduce an element of cost sharing, even among pensioners. Japan, for example, where until recently all medications and medical care were free of charge to persons over age 70, now requires a small co-payment.[22]

Health care systems also differ in the extent of their coverage of needs. In Sweden, medical aids of various kinds, including their repair and maintenance, are available free of charge simply on the basis of need. In the United Kingdom, the National Health Service makes prescription drugs, optical and aural equipment, dental care, and chiropody available to the elderly at little or no charge. In the United States, none of these items is covered under Medicare unless related to a hospital stay.

Long-term care, whether in institutions or the community, is another area where health care systems in different countries diverge. In the United States Medicare coverage for either nursing home or community care is very limited, and one must be pauperized before Medicaid begins to cover nursing home care. At the other extreme are countries like the Netherlands, where the Exceptional Medical Expenses Compensation Act covers many forms of institutional care for both mental and physical infirmities from the day of admission, regardless of the individual's income. Individuals are asked to contribute part of their pensions towards their care in nursing homes only after the first six months of residence.[23] This coverage is financed through a payroll tax of about 3 percent a year paid entirely by employers. In France, nursing home or retirement home residents are expected to pay for or contribute towards their room and board; their health care, however, is picked up by health insurance.[24] Other European countries charge according to ability to pay for institutional care, but in no circumstances are all the individuals' savings or entire pensions forfeited. And in New Zealand and Denmark, no one must dispose of his or her assets in order to obtain quality long-term care.[25] In Denmark, at most, nursing home residents with savings have to pay 60 percent of their interest income towards their care, but their assets remain intact.[26]

Long-term care through community health services, such as home nursing and day hospitals, is also usually available to individuals at little or no out-of-pocket expense in many of the industrialized countries.[27] The social care services, on the other hand, such as home help assistance, are usually available on a graduated fee basis, based on ability to pay, but some jurisdictions, such as the provinces of Saskatchewan and Manitoba in Canada, also provide these free, in the belief that they are crucial to keeping individuals out of more costly hospitals and nursing homes.[28]

Along the same lines, Israel recently enacted legislation establishing eligibility for "nursing" insurance for any person entitled to old age or survivors' benefits.[29] As yet the term "nursing" insurance has no specific meaning, and it may eventually be interpreted to cover all aspects of long-term care. The specific nature and extent of benefits is now being determined by a national commission appointed for the purpose. The collection of .2 percent of the social security wage base has already been started in order to build up a reserve fund for the "nursing" needs of Israel's rapidly growing older population.

Just a brief word about the costs of national health insurance systems or health services which seem to provide more generous coverage and benefits than is the case in the United States. A national health service or insurance system is not necessarily more expensive than one essentially run under private auspices, as in the United States. Of the industrialized countries, very few come close to spending the same proportion of their gross national product (GNP) on health care as does the United States which in 1981 spent 9.8 percent of its GNP on health care.[30] The United Kingdom, for example, whose national health service is the largest employer in Western Europe, spends less of its GNP on its health service than does the United States for health care, yet indicators of health status on most measures are comparable, if not better, than in the United States.[31] The fact that health care is free at the point of delivery has not resulted in abuses, such as large numbers of unwarranted physician visits.[32] Cost controls are obtained, however, by limiting the number of health facilities available. This results in reduced ability to meet non-emergency needs and long waiting lists.

Similarly, Canada, which has a national health insurance system, kept its health care costs virtually stable at about 7 percent of GNP during the 1970's.[33] Cost savings result, in part, from greater efficiency. For example, administrative costs for Canada's national health care program come to less than 3 percent of total costs, while comparable figures in the United States run about 10 percent.[34] Greater rationalization could also be obtained in the sharing of services, the appropriate use of new technologies, and the expanded use of generic drugs. And during this time, measures of health status improved.[35] Infant mortality was sharply reduced and life expectancy continued to improve. (Life expectancy is about two years longer for all ages than it is in the United States.)

COMMUNITY HEALTH SERVICES

The array of community health services serving the elderly is great. They range from payments to family members and neighbors who care for an older person to "hospitals-at-home," which extend practically all the services that can be provided in an acute care hospital, except for surgery, to the patient's home.

Countries such as Sweden, Norway, the Federal Republic of Germany and the United Kingdom encourage family care of sick older persons through the provision of special allowances paid either directly to the older person or to the family member. In Denmark, for example, such assistance is available to family members other than spouses if they spend more than sixteen hours a week caring for a sick person.

Other services which are becoming increasingly common in supporting families of sick older persons are respite care and "night sitting" services. These, as well as the financial support described above, will be discussed in greater detail in Chapter 8. Support to family caretakers can also take the form of training in basic nursing skills. This is available in Sweden, and in other countries the Red Cross has taken the initiative in providing short training courses in care of the elderly to family members and other interested individuals.[36] Families and older individuals can also benefit from the provision or loan of nursing aids or special equipment designed to help the elderly become more independent. Norway, for example, has some 2,000 centers throughout the country which make such aids available.[37] Most are run by voluntary organizations, but are subsidized by government.

General practitioners are often the first point of contact for older persons requiring assistance, but they have generally been neglected in health care planning for the elderly. It is the general practitioner upon whom the burden often falls of linking up the health and social services needed to support the older person in the community, but often his knowledge and training may be inadequate to the task.

The growing trend towards group practices can also diminish the quantity and quality of contacts between older people and their physicians because of the need to travel greater distances and the reduced likelihood of always being able to see the same physician.

Older people also suffer from the practical elimination of home visits by physicians. These are particularly important for the elderly because of their reduced mobility and the need to examine how the older patient's social and physical environment may influence his or her health status. The United Kingdom and the U.S.S.R. are two countries where home visits to older persons are still common. In the U.S.S.R, for example, persons over age 50 account for more than 50 percent of physicians' home visits, and in Britain, two-thirds of persons 75 and older obtain medical consultations at home.[38]

In an effort to improve primary care to the elderly, Bulgaria, Romania and the U.S.S.R. have established special "geriatric rooms" in their larger towns and geriatric consultations within out-patient departments of clinics and hospitals.[39] These are often staffed by retired physicians, who are thought to be able to provide a more attentive ear to the complaints of older persons.

Home nursing is one of the oldest of community services. It exists in all of the developed countries, although with greatly differing degrees of adequacy and availability. In New Zealand, for example, home nursing is provided free of charge, often on a seven-day-a-week basis.[40] France, on the other hand, has only recently begun to expand its home nursing service to better serve the elderly.[41]

Home nursing can provide support to both the caring family and the individual living alone. A home nurse's functions can include direct nursing, education in elementary nursing techniques and hygiene for patients and family members, and coordination with other health and social services. In New Zealand, night nursing for the terminally ill is also becoming more common.[42]

Home nursing is one of the health services required on the part of local governments in both the United Kingdom and Denmark. In both countries, official guidelines call for one home nurse for about each 350–400 persons 65 or older.[43] In some local districts, physicians and home nurses share a common clientele in order to facilitate the exchange of information between the two. And in both countries, home nursing is a service provided free of charge upon a physician's recommendation.

Czechoslovakia has introduced the profession of "geriatric nurse" a nurse who works closely with two primary care physicians. The nurse is responsible for home nursing and identifying older people in the community who require assistance—much like the "health visitor" in Scotland. In this connection, she works closely with the local social worker and visits old people living alone in order to monitor their changing needs. Where appropriate, the nurse can arrange for domestic help or placement in an institution, and she also works closely with the hospital social worker when an elderly patient is discharged. The geriatric nurse's catchment area includes about 7,000 persons.[44]

A health care professional somewhat neglected in the United States but of crucial importance to the continued mobility of the elderly, is the chiropodist or podiatrist. Chiropody services are commonly made available as a community health benefit to the elderly—and in their own homes, if necessary. In the United Kingdom, chiropodists, along with home nurses, health visitors and general practitioners, are legally required services that must be provided by all municipalities.[45]

The United Kingdom pioneered in day hospitals for the elderly in an attempt to separate the custodial from the medical aspects of care. The idea has now caught on in other countries as well. Sweden, for example, now has 4,000 places in day hospitals and plans to increase the number available yet further.[46]

Day hospitals provide medical care and rehabilitation while permitting patients to return home in the evening. They are used by people recently released from hospitals or by persons seeking to avert hospitalization. Day hospitals also provide opportunities for socializing, and sometimes the line separating day hospitals from other forms of day care becomes quite thin.

Day hospitals can be free-standing but are more typically situated in a hospital or nursing home. This is the case in the Netherlands, where the existence of day hospitals in nursing homes has accelerated patient turnover.[47] Transportation to day hospitals is usually provided through taxi services, special vans or (in the United Kingdom) ambulances.

In the United Kingdom, there are now some 300 day hospitals, about one-third of which cater to the elderly mentally ill.[48] National guidelines call for two day-hospital places per 1,000 elderly.[49] Day hospitals serve an average of 10–20 patients a day at a cost of approximately $45 a day per patient.[50] While this is cheaper than institutional care for patients attending day hospitals three times a week or less, it becomes less competitive with institutional care if attendance at the day hospital is five days a week and the hidden costs of home care and housing are also taken into account.[51] However, of the persons discharged from day hospitals, about 50 percent are regarded as improved and 17 percent are referred on for social care at day care centers (the equivalent of U.S. senior centers).[52] Despite the day hospitals' recognized achievements, there is still a shortage of places, especially for the elderly mentally ill, and arranging for transportation has remained a vexing problem.

The most sophisticated form of community home health care is probably the "hospital-at-home," now being experimented with in France, the United Kingdom and several other countries.[53] Practically all forms of hospital care, except for surgery, can be made mobile and brought to the patient's home if called for. "Hospitals-at-home" cost less than full hospitalization and may often be considered desirable over hospitalization in certain circumstances—for example, where older spouses have been taking care of each other and hospitalization of one may precipitate a sudden deterioration in the other who has been left at home.

In many of the developed countries, the community health services described above are provided at little or no charge to the client. Eligibility is usually open to all in need; means tests are rarely imposed. Where scarce resources limit the availability of services, priority is usually given to low-income individuals. In most countries with advanced welfare systems, health services are viewed as a right—lack of funds does not constitute a barrier to service.

INSTITUTIONAL CARE

It would be hard to find an industrialized country that is not expanding its community services in order to avert inappropriate institutionalization—in recognition of both the desire of older people to remain in their own homes and what are believed to be the lower costs of non-institutional care. Yet, at the same time, most countries are finding it necessary to expand the number of long-term care beds because of the growing numbers of the very old and frail elderly and increased labor force participation by women who are no longer free to serve as "caretakers." It is people over 80 years of age who are most at risk of being institutionalized, and this is one of the fastest growing age groups in almost all industrialized countries.[54] In Sweden, one-half of the patients in somatic long-term care are 80 or older.[55] Countries which have not had a nursing home level of care per se (other than long-term care wards in hospitals), such as the United Kingdom and France, are seriously considering instituting one.

The percentage of the elderly population 65 and older living in long-term care wards or institutions roughly equivalent to American nursing homes ranges from a low of 1.5 percent (in Japan, where co-habitation with an adult child is still the rule) to a high of about 6 percent as in New Zealand.[56] The common range lies between 4 and 6 percent—comparable to the experience of the United States.[57] The Netherlands, for example, which has a well-developed system of community services, estimates it needs enough nursing home beds for about 3.5 percent of its elderly population, who suffer from either serious physical impairments (2 percent) or moderate to serious mental confusion (1.5 percent).[58] Norway, by contrast, estimates a nursing bed need for 7 percent of its population over age 70.[59] Such estimates will, of course, depend on the age and health profile of the population, the adequacy of community services, the extent of family support available, and so on.

Some differences among countries in financing long-term institutional care have already been mentioned. Another important difference is that of the auspices under which they are managed. Only in the United States, Canada and Israel does the private for-profit sector play an important role in providing long-term care beds. In other countries, nursing homes or skilled nursing facilities are managed predominantly by the public sector or non-profit organizations. Profit-making is generally considered incompatible with long-term care. In fact, it was dissatisfaction with the quality of private nursing homes that led Denmark in 1964 to enact legislation providing public subsidies only to public and non-profit homes.[60] In addition, all new homes had to follow certain guidelines and win the approval of government planners. The net result has been that privately run homes have largely disappeared in Denmark.

The quality of care is generally higher in the public and non-profit homes than in for-profit homes. For one thing, the ratio of staff to patients is larger and staff turnover is less because staff members are paid at comparable rates to medical personnel in hospitals and other health-related institutions. In the Netherlands, a full-time physician, often with a specialty in long-term care medicine, must be in attendance in all nursing homes.[61] Great emphasis is placed on the maintenance of skills and rehabilitation in Dutch nursing homes—few patients are seen in bed during the daytime. In fact, several nursing homes in the Netherlands are called "geriatric clinics" or "reactivation centers" because of their emphasis on bringing the disabled back to community life.[62]

And in both the Netherlands and Denmark, nursing aides or "nursing home assistants," who have had as much as two years' training in long-term care, are essential personnel in nursing homes and in homes for the aged.[63] In Denmark, these nursing aides are trained to respect the patients' privacy and dignity. They are taught to treat patients as if they were still in their own homes, controlling their own affairs within the limits of their disabilities and having the right to withdraw from institutional life to their own private rooms.

The economic prosperity of the 1960's made it possible for countries like Denmark to establish private rooms with bath and access to the outdoors as the standard of provision in all new nursing homes.[64] Even in today's economic circumstances, Norway is moving towards providing private rooms in all new home construction.[65] And in Sweden, emphasis is now being placed on building new homes near patients' former neighborhoods.[66] Efforts are being made to give homes a personal character through the adaptation of furnishings and equipment to suit individual needs. This feeling of being in one's own home is significantly enhanced by the right of patients in countries such as the Netherlands, Denmark and Sweden to bring some of their own furnishings and personal effects to the nursing home or even hospital ward.[67]

Two observers of long-term care in other countries, Robert L. Kane and Rosalie A. Kane, also found a greater tradition of service in European countries, where the performance of menial duties did not preclude the development of warm and compassionate relationships with patients.[68] On a more measurable level, the Kanes found that the usual approach to quality care was a structural one—''One senses an almost tacit assumption that if adequate resources are provided (such as good facilities and staffing patterns), good care will result.''[69] Intangibles have not been neglected, however, as witnessed in the enactment of legislation in several countries requiring the establishment of elected councils of residents in all nursing homes and homes for the aged to advise management on issues affecting residents.[70]

The net result of measures such as those described above is that less abuse is reported in the public and non-profit nursing homes than in the for-profit ones.

Current Policy Issues

Most countries continue to be concerned with the issue of inappropriate institutionalization. Examples of this can be found practically everywhere. As in the United States, pressure to institutionalize an individual who may not need that intensive a level of care may result from the way financial incentives are structured. When funding for different kinds of care emanates from more than one source—an almost universal situation—incentives may be created to assign individuals to a greater or lesser level of care than required because it results in less out-of-pocket expense for either the individual or the authority responsible for that individual's well-being.

One response has been the establishment of geriatric assessment teams to rule upon all applications for institutional care. This has been done in municipalities in both Denmark and the Netherlands.[71] These interdisciplinary teams have been effective in diverting many older people from institutional forms of care, allowing them to stay on in their own homes with appropriate community services. In Denmark, all applications for long-term care placement must be accompanied by a report from the family physician, from a visiting nurse regarding the applicant's home situation, and from a long-term care physician who, ideally, has had an opportunity first to assess the applicant within a long-term care unit.[72]

As an additional economy move, some countries are experimenting with the use of skilled nursing facilities to deliver services to the elderly in the community in order to use the existing capital plant more efficiently.[73] It is hoped that such measures will also broaden residents' contacts with the community and lessen fear among the community-dwelling elderly about one day entering a home. Another advantage is that care from a nursing home or similar institutional facility can be offered on a seven-day-a-week basis.

In the Netherlands, one-third of nursing homes now provide day care.[74] And in Denmark, all new nursing homes must provide "day nursing homes" to both the physically and the mentally frail elderly living in the community.[75] Individuals attend an average of two to three times a week and are eligible for all the services available to residents of nursing homes. One risk involved in institutionally based outreach, however, is the reluctance on the part of many community-dwelling elderly to use services emanating from a nursing home—for fear of being identified with its residents.

One particularly imaginative use of an "old people's home" in Pendleton, England, has been to make available three "revolving" beds for one-month periods to persons who are on the waiting list for admission to the home in order to maximize the individual's ability for independent living upon return to the community.[76] This program was developed in the face of bed shortages and the growing number of frail older persons seeking placement in institutional care.

Upon entering the home, the temporary placements are given a full examination, and goals to be achieved during the month in nutritional intake, improved agility and so on are determined. Just before discharge, personnel of the home meet with the client's relatives and health and social services representatives of the community to ensure that there will be sufficient supports available upon the individual's return home. The Pendleton home has achieved some success in postponing the need for permanent institutionalization through such temporary placements.

Another issue of concern to most countries is the extent to which long-term care beds should be made available in retirement homes and other sheltered housing facilities as residents become infirm. It is generally recognized that older people do not wish to move far from their familiar environment; yet creating small nursing-home-like units within essentially residential facilities is not always economical. One result has been the expansion in Europe of multi-level care complexes, which combine independent living units with sheltered housing and skilled nursing care units, to which residents can move as necessary without having to be displaced very far. A disadvantage is that such large complexes need considerable space, which is not often available in the hub of town where most community facilities and amenities are located. If they must be located outside of town, the possibilities for integrating the elderly into the general community are lessened. It is the fear of segregating large numbers of older people that has prevented France from moving rapidly ahead with its planned regional geriatric centers.

As an alternative, France is encouraging existing retirement homes to set up medical departments which can provide regular medical supervision and routine care to residents as they become more infirm in order to avoid the need for transfers to other institutions.[77] However, a home cannot have more than 25 percent of its beds in the medical department—otherwise, it is feared, the character of the home would be changed.

Geriatric Medicine

While, typically, the elderly are not differentiated as consumers for health care coverage in most countries, the fact remains that they are disproportionately large consumers of health care and often present complex symptomology. In some countries—such as the Netherlands, New Zealand, Sweden, the United Kingdom and the U.S.S.R.—this has resulted in the development of geriatric medicine or long-term care as a separate specialty.

The need for a geriatric or long-term care specialty was seen to arise from the multiple pathologies often experienced by older people, making diagnosis an especially difficult task, and from the close interrelationship of health and social problems commonly found among many elderly persons. Solutions require an interdisciplinary approach, and geriatricians and long-term care physicians have learned to cooperate with other health care and social services personnel.

Geriatricians usually serve as consultants to general practitioners and work in geriatric departments of general hospitals. They provide acute, rehabilitative and some long-term care. Most geriatric departments also provide day hospital and out-patient facilities. Geriatricians also usually serve as the gatekeepers for admission to institutional long-term care, and in some countries, such as the United Kingdom, few people are placed in long-term care until all community alternatives have been exhausted.

Geriatricians, unlike general practitioners in many countries, recognize the importance of visits to the homes of patients in order to determine, for example, the extent of the social supports available following hospital discharge. Once a thorough assessment is made—either in the patient's home, in a day hospital or in the geriatric unit itself—a patient is either admitted to the hospital or a case conference is called with the patient and his or her relatives to discuss community alternatives, including support by family and friends and supports to family members, such as respite care, home nursing and knowledge about whom to call for further assistance.

Britain's Department of Health and Social Security (DHSS) has recommended ten geriatric beds per 1,000 population 65 and older.[78] However, this goal has not yet been realized, and progress in placing geriatric beds within general hospitals has been slow. While Britain's goal is to bring geriatric, psychiatric and acute hospital services together within the general hospital, there has been resistance to doing so; geriatric medicine still suffers from a low status within the medical profession.[79] This is also true in other countries, where, in addition, geriatric services may not be as fully covered by national health insurance systems. Nevertheless, even in countries which have not established a specialty in geriatric or long-term care medicine, a need for such a specialty is being felt, and many doctors train in other countries in order to obtain the needed skills.

A geriatric specialty probably leads to better diagnosis, treatment and after-care. A study conducted by Britain's National Corporation for the Care of Old People found that the quality of aftercare for older patients following hospital discharge was much better in hospitals with geriatric departments than in those without such a specialty.[80]

A geriatric specialty promotes geriatric research and provides improved opportunities for education and training in long-term care. There is also evidence that the existence of a geriatric unit reduces waiting lists for hospital admission, lessens the demand for long-term care by preventing irreversible deterioration, and prevents the blocking of acute-care hospital beds.[81]

It should be noted that, even in countries with a specialty in geriatric medicine, only a minority of the elderly ever pass through a geriatrician's hands. Older persons suffering from simple or easily diagnosed illnesses that are common to all age groups do not obtain segregated medical treatment. It is only those cases deemed particularly difficult because of complicated and interacting health and social problems that are passed on to the expert geriatrician. Thus, only 14 percent of the hospital beds in Britain are geriatric beds (although, admittedly, an acute shortage exists).[82] A complementary effort is being made in a number of countries, including the United Kingdom, to include some training in geriatric medicine as part of the general medical school curriculum for everyone. The U.S.S.R. now provides extensive training in geriatric medicine to all levels of health care personnel.[83]

Some countries have established a specialty in long-term care rather than geriatric medicine. It operates to some extent like a geriatric specialty but is not limited to care of the elderly, although, not surprisingly, older people still account for the bulk of the caseload. In Denmark, specialists in long-term care study a combination of internal and geriatric medicine. Unlike British geriatricians, Danish long-term care specialists are not responsible for custodial care or home assessment and do not become involved in acute care cases.[84] These remain the province of the general practitioner and other health care specialists.

In Denmark, every county hospital must establish a long-term care unit for patients requiring one to three months of care. Denmark presently has some 1,000 long-term care beds, about one-quarter of the estimated need.[85] Long-term care units also provide day hospitals and are strongly represented on the geriatric assessment teams which are required by law in all local authorities in Denmark to determine the need for various forms of institutional care by individual applicants. While such assessment teams are not yet universally consulted, where they have been, as many as one-half to two-thirds of those applying for admission to long-term institutional care are found to require a less intensive level of provision.[86]

As in the British experience, Danish long-term care departments are still given low priority in hospital settings despite their demonstrated effectiveness and the fact that a long-term care bed costs less than half as much as an acute care bed.[87] According to evaluations that have been done of long-term care units, approximately 40–60 percent of patients benefit from their stays; these average forty days.[88] The number of patients totally dependent on staff has been halved; in fact, some 40 percent of those admitted can be referred to a less intensive level of care than was originally proposed at the time of admission.[89] About 60 percent of the patients admitted are discharged back to their homes; 30 percent are sent to nursing homes; and 10 percent die.[90] Most of the patients admitted to long-term care units are in their 80's, but physicians have found that neither age nor sex is relevant when considering possibilities for rehabilitation.

PREVENTIVE HEALTH MEASURES

Primary Prevention

Most countries have adopted measures which, either narrowly or broadly defined, could be considered means of preventing or delaying illness. In the face of escalating health care costs, emphasis on such measures is increasing almost everywhere.

Nevertheless, relatively little is known about what constitutes adequate health promotion or how best to convey this kind of information. Among the alternatives suggested at a World Health Organization (WHO) meeting, those which could constitute part of a health promotion campaign directed to older persons are periodic medical screenings, continued physical activity, meaningful participation in work and leisure activities, good nutrition, moderation in the use of tobacco and alcohol, and opportunities to remain physically and mentally active.[91]

Social security administrations, which, in a number of countries, administer national health insurance programs, have begun to inform their beneficiaries about the need to form good health habits, especially with regard to moderate intake of food, alcohol and tobacco. Similar educational campaigns are conducted regularly through senior centers and the media.

A valuable educational function is performed in the United Kingdom and especially in Scotland, by the health visitor, who calls upon older persons in the community to provide general health education and detect early stages of illness. The health visitors may be attached to general medical practices, but they work in an advisory and supportive role. Health visitors are knowledgeable about community services and can provide the essential liaison between an older person and the bureaucracy—much like the "geriatric nurse" in Czechoslovakia. In parts of Scotland, health visitors regularly visit everyone over 70 years of age.[92]

The U.S.S.R. uses its "geriatric consulting rooms" to provide not only direct medical treatment, but also instruction on preventive health measures. Physicians may further refer older patients to "health groups," where they obtain information on hygiene and maintaining health, learn first-aid techniques, and are encouraged to exercise.[93] In addition, "universities of health and longevity" in some of the major cities offer classes and lectures on hygiene and other health issues of interest to older people.[94]

In the Federal Republic of Germany, one state has developed a model health center which combines the skills of both physicians and social workers. Among its priorities is to provide information to older people on common health problems they may face and arrange for the provision of care in case of chronic illness. The center's personnel have found it necessary to do much home visiting, since older people rarely come to the center seeking advice. It is expected that this health care outreach model will be adopted in other parts of Germany as well.[95]

In Sweden, where study circles are the most popular form of adult education, the focus of some of these informal groups is on diet and other measures to promote health. And Finland is now developing some national models for health education of the elderly.[96] It is hoped that such programs will facilitate contacts between older people and health care personnel.

The importance of exercise in health promotion is increasingly being recognized, and exercise programs for the elderly are expanding in many places. In Switzerland, the Swiss Union for Gymnastics for the Elderly has over 50,000 active participants and forms the largest organization within the Swiss Association for Physical Exercise.[97] In the Federal Republic of Germany, the Red Cross has trained 1,500 leaders to conduct gymnastics classes for the elderly at their request.[98] Similarly, 2,000 dance teachers have been trained for work in institutions and senior centers.[99] In the Netherlands, a national foundation has been formed to promote exercise among the elderly.[100] It is subsidized by government, which has also appointed counselors at the provincial level to help the foundation develop its programming.

The effectiveness of such health surveillance in the workplace is attested to by a Swedish study involving eight firms with more than 20,000 workers. Some 60 percent of older workers whose working capacity had been reduced because of ill health were able to continue at work thanks to the medical service and suitable placement. "Surveillance of the health of older workers is based on medical examinations prior to assignment, periodic examinations, and special examinations after absence due to sickness or accident."[101]

In Grenoble, France, the Association Sportif du Troisième Age (ASTA) has trained over 1,500 persons between the ages of 65 and 80 to participate in such strenuous sports as skiing, tennis and cycling.[102] The emphasis is on training older people in groups so that they can draw confidence from each other and improve their performance. ASTA also trains persons who work directly with the elderly in retirement homes and clubs.

ASTA found it could dispense with the screening programs it originally required to determine whether participants were suffering from some health problem that might be aggravated through physical activity. Experience showed these fears to be unjustified. Among the active elderly, there were almost no conditions which would be worsened by exercise—on the contrary, they could only benefit from regular physical exercise. ASTA does, of course, take strict precautions to avoid unusual dangers and hardships in the sports it selects.

Campaigns to improve traffic safety must also be considered an important tool of health promotion. In many countries, elderly pedestrians and drivers constitute a disproportionate number of traffic fatalities. In the Federal Republic of Germany, traffic safety officials have found that one effective way to reach seniors is to take them out into traffic situations as a group and teach them alternative forms of behavior.[103] Simultaneously, measures must be taken to reduce traffic hazards for the elderly, such as overly short traffic signals which prevent anyone but a quick pedestrian from crossing the street in one stage.

Secondary Prevention

The early detection and treatment of illness also form an essential part of a set of preventive health measures. If ill-health is to be avoided in old age, it is important that such screenings begin earlier in life. Some Eastern European countries have introduced special dispensaries or gerontological centers within large firms or factories to provide preventive health services to older workers. In Romania, for example, such centers exist in 219 firms, for workers 45 or older.[104] In the German Democratic Republic, special dispensaries are available to workers starting ten years before retirement.[105] Some large firms in the U.S.S.R. also provide rehabilitation facilities to their older workers.[106]

In Finland, health screening and counseling for persons over age 65 are conducted through neighborhood health centers staffed by physicians, nurses and physiotherapists.[107] Consultations are also available with psychologists and representatives of the local social welfare authority. Very thorough medical checkups, which include inquiries regarding the individual's economic and social circumstances, are provided every two to three years. Besides various forms of rehabilitation, the centers also offer small-group activities in order to encourage the social interaction that is so necessary to mental health.

The early detection of illness is an important function of the health visitors deployed in the United Kingdom. Some localities establish special registries for older people considered "at risk," who are then visited regularly by health visitors or district nurses.

Early warning systems can be provided by persons other than traditional health professionals. Sweden makes use of postmen, especially in rural areas, to check on the well-being of older persons on their routes and to dispense information about available services.[108] In many of the countries of Eastern Europe, young volunteers are assigned to watch over elderly people within specific blocks; they also check on the older people's well-being, run errands for them and inform authorities of unmet needs.[109] Similar "neighborhood watch" programs have been run successfully for many years in the United Kingdom.[110] Such measures are generally not viewed as an inappropriate invasion of individual privacy.

To facilitate the treatment of chronic conditions, the most common health complaint among the elderly, the Soviet Union has established special dispensaries for the treatment of particular illnesses, such as cardiovascular and gastrointestinal disease, from which older people suffer in disproportionate numbers.[111] Patients are encouraged to visit frequently in order to avert any deterioration in their condition.

And both the U.S.S.R. and the Federal Republic of Germany make considerable use of "health zones" or spas to assist individuals in maintaining or restoring their health.[112] Individuals attending these facilities are prescribed a course of treatment, perhaps including various therapies, medications, exercise or special diets—all under the supervision of a physician. In Germany, these spas are mainly run by voluntary organizations, but the care may be subsidized by national health insurance funds as a form of "preventive" health.

Despite these increasing activities along the prevention front, it should be pointed out that little is really known about the efficacy of various alternatives. Annual medical checkups, for example, have recently been called into question in the United States as expensive and unnecessary procedures.[113]

MANPOWER AND TRAINING

Countries with a broad array of community services and quality institutional care have invested considerable amounts in staff training. Mention has already been made of the two years' training in long-term care received by nurse's aides in Denmark and the Netherlands. Similarly, registered nurses, more and more, are receiving special instruction in geriatric medicine. In the United Kingdom, student nurses are now required to take some geriatric training, and Denmark offers a certificate in geriatric nursing.[114] In Bulgaria, Hungary and Poland, nurses and para-medical personnel receive one to two years of training in social gerontology and the basic care of elderly patients.[115] Even home help aides, in countries such as the Netherlands, the Federal Republic of Germany and Sweden, receive extensive training (sometimes up to two years), including training in the care of the aged.[116]

Interestingly, it is only recently that long-term care and geriatric medicine have begun to be incorporated into the general training of medical students— considerably behind the training of the other helping professions. Such training for medical students is rarely mandatory; nevertheless, progress is evident. In Sweden, all medical schools now have chairs in geriatrics.[117] And geriatrics is becoming a popular field of study for post-graduate and in-service training in many countries, as practitioners become aware of the large proportion of their caseload comprised of older persons.

Despite the better circumstances under which long-term care personnel work in some other countries, concerns about meeting future manpower needs exist. All industrialized countries are faced with large increases in their population over 80, the group that is most likely to require long-term care, but long-term care as a profession is still not as attractive a career alternative as other helping vocations. Options that are being looked at to deal with possible personnel shortages are attraction of more males and volunteers to the caring professions and wider experimention with part-time jobs in order to keep married women in the labor force.[118] Strong appeals are also being made to the "natural support" systems—family, friends and neighbors.

SOME POLICY IMPLICATIONS FOR THE UNITED STATES

There is a remarkable convergence of views among experts in the field in industrialized countries about the components of a sound health care policy for the elderly. According to the World Health Organization,

It is now more widely accepted that public policies should aim at maintaining elderly people at home with dignity and maximum independence and that admission to a nursing home or similar institution should be a consideration only when constant professional nursing supervision or other intensive levels of service are necessary. In this context, multi-disciplinary geriatric assessment and rehabilitation services are being seen as essential elements of any comprehensive system of service provision for frail and disabled people. It is also being recognized that these services need to be well supported by domiciliary services and institutional facilities which offer medico-social services of varying intensity, e.g., inpatient rehabilitation services, day hospital facilities, long-term home nursing services and respite beds.[119]

The implementation of such policies is difficult and expensive, and the health care systems of other countries are, in many ways, as fraught with problems as is that of the United States. Escalating costs, inadequacies in coverage, and personnel shortages are common throughout the industrialized world. Nevertheless, the experience of other countries still holds important lessons for the United States.

Perhaps the most significant is that it is possible to shape a health care system which provides almost everyone access to quality care regardless of income level at a total systems cost no larger than the present U.S. expenditure for health care. And, by and large, the countries discussed in this chapter already have considerably larger proportions of older people in their population than does the United States.

How is this accomplished? In large part through a significant role for the public sector in providing or insuring health care and a negligible role for the for-profit sector, especially in providing long-term care. However, at the same or smaller cost (calculated as a percentage of GNP), other countries have been able to provide a broader range of community services and higher quality institutional care than does the United States. Such services include home nurses, health visitors, chiropodists, the loan of special aids and equipment, day hospitals and specially trained staff to deal with the long-term care needs of people who are institutionalized. While examples of all these services can also be found in the United States many only exist on an ad hoc, experimental or demonstration basis. In some countries of northern Europe, such services are commonly available to everyone in need and at little if any out-of-pocket expense to the client. Functional need, rather than financial means, is the major criterion for service eligibility. People are not required to become paupers in order to have their long-term care needs met, whether in the community or in an institution. Fees, where they are charged, are usually based on an "ability to pay" basis. Such policies reflect a recognition that chronic illness afflicts rich and poor alike.

To be sure, countries may be able to provide such services only at the expense of other kinds of health care provisions. For example, in the United Kingdom, kidney dialysis is usually not performed through the National Health Service on patients over a certain age.[120] And the broad range of services permitted by a high technology medical care system may simply not be available.

While hard evidence is sparse regarding the effectiveness of community services in preventing inappropriate institutionalization, they certainly are widely believed to be effective, and countries continue to place high priority on their expansion. An eye to economy is leading some to consider utilizing existing long-term care facilities to deliver services to the community-dwelling elderly in order to maximize the capital investment made in these institutions. Certainly, the experience of multidisciplinary geriatric assessment teams, where they have been created to determine the actual need of applicants for institutional care, has been that many applicants do not need this intensive level of care and can continue to manage in the community with appropriate supports. The effectiveness of such teams is, of course, predicated on the availability of adequate community services if alternative strategies are recommended.

The availability of "at risk" registers on which all older persons who are vulnerable for health reasons are inscribed, annual visits to persons over 70 or 75 years of age by "health visitors," and the mobilization of youth, neighbors, postmen and tradesmen are, in addition, relatively inexpensive ways of monitoring the well-being of frail older persons and serve as valuable early warning systems for appropriate intervention in order to prevent a further deterioration in health.

The availability of a geriatric medical specialty and geriatric departments in general hospitals seems to be an efficient and cost-effective way of concentrating a variety of expertise and resources on older persons suffering from a complex interaction of health and social problems. Geriatric consultants do not replace general practitioners, but serve in a complementary role. Where geriatric medicine is practiced, the quality of both care and after-care following discharge from the hospital seems to be higher because of the team approach that is followed and the close coordination with the social services—a skill that the medical profession at large is not noted for. This service too helps minimize cases of inappropriate institutionalization.

Finally, stress is being placed everywhere on preventive measures that may slow down pathological aging processes. Areas of promise lie in nutrition, exercise and education regarding "self-care."

NOTES

1. *Ageing in Australia*, report prepared for the World Assembly on Aging (Canberra: Australian Department of Social Security, 1982), p. 19; *Aging in Finland*, report prepared for the World Assembly of Aging (Helsinki: Ministry of Social Affairs and Health, 1982), p. 14.

2. See, for example, *Epidemiological Studies on Social and Medical Conditions of the Elderly* (Copenhagen: World Health Organization (WHO), Regional Office for Europe, 1982), pp. 11–12.

3. See, for example, Ethel Shanas, "Health Status of Older People," *American Journal of Public Health* 64, No. 3 (March 1974):262.

4. Ibid.

5. Ibid., p. 263.

6. Ibid.

7. *Aging in Norway*, report prepared for the World Assembly on Aging (Oslo: Ministry of Health and Social Affairs, 1982), p. 19; *Aging in Finland*, p. 22.

8. Ole Zeuthen Dalgaard, "Care of the Elderly in Denmark: Special Aspects Including Geriatrics and Long-Term Medicine," *Danish Medical Bulletin* 29, No. 3 (March 1982): 132; *Ageing New Zealanders*, report prepared for the World Assembly on Aging, 1982, p. 82; *Aging in Norway*, p. 19; *Ageing in the United Kindgom*, report prepared for the World Assembly on Aging (London: Department of Health and Social Security, 1982), p. 20.

9. *Just Another Age*, report prepared for the World Assembly on Aging (Stockholm: Ministry of Health and Social Affairs, 1982), p. 20.

10. Dmitri F. Chebotarev, Nina N. Sachuk and N. V. Verzhikovskaya, "Status and Condition of the Elderly in Socialist Countries of Eastern Europe," report prepared for the World Assembly on Aging (Kiev: Institute of Gerontology, 1982).

11. Gert Almind, "Primary Health Service for the Elderly," *Danish Medical Bulletin* 29, No. 3 (March 1982):128–129.

12. United Nations, *Health Policy Aspects of Aging*, Report of WHO (A/Conf. 113/19, March 26, 1982), p. 31.

13. *Social Security and the Elderly* (Geneva: International Social Security Association, 1982), p. 29.

14. *Just Another Age*, p. 18.

15. Abraham Doron, *Social Services for the Aged in Eight Countries* (Jerusalem: Brookdale Institute of Gerontology and Adult Human Development, 1979).

16. *Report from Ireland*, report prepared for the World Assembly on Aging (Dublin: National Council for the Aged, 1982), p. 6.

17. *Report on the Situation of the Elderly in the Federal Republic of Germany*, re-

port prepared for the World Assembly on Aging (Berlin: German Center of Gerontology, May 1982), p. 12.

18. *Ageing in the United Kinqdom*, p. 13.

19. *Ageing New Zealanders*, p. 77.

20. *Developments and Trends in Social Security, 1978–1980*, report of the Secretary General (Geneva: International Social Security Association, 1981).

21. *Social Security and the Elderly* p. 32.

22. *Asahi Shimbun*, August 10, 1982.

23. Robert L. Kane and Rosalie A. Kane, *Long-Term Care in Six Countries: Implications for the U.S.* (Rockville, Md.: U.S. Department of Health, Education, and Welfare, Public Health Service, National Institutes of Health, 1976), p. 116.

24. *Aging in France*, report prepared for the World Assembly on Aging (Paris: Ministère des Affaires Sociales et de la Solidarité Nationale, 1982), p. 30.

25. *Ageing New Zealanders*, p. 77.

26. Esther Ammundsen, "The Future of Health-related Care for the Elderly in Europe," in B. Herzog (ed.), *Aging and Income: Programs and Prospects for the Elderly* (New York: Human Sciences Press, 1978), p. 268.

27. A. Gommers, B. Hankenne and B. Rogowski, "Help Structures for the Aged Sick: Experiences in Seven Countries," in Morton Teicher et al. (eds.), *Reaching the Aged: Social Services in Forty-Four Countries* (Beverly Hills, Calif.: Sage Publications, 1979), p. 124.

28. E. Thompson and C. Motuz, "The Manitoba/Canada Home Care Study: Some Preliminary Findings" (paper presented at the annual meeting of the Canadian Association on Gerontology, Halifax, Nova Scotia, November 1979), p. 3.

29. *Ageing International* 8, No. 1 (Spring 1981):13.

30. Victor W. Sidel and Ruth Sidel, *A Healthy State* (New Pantheon Books, 1977), p. 27; Robert M. Gibson and Daniel R. Waldo, "National Health Expenditures, 1981," *Health Care Financing Review* 4 (September 1982), p. 1.

31. *A Healthy State*, pp. 14, 16, 19.

32. Ibid., p. 145.

33. Maureen Law, "The Canadian Health Care System" (paper presented at the National Conference on Social Welfare, Boston, April 1982), p. 8.

34. Ibid.

35. Ibid., p. 11.

36. *Ageing International*, 3, No. 1 (Spring, 1976):3.

37. Gommers, Hankenne and Rogowski, "Help Structures for the Aged Sick," p. 124.

38. Dmitri F. Chebotarev and Nina N. Sachuk, "A Social Policy Directed Toward the Health and Welfare of the Aged in the Soviet Union," *Journal of the American Geriatrics Society* 27, No. 2 (February 1979):51; Kane and Kane, *Long-Term Care in Six Countries*, p. 8.

39. Chebotarev, Sachuk and Verzhikovskaya, "Status and Condition of the Elderly in Socialist Countries," p. 32.

40. *Ageing New Zealanders*, p. 79.

41. *Ageing in France*, p. 32.

42. *Aging New Zealanders*, p. 79.

43. Henning Friis, "The Aged in Denmark: Social Programmes," in Teicher et al., *Reaching the Aged*, p. 205.

44. *Ageing International* 5, No. 1 (Spring 1978):4.

45. Sheila B. Kamerman, "Community Services for the Aged," *Gerontologist* 16, No. 6 (December 1976):534.

46. *Just Another Age*, p. 22.

47. Gommers, Hankenne and Rogowski, "Help Structures for the Aged Sick," p. 119.

48. John C. Brocklehurst, "A Different Dimension," *Health and Social Service Journal* (May 9, 1980):616.

49. Marion Hildick-Smith, "Geriatric Day Hospitals: Practice and Planning," *Age and Ageing* 9 (1980):38.

50. Brocklehurst, "A Different Dimension," p. 616.

51. Ibid., p. 617.

52. Ibid., p. 616.

53. Stephen Cang, "Why Not a Hospital-at-Home Here?" *Age Concern Today* (Winter 1976/1977):9–11; F. Guyot, "L'hospitalisation à Domicile," *Gérontologie* (December 1976):33, 51–56.

54. United Nations, "Demographic Considerations," introductory paper prepared for the World Assembly on Aging (A/AC. 208/8, January 15, 1982), p. 8.

55. *Just Another Age*, p. 23.

56. See individual country reports issued for the U.N. World Assembly on Aging, 1982, cited in notes, 1, 7–10, 16–17, 24 and 71 of this section, note 7 to Chapter 6, and note 180 to Chapter 8.

57. WHO, "The Well-Being of the World's Aging Citizens: A Status Report," background paper prepared for the WHO preparatory conference for the U.N. World Assembly on Aging, Mexico City, December 8–11, 1980, (IRP/ADR 101/10, October 24, 1980), p. 5.

58. R. J. van Zonneveld, "The Netherlands," John C. Brocklehurst (ed.), *Geriatric Care in Advanced Societies* (Baltimore: University Park Press, 1975), p. 75.

59. *Aging in Norway*, p. 23.

60. Esther Ammundsen, "The Transition from Private to Public Provision of Nursing Homes in Denmark," *Danish Medical Bulletin* 29, No. 3 (March 1982):153.

61. R. J. van Zonneveld, "Long-Term Care for the Elderly in the Netherlands," *Z. Gerontoloqie*, No. 11 (1978):265.

62. Van Zonneveld, "The Netherlands," p. 76.

63. Ibid., p. 78.

64. Ammundsen, "Transition from Private to Public Provision of Nursing Homes in Denmark," p. 154.

65. *Aging In Norway* p. 23.

66. *Just Another Age*, p. 23.

67. See, for example, Chloe Refshauge, "A Nursing Home in Denmark," *Growing Older* (September 1976):20.

68. Kane and Kane, *Long-Term Care in Six Countries*, p. 177.

69. Ibid., p. 178.

70. Charlotte Nusberg, "Formalized Participation by the Elderly in Decision-making a Growing Trend in Western Countries," *Ageing International* 7, No. 1 (Spring 1980):17–18.

71. Jorgen Worm, "Effect of Long Term Medical Therapy," *Danish Medical Bulletin* 29, No. 3 (March 1982):148; and *Netherlands National Report on Aging Policy*,

report prepared for the World Assembly on Aging (Rijswijk: Ministry of Cultural Affairs, Recreation and Social Welfare, 1982), p. 13.

72. Dalgaard, "Care of the Elderly in Denmark," p. 133.

73. U. Braun and R. Hauri, "Centres for the Elderly in Switzerland," *EURAG Newsletter* (September 1978).

74. *Netherlands National Report on Aging Policy*, p. 14.

75. Raymond Glasscote, Jon E. Gudeman and Donald Miles, *Creative Mental Health Services for the Elderly* (Washington, D.C.: Joint Information Service of the American Psychiatric Association and the Mental Health Association, 1977), p. 55.

76. *Ageing International* 6, No. 2 (Summer 1979): 8–9.

77. *Ageing International* 7, No. 1 (Spring 1980): 9.

78. U.K., Department of Health and Social Security, *Priorities for Health and Personal Social Services in England* (London: Her Majesty's Stationery Office, 1976), p. 40.

79. John C. Brocklehurst, "Great Britain," in Brocklehurst (ed.), *Geriatric Care in Advanced Societies*, p. 34.

80. *Organising Aftercare* (London: National Corporation for the Care of Old People, 1979).

81. U.K., Department of Health and Social Security, *Priorities for Health and Personal Social Services*, pp. 42–43.

82. Age Concern England, *Information Circular* (October 1977).

83. Chebotarev and Sachuk, "Social Policy Directed Toward the Health and Welfare of the Aged in the Soviet Union," p. 52.

84. Dalgaard, "Care of the Elderly in Denmark," p. 131.

85. Worm, "Effect of Long Term Medical Therapy," p. 148.

86. Dalgaard, "Care of the Elderly in Denmark," p. 134.

87. Worm, "Effect of Long Term Medical Therapy," p. 148.

88. Ibid., p. 150.

89. Ibid.

90. Ibid.

91. R. J. van Zonneveld, "Planning and Organization of Geriatric Services" (background paper prepared on behalf of WHO for a U.N. Expert Group Meeting on Aging, New York, May 1974), p. 10.

92. Ferguson Anderson, "Modern Practice of Geriatric Medicine" (paper presented at a George Washington University Medical Center Conference, "Current Concepts in Care of the Elderly," Washington, D.C., October 1978), p. 5.

93. R. G. Revutskaya, "The Union of the Soviet Socialist Republics," in Brocklehurst, *Geriatric Care in Advanced Societies*, p. 133.

94. Dmitri F. Chebotarev and Nina N. Sachuk, "Social Policy Directed Toward the Health and Welfare of the Aged in the Soviet Union," p. 57.

95. *Report on the Situation of the Elderly in the Federal Republic of Germany*, p. 12.

96. *Aging in Finland*, p. 17.

97. *Zeitlupe* (June 1975).

98. *Presse- und Informationsdienst des KDA* (October/November 1977).

99. *Altenpflege* (November 1977).

100. *Gérontologie* 2 (1981).

101. International Labour Organisation, *Problems of Employment and Occupation of*

Older Workers, report prepared for the World Assembly on Aging (A/Conf. 113/15, February 17, 1982), p. 35.

102. *Help Age International* (March 1977).

103. *Presse- und Informationsdienst der KDA* (October/November 1980).

104. Chebotarev, Sachuk and Verzhikovskaya, "Status and Condition of the Elderly in Socialist Countries of Eastern Europe," p. 33.

105. Ibid.

106. Ibid.

107. Esko Kalimo, Timo Klaukka and Kauko Nyman, "Health and Health Care of the Elderly Population in Finland," *Geron XXII Yearbook 1978–79* (Helsinki).

108. *Just Another Age*, p. 33.

109. *Ageing International* 4, No. 2 (Summer 1977): 5.

110. Ibid., pp. 5–6.

111. Sidel and Sidel, *A Healthy State*, p. 179.

112. Revutskaya, "The Union of the Soviet Socialist Republics," pp. 133–134.

113. Proceedings of the American Medical Association, House of Delegates, June 1982.

114. *Ageing in the United Kingdom*, p. 15; Dalgaard, "Care of the Elderly in Denmark," p. 133.

115. Chebotarev, Sachuk and Verzhikovskaya, "Status and Condition of the Elderly in Socialist Countries of Eastern Europe," p. 37.

116. Dalgaard, "Care of the Elderly in Denmark," p. 133.

117. Ibid.

118. *Die Altersfragen in der Schweiz, Neuarbeitung* (Bern: Bundesamt für Sozialversicherung, 1979).

119. WHO, background paper prepared for the World Assembly on Aging, 1982, p. 20.

120. William A. Glaser, "Services for the Aged: Foreign Lessons for the United States," *Aging: An International Perspective*, proceedings of a conference of the same name organized by the Brookdale Institute on Aging and Adult Human Development (New York: Brookdale Institute of Aging and Adult Human Development and the School of International and Public Affairs, 1982), p. 62.

5

MENTAL HEALTH

Sheila Peace

Since the 1971 White House Conference on Aging there have been a number of important initiatives in the field of mental health and aging. In August 1975 the National Institute of Mental Health established a new center, the Center for Studies of the Mental Health of the Aging, and during its first year of operation of the center three national planning conferences were held devoted to the areas of research, training and services.[1] The themes of these meetings were to be taken up again by three important committees which met during the late 1970's— the President's Commission on Mental Health: Task Panel on the Elderly, the Secretary of Health, Education and Welfare's Committee on the Mental Health and Illness of the Elderly, and the Select Commmittee on Aging's National Conference on Mental Health and the Elderly.[2] The recommendations and opinions expressed by these various groups revealed certain common areas of concern, and it is these themes which form the basis for this international perspective. They include innovations in service delivery, service integration and coordination, and options in long-term care, personnel and training, and the promotion of mental health.

MAKING SENSE OF THE STATISTICS

The World Health Organization (WHO) has estimated that in developed countries the overall prevalence of mental disorder in those over 60 years of age may be as high as 30–35 percent.[3] However, severe and irreversible disorders, such as senile and arteriosclerotic dementia, affect a much smaller proportion of this age group—only 3–6 percent.[4] The incidence of dementia does increase with age, though. A study by D.W.K. Kay and others in Newcastle, England, found 22 percent of those over 80 suffering from organic mental illness.[5]

However, by far the largest category of mental morbidity in old age "consists of neurotic and depressive disorders and of ill-defined mild mental deterioration, which often has a neurotic overlay, and whose significance may be more social than medical."[6] The pattern of depressive and neurotic disorders is therefore similar to that seen in younger people and contrary to popular belief, much of the mental illness in old age is either treatable or partly preventable. Yet only a fraction of these cases is likely to be known to community psychiatric services. "While the over–65 age group is generally over-represented among psychiatric in-patients, it appears to be distinctly under-represented among the patients of psychiatric extramural services."[7]

Some professionals believe that the incidence of mental disorders in old age may be influenced by cultural factors. Table 5.1 provides the results of several epidemiological studies of psychiatric disorders among the aged in the community, which show a sharp contrast between Japan and many of the Western European countries. In his discussion of community health care for the elderly in Japan, Kazuo Hasegawa points to the low incidence of functional disorders among the older Japanese and the importance of cultural factors, such as respect for the elderly and parent-child relationships in maintaining the well-being of older people.[8] He points out that in 1975, 75 percent of elderly Japanese were living with their children, as opposed to 20–30 percent in western countries, and concludes that:

the fact that the frequency of functional disorders is low in Japan should not be attributed solely to differences in diagnostic criteria; it seems to be due to differences in the socio-cultural conditions that surround the elderly in Japan and the West, in particular, the differences in family structure.[9]

Others point to the possible relationship of mental illness among the elderly with socio-economic class. For example, in Mannheim, West Germany, a concentration of mental disorders, both functional and organic, was found among the lower socio-economic groups.[10] Interestingly, this group was also more subject to chronic physical disease and impairment, and the correlation between physical and mental impairments was high.

Also, contrary to the Hasegawa hypothesis, the frequency of family contacts did not differentiate mentally ill older persons from healthy ones in the Mannheim study. The frequency of contacts outside the family, however, was important. The highest rate of mental illness was found among those who had few social contacts and complained of severe loneliness. These were not necessarily the extreme isolates, but "those who in terms of numbers of contacts evinced a moderate degree of isolation."[11]

For many countries throughout the world, the most dramatic increase in numbers of older people occurs amongst the very old, those over 80 years of age. United Nations statistics indicate that among the more developed regions of the world, where the percentage of the population over 60 years of age is

Table 5.1
Comparison of Epidemiological Studies of Psychiatric Disorders in the
Aged

AUTHOR	COUNTRY	YEAR	NUMBER OF SUBJECTS	DEMENTIA (in percentage)	FUNCTIONAL DISORDERS (in percentage)
Sheldon	England	1948	369	3.9	9.4
Bremer	Norway	1951	119	2.5	9.2
Essen-Moller	Sweden	1956	443	5.0	2.5
Primrose	Scotland	1962	222	4.5	11.4
Nielsen	Denmark	1963	978	3.1	7.7
Kay et al.	England	1964	297	5.6	11.3
Hasegawa et al.	Japan	1974	4,716	4.5	2.4

Source: Kazuo Hasegawa, "Aspects of Community Mental Health Care of
the Elderly in Japan," International Journal of Mental Health
(Fall/Winter 1979/1980).

expected to increase by 31 percent between the years 1975 and 2000, the proportion aged 80 or over is expected to increase by 58 percent.[12] The rate of
increase will be even higher for the United States. By the year 2025, the United
States is projected to be one of only seventeen nations in the world with more
than 1 million persons 80 years of age or older.[13]

In all countries this demographic phenomenon has a direct bearing on health
services, because it is those over 80 years of age, the majority of whom are
female, who are most likely to become dependent on some form of service,
whether provided by family, neighbors or organized agency. For those suffering from some form of mental illness, the incidence of organic psychoses increases with advanced age, and it is important to recognize that, at present, this
relatively small percentage of older persons places a great demand on both health
and social services and will continue to do so.

The changing demographic profile of the aging population is more likely to
focus our attention on a small minority suffering from certain types of mental
illness, the management of which is most demanding. In so doing
we run the risk of neglecting the general well-being and mental health of the
older population as a whole. Therefore, in considering the maintenance of mental health and the management of mental illness amongst the elderly, a number
of factors should be considered:

1) The vast majority of older people are mentally healthy. However, many are "at
risk" because of poor housing, low income or poor physical health. These factors can
all contribute to a decline in self-esteem and constitute target areas for prevention.

2) The vast majority of older people suffering from some form of mental disorder live
in the community, thanks largely to the support of family members.

3) The misdiagnosis of both functional mental illness, such as depression, and organic mental illness, such as acute brain syndrome or chronic brain failure, amongst older people can lead to inappropriate admissions to residential facilities.

4) In many of the developed countries old people still constitute a high percentage of the patients in mental hospitals. Robert N. Butler and Myrna Lewis state that in 1976 "there were 171,497 resident patients in state and county mental hospitals in the U.S.— of that number 28.7 percent were older persons (59.5 percent of these were women)."[14] Many of these long-stay patients could be supported in the community, given sufficient rehabilitative and supportive services, but it seems inappropriate to deinstitutionalize any psychiatric patient if the outcome is merely another form of custodial care within "the community" or no care at all.

The mental health needs of the elderly therefore must be viewed in relation to four groups of individuals: the mentally healthy; those with a functional disorder who can be treated and maintained within the community; those with organic psychoses who may need a range of in-patient, out-patient and community services; and those who are long-stay psychiatric patients.

SERVICE INTEGRATION AND COORDINATION

In most of the developed countries, provision of services for the elderly mentally ill falls within the responsibility of three sectors—health, social services and housing. In the majority of cases, an integrated model of care begins from the basic premise of allowing older persons to remain in their own homes for as long as possible. This can only be achieved through coordinating the various agencies involved and allowing for flexible use of both personnel and services. Such a coordinated system should be able to offer support along a continuum from the most open form of care—care in the community—to the most closed— long-stay institutional care. Within this continuum we see various combinations of service provision at work—for example, an elderly person suffering from organic mental illness may be maintained at home, where he or she is looked after by caring relatives who are supported through the provision of day care and periodic respite care. Such a program involves the patient, the relatives, the family practitioner, medical specialists, social workers and home care workers. The responsibility for planning a package of care may fall either to the medical service or to the community agencies. Such an integrated system can only be achieved where professionals have a common goal and understand the day-to-day activities of the other agencies involved.

The following discussion looks at how four countries—Sweden, the Netherlands, the United Kingdom and the U.S.S.R.—have attempted to foster collaboration between agencies in order to serve the needs of the elderly mentally ill.

Sweden

A comprehensive network of services for the elderly mentally ill in Sweden is still very much in its infancy.[15] The specialty of long-term care, which was developed in the 1960's, is primarily concerned with chronic somatic cases. Those patients who are agitated, disturbing to others or confused to such an extent that they require in-patient care are relegated to the psychiatric services, which in most cases results in hospitalization or a place in a special nursing home. Only those whose primary diagnosis is a somatic complaint are accepted in long-term care clinics, which usually have excellent resources for social and medical rehabilitation and offer a combination of in-patient, out-patient and day care services. No specialty at present takes clear responsibility for those older people suffering from mild or moderate dementia. These persons are being cared for either at home or in homes for the aged.

In the future, it is expected that the somatic long-term care specialty will assume responsibility for the care of persons with organic psychoses, and already a number of psychiatrists have been appointed to long-term care facilities who have both a specialization in long-term care and a primary interest in senile dementia. However, other elderly persons requiring psychiatric treatment will still be cared for by the traditional psychiatric services, which heretofore have neglected the special needs of the elderly.

At present, examples of progressive patient care for the elderly mentally ill in Sweden are still few and far between. There are, however, a few exceptions. The Langbro Hospital, a major psychiatric hopsital in Stockholm, has developed a comprehensive service for elderly people, including a large amount of day care, home visits, out-patient care and, when necessary, hospitalization.[16] The aim of the service has been to enable as many elderly people as possible to live in the familiar surroundings of their own homes and also to reach out to those older people in the community who have mental health problems but traditionally have been underserved.

Coordination and collaboration between agencies provided the basis for developing this service, and the consultant psychiatrist responsible for the elderly, Krantz, sought out and developed close relationships with the other key medical and social service staff in her area, asking for their ideas about how best to develop the service. One of the primary needs was day care, and Krantz and her associates have developed a progressive program of assessment, treatment and rehabilitation within the day care setting.

The Netherlands

In the past forty years, a great change has occurred in the care of the elderly mentally ill in the Netherlands. Formerly, many places in mental hospitals were used for the elderly, who were cared for but given very little active treatment. However, in the 1950's, a few physicians and psychiatrists began taking a more active approach to such patients. In a number of mental hospitals special geriatric departments were created, and through various measures, such as drug treatment; physical, occupational and recreational therapy; and group psychotherapy, they have been able to either return people to their own homes or discharge them to old people's homes or special nursing homes for the mentally confused elderly.

Special nursing homes for the mentally confused have been in existence since the 1950's, and in 1974, of 33,000 nursing home beds, 9,000 were allocated to the mentally ill.[17] Studies have shown that a need exists for nursing home places for the moderately confused for about 1.5 percent of the elderly population in the Netherlands.

While viewing the nursing home as an alternative to hospitalization, the Dutch also recognized that such a home must not become an isolated long-stay annex, divorced from the hospital and the community. Efforts are now also being made to develop "observation departments" within the psychogeriatric service, which allows a multidisciplinary team of both health and social service professionals to assess and treat patients and ensure that they are placed in the most appropriate accommodations.[18]

Hospitals and nursing homes in the Netherlands are independent and mostly run on a non-profit basis by private secular or religious organizations. However, both adhere to a fee system approved by the central government and are heavily subsidized by the government as well.

Great Britain

Although there are still a large number of severely mentally ill elderly patients being cared for in psychiatric hospitals there, one of the most advanced systems of coordinated care for the elderly mentally ill within the community is that which is emerging in Great Britain. (Figures for 1976 show that 49 percent of the patients resident in British psychiatric hospitals were 65 and older, and 26 percent were 75 and older.[19]) Britain now has some 120 psychiatrists who have assumed a responsibility for the elderly, and geriatric psychiatry is gradually becoming a recognized field.[20] Indeed, the Royal College of Psychiatrists has established a working group concerned with the psychiatry of old age. Such specialists work either in psychiatric hospitals or in general hospitals within a district health authority, the basic administrative area of the National Health Service.

There are many local variations in the components which go to make up a district-based mental health service for the elderly. However, certain features are common to most. The team, led by the psychiatric consultant, is multidisciplinary—including a medical social worker, community psychiatric nurses, therapists and nursing and medical staff. Depending on the type of area served, there may be a greater emphasis on certain key workers, such as community psychiatric nurses in rural areas. The initial referral, most commonly from a general practitioner or a social service agency, normally results in a home visit. The home visit is justified by most British consultants working with the elderly as a way to obtain a complete medical and social history in surroundings most familiar to the patient.

The second step is often to ask the patient to attend a day hospital or outpatient clinic, where a thorough assessment can be carried out. At this stage, other geriatric specialists may be invited to examine the patient if it is felt that the problem may be more physical than mental. The result of the assessment is discussed at a case conference attended by the patient and, if possible, a relative. At this meeting various options for patient care are discussed and every effort will be made to maintain the older person in the community. This often involves support to families through day hospital attendance and respite or short-stay care, as well as the security of learning who the professionals are and where to go for help. If in-patient care is needed, then, in most cases, both short-stay and long-stay hospital care are usually available. If residential accommodation is necessary, links can be made to the appropriate social service agency, which will make the necessary arrangements.

In 1970, the Department of Health and Social Security offered guidelines for establishing psychogeriatric assessment units.[21] It was suggested that a unit of this kind should be set up in each proposed district general hospital; that it should consist of between ten and twenty beds for a population of 250,000 people, and that the maximum length of stay should be four weeks. The unit was to be managed through close cooperation between the geriatric physician and the psychiatrist with special responsibility for the elderly, but the unit should remain the clinical responsibility of only one of these consultants. In a number of districts, such assessments units have been developed, but in other areas it is felt that the development of a special unit is not the only way to foster collaboration between specialties and that assessment is best carried out either in the elderly person's home or in a day hospital.

Despite these differences, there is a general consensus that the growing needs of the elderly mentally ill do not necessarily mean an increase in that scarce resource, the long-stay bed. In a review of service provision for the elderly mentally ill, the National Association for Mental Health (MIND) concluded that the area of greatest promise lay in the use of hospital and local authority residential home places for short-term admissions, whether for assessment, rehabilitation or respite care.[22] One Southampton psychiatrist, Colin Godber, found that by using his assessment unit for these purposes, he was able to do away with long waiting lists for admission completely and that, of more than 500 admissions in three years, only about twenty older persons had to be transferred to permanent long-term care.[23] " 'Dumping' of older people has almost completely disappeared as relatives and other caregivers in the community know that admissions can usually be arranged without difficulty. At the point of admission, discharge is negotiated with the relatives.''[24]

So far the British have not developed a public nursing home level of care, and although residents in old people's homes are becoming increasingly frail, the general trend is toward diversifying present levels of care in order to minimize moves between facilities. (The Department of Health and Social Security is, at present, initiating a pilot project of three public-sector nursing homes.) There are, of course, problems and many consultants recognize that without active cooperation between the geriatric psychiatrist, geriatrician, social services staff and the patient's family scarce resources cannot be utilized in the most efficient way.

The U.S.S.R.

According to one observer, "The main features of the Soviet Health Services are their governmental character, their emphasis on prevention, their availability and proximity to the population."[25] The Soviet health care system emphasizes the provision of readily accessible primary health services. At the neighborhood (*uchastok*) level, comprising about 4,000 people, a polyclinic serves as the center for physical health needs; mental health is the responsibility of the psychoneurological dispensary based at the district (*rayon*) level. The psychiatrist/population ratio covered by the dispensaries is one psychiatrist to 30,000 to 40,000 of the general population.[26]

The district psychiatrist is responsible for mental health services to the elderly and for treating those whose condition and social circumstances allow them to remain in the community. As there is no such position as a psychiatric social worker, the psychiatrist and his psychiatric nurse are also responsible for all forms of support to the patient and his or her family, including liaison with other welfare services.

Patients with acute psychotic conditions are usually referred to a mental hospital in the catchment area. If the psychotic state is accompanied by severe physical disorders, then the patient will be referred to the psychiatric ward of a general hospital. In cases of severe dementia, patients can be admitted to homes for the "invalid" elderly, while those with mild mental deterioration are cared for in other homes for the elderly.

Clearly, a large number of the elderly mentally ill are still being treated in institutional settings when they could be maintained within the community. As the number of older people has increased, with concomitant increases in mental health problems, the Soviet mental health system has seen the need for training specialists in geriatric psychiatry and the creation of specialist geriatric departments within the framework of the psychoneurological dispensary in order to improve services to the elderly. In this way it is hoped to centralize services, making them more accessible, and to improve screening, assessment and treatment facilities.

SOME COMPONENTS OF COMMUNITY CARE FOR THE ELDERLY MENTALLY ILL

As can be seen from this brief look at service delivery for the elderly mentally ill, such services are still in their infancy. However, some innovations can be seen even within this developmental stage, and some old ideas are being adapted to serve a different population.

The Community Psychiatric Nurse

Although district nurses and geriatric nurses attached to primary care teams have been working within the community for some time now—in Britain, the

Netherlands, Sweden, Denmark and more recently Czechoslovakia, to name but a few—the role of the community psychiatric nurse (CPN) is relatively recent. In countries such as Sweden, psychiatric nurses who are hospital based are now an important part of the assessment team, often visiting an elderly person in the community. In Britain, community psychiatric nurses have been employed since the 1950's. The role of the CPN has traditionally been "generic," with the elderly forming only part of the caseload. However, in recent years, specialist teams of CPN's have been set up, often in relation to a new psychogeriatric service. A specialist team may be in a better position to negotiate for a range of services to support the elderly mentally ill person, by fostering specific contacts and gaining knowledge concerning services for the elderly. Thus the CPN's provide an effective link between specialist hospital services and the community. Although the general practitioner retains overall medical responsibility for the patient, the CPN acts as a facilitator and, if necessary, mobilizes further medical treatment and social support. She will also monitor medication and often provide vital counseling to caregivers.[27]

One example of such a team is in Buckinghamshire. Here the service, which is jointly funded by the county council and the health authority, uses a team of registered qualified psychiatric nurses. The service was initially set up by two nurses with differing backgrounds, one having been a psychiatric hospital ward sister and the other a district nurse. This provided a useful pooling of experience from both hospital and community. The service now employs eleven nurses. They offer a range of help that includes providing counseling and advice to elderly people and their relatives, maintaining a liaison with health visitors, arranging for respite care, taking part in initial assessments, giving medication, and generally acting as the link to secure other necessary services.[28] In rural areas, such as Gloucestershire, the CPN's operate a radio car service and can be called out to cover any part of this widespread county on a twenty-four hour basis. When hospital facilities are centralized and the client population is widely dispersed, this becomes essential.

Respite and Short-Stay Care

The use of respite care and short-stay beds is becoming a vital part of any comprehensive service for the elderly mentally ill. The rationale for this type of care is twofold. First, success in keeping frail older persons in the community for as long as possible often depends on the degree of support given by professionals to family members. Research has shown that it is those mentally ill elderly living with family who are most likely to survive within the community, whilst those living either with an elderly spouse or alone are the most vulnerable to being institutionalized.[29] Assurance of respite care and support in times of crisis become key factors in assisting carers to go on caring. Second, in-patient beds and residential places are becoming scarce commodities. Thus, in order to prevent the blocking of much-needed long-stay places, innovations in short-stay care are imperative.

As already noted, Godber in Southampton negotiates the time of discharge for a patient at the point of admission. For example, the family may take care of the patient for a four-week period, followed by his or her admission to a "respite" bed for two weeks. A similar policy is pursued by Dr. Alex Baker, a physician at Coney Hill Hospital in Gloucestershire, who combines short-term stays with active treatment. Reasons for hospitalization include

the suspicion that further diagnosis may uncover reversible illness; to prepare a person for subsequent referral to a day hospital; when the patient's behavior is beyond the family's management; when family members are in important need of a respite or when a patient who is about to die cannot do so in reasonable comfort in her community setting."[30]

The practice of using short-term stays is an efficient one in that a single bed may be made to serve a number of patients each year.

Short-stay places and respite care are now becoming available in both nursing homes and homes for the aged throughout most of Northern Europe.

Day Hospitals and Day Care

Day care, whether its major emphasis is medical or social, is a necessary part of any service for the elderly mentally ill and their families. It is one of the key components in any service which hopes to maintain frail older people within the community for as long as possible.

Although general psychiatrists were at the forefront of the day hospital movement in Britain, its potential for the elderly was to a large extent pioneered by geriatricians. As a focal point for both medical assessment and treatment, rehabilitation, socialization and companionship, the day hospital has become the hub of many geriatric services in Britain.[31] Its value is now being recognized in the psychogeriatric day hospitals in England and Wales.[32]

A recent study by Peace (1980) examined twenty-seven day hospitals for the elderly mentally ill in Britain, showing how the day hospital can be used to the benefit of both patient and relatives, providing stimulation for the former and respite for the latter.[33] The report, however, also pointed to the lack of sufficient therapy, the fact that most services were not open on weekends; and the acute dependency on an overworked ambulance service for transportation. Nevertheless, the day hospital provides a valuable link between the patient's home and the in-patient service. It is also seen as the most active part of the hospital-based service for the elderly mentally ill. These qualities all serve to enhance the morale of staff, who can experience a sense of progress in their patients' well-being. Finally, it is interesting to note that in every service reported in this study, the initiative for setting up the day hospital rested with individual consultants—many of whom fought hard for scarce resources and even harder to retain them.

In Copenhagen, Denmark, the medical community is optimistic about its ability to keep the number of beds in gerontopsychiatric hospitals down to 1.23 per 100 inhabitants 65 and older because of the good results obtained through two day hospitals connected with two of these long-term care facilities.[34] In a large number of cases of persons admitted in quite serious condition to day hospitals, hospitalization or placement in a nursing home has been avoided. These results were obtained by improving the patients' general condition through good nutrition and adequate fluids, psychopharmacological treatment, home nursing, food delivery on weekends, assistance in the administration of medicine and treatment of physical diseases. The possibility of respite care and short-term hospitalizations is also available to family members. In fact, it is the impression of medical personnel that persons who have tried short-term hospitalizations to provide relief to their families adjust more easily to long-term care should this become necessary.[35]

Other forms of day care are also important. In many countries we are seeing innovations in the use of alternative settings for day care. Since the early 1970's, regulations have required that all newly built Danish nursing homes have a "day nursing home," to which those living in the vicinity may come and receive the same treatment and services offered to nursing home residents.[36] In many cases, the day nursing home may be open seven days a week, although the majority of participants come only two or three times a week. Whilst day nursing homes are used primarily by those with somatic illnesses, in some facilities at least half of the members suffer from organic brain disease.[37]

The day nursing home usually occupies a special wing of the nursing home and can include an activities room, a dining area, a bathing area, a physical fitness and physical therapy room, an occupational therapy room, a chiropody room and lounge space.

At the Herman Kock Garden, a nursing home in Copenhagen, attendance at the day nursing home on a given day is approximately twenty-five and in the course of a week about eighty-five.[38] Some participants are telephoned every morning, whether they are to come in that day or not, to help orient them. Problems of transportation are overcome by contract arrangements with taxi firms which regularly bring in day care members. Indeed, some firms have specially outfitted minibuses for people who are confined to wheelchairs.

Finally, in some countries both public and voluntary agencies are beginning to develop day centers specifically for the elderly mentally ill. For example, in Britain, Age Concern Berkshire, a local voluntary association for the elderly, runs a center in Bracknell for twelve very confused elderly persons who, because of their disruptive and unpredictable behavior, could not be placed in other day care centers. The main aim of the center is "to provide kindly containment, to make the clients comfortable and to provide relief to families."[39]

The center is run from a ground floor apartment which was allocated rent free to Age Concern by the housing department. Furnishings were provided by voluntary effort. Because of their special needs, a one-to-one ratio of volunteers to clients is necessary, and all the volunteers, who have to have had some experience of working with the elderly, are carefully selected by Age Concern's organizer, who offers support and some training. The team works closely with the local health care team, psychiatric nurses and social workers.

"Psychogeriatric" Home Help

As the backbone of community-based social services, the home help is often called on to assist an older person who has some degree of mental frailty. Yet only in recent years have some countries seen the need to train homemakers to cope with tasks which fall outside their normal duties.

In 1979, a pilot scheme was established in Cardiff, South Wales, to provide an intensive home help service to confused elderly people living alone or with another elderly person.[40] The service is offered evenings and weekends in addition to weekdays and includes the normal home help tasks of shopping, cooking, dressing, housework and companionship. The project is jointly funded by the district health authority and the local social services department. There is a full-time home help organizer who coordinates the scheme. This is just one example of a number of programs underway in Britain at the present time. However, most services are yet to be evaluated.

The homemaker provides one of the most practical and often most routine services for elderly people, and because of this she frequently possesses much more knowledge concerning her client than many other professional workers, whose contacts with the elderly person are often brief. However, such knowledge often goes untapped. There is still a need for greater integration of homemaker services with other personal health and social services.

Supports to Relatives of the Elderly Mentally Ill

Many of the supports that are critical to whether or not family members continue to maintain in the community their older relatives suffering from mental illness are quite similar to those needed by families caring for the physically ill. They include respite care and the availability of day care and other community services. These and others will be discussed more extensively in Chapter 8 on family care. Here we will only look at programs designed to promote the mental health of the carer.

All too often, psychological support for carers is neglected—relatives of the elderly mentally ill may find themselves the victims of feelings of guilt and despair, yet without someone to turn to. This is one area where self-help groups and action by voluntary agencies can come into their own. In the United States the Alzheimer's Disease and Related Disorders Association (ADRDA) was founded in 1979, originating from a small network of seven family support groups across the country. The aims of the organization are to support research, share information and promote education, patient care and advocacy.[41]

A similar, though more modest, example of innovation in self-help comes again from Britain. In 1977, a community psychiatric nurse and a medical social worker at the Southmead Hospital, Bristol, Avon, decided to initiate a "relative's support group" for any relative who cared for someone with a mental disorder. They felt they could help relatives become more informed about available resources.

Initial meetings showed that a mixed group of relatives—those caring for relatives of any age—would not work successfully, so they decided to concentrate on those relatives caring for the elderly mentally ill. They then structured their meetings into six sessions, one every two weeks. Each session was to focus on a particular topic, and professionals in various fields were invited to speak. The sessions included topics such as mental health problems in old age; what your social services department can do for you; what it is like living in an old people's home. Thus, relatives came to know the professional workers in health, social and voluntary agencies.

Every effort was made to ensure that relatives could attend; transportation was available, and if no one else was able to care for their elderly relatives, then they too came and were looked after by volunteers while the carers joined the meeting. The group proved to be a considerable success.

At the end of the group sessions, some relatives wanted to continue meeting and form a self-help and advocacy group. Thus, Support the Elderly Mentally Infirm (SEMI) was formed in 1978. The two groups continued in parallel for some time, and at the end of each "relative's group" session, new members joined SEMI. SEMI's aims are to increase public awareness concerning the problems of the elderly mentally infirm and those who care for them; to provide support, fellowship and information for carers; and to develop educational information leaflets. Members have appeared on local television and radio, as well as at conferences. In 1981, it obtained funding for a part-time coordinator, and plans are afoot for a flexible sitting service and a new day center for the elderly mentally infirm.[42]

TRAINING OF PERSONNEL

Services for the elderly mentally ill are probably understaffed in all countries. All too often staff report that they do not enjoy treating the elderly, experiencing feelings of pessimism concerning outcome and doubt as to whether or not their efforts are really worthwhile. Staff are just as likely to share the familiar stereotypes and prejudices concerning older people and the mentally ill as the rest of society. The need for training is great, and recent developments in some countries, increasing the scope of geriatric medicine, need to be mirrored by parallel developments in geriatric psychiatry.

In most countries, the majority of psychiatrists care for some elderly mentally ill persons as part of their normal case load. Yet very few would consider themselves to be specialists in the mental health problems of old age. The need to develop a sub-specialty in geriatric psychiatry is subject to debate in many countries; indeed, many psychiatrists would agree that the clinical content of work with elderly patients does not justify a separate specialty in psychiatry.

However, there is a need for identifiable individuals to serve as a specialist resource for others and to mobilize services for the multiple needs of older people. The geriatric psychiatrist has to be something more than a competent cli-
nician; he or she is also an administrator, organizer, coordinator and innovator,
with duties far broader than simple responsibility for diagnosis and treatment.

In a study by WHO (1979), reporting on services for the elderly mentally ill
in ten countries, only four—Bulgaria, Finland, Ireland and the United Kingdom—offered training in both geriatric medicine and geriatric psychiatry within
their medical schools at the undergraduate level.[43] Postgraduate training specialization was more commonly available in Bulgaria, Czechoslovakia, Finland, Ireland, the United Kingdom and Yugoslavia.

In the United Kingdom, it is now the policy of the Department of Health and
Social Security that there should be at least one consultant psychogeriatrician
in each health district (there are 200 in England and Wales), and the Royal College of Psychiatrists' working group for "The Psychiatry Old Age" has recently established guidelines for the appointment of such posts.[44] Other countries, however, view the consultant as a pure specialist rather than as a community
resource and seek to develop centers of excellence which can provide training
for other key personnel.

The need for training varies widely, from sophisticated education at the highest academic level to more modest kinds of training which cover a broad range
of subject matter and which can be adapted to the differing needs of personnel
working with the elderly. These personnel include general practitioners, nurses,
social workers, therapists, nursing home administrators, nurses' aides, care staff,
homemakers, relatives and volunteers, to name but a few.

The group recognized by all countries as being a central figure in care of the
elderly person is the general practitioner, the first port of call in terms of primary care. The general practitioner is also in many cases the only source of
contact for the elderly mentally ill. In the Mannheim study of the elderly mentally ill resident in the community, the large majority had no contact with either
a psychiatric or social service agency.[45] The large majority had, however, seen
a general practitioner within the past few months. Yet all too often the general
practitioner has little or no training in the psychiatry of old age. Few refer their
patients on to community psychiatric programs. Refresher courses and weekend
and week-long residential courses for general practitioners have worked well
for training in geriatric medicine; such courses could also be developed for geriatric psychiatry.

Little is known about specialized training for psychogeriatric nurses. In Ireland and Yugoslavia a small number of hours are devoted to such training, while
in the United Kingdom eight weeks' practical experience in psychogeriatrics is
provided for student psychiatric nurses.[46] In some European countries, however, there is no specialization in psychiatric nursing, let alone psychogeriatric
nursing. Yet services for the elderly mentally ill frequently require care rather

than cure. The nursing service is especially important in such cases and should become an important focus for training efforts.

Toronto, Ontario has developed an innovative approach to improving the training of nurses in psychogeriatrics in both community and institutional settings. Through its community Psychogeriatric Service, Toronto makes available to a catchment area of 450,000 the consulting skills of two full-time clinical nurse specialists who have obtained their masters' degrees in psychiatric/community mental health nursing.[47] These clinical specialists have been trained by a psychiatrist who works for the service on a part-time basis. Each specialist provides consultation, education, coordination and collaborative services in the care of the mentally ill elderly to those directly responsible for the on-going care of the client. The clinical specialist remains as mobile as possible so that consultation can be provided wherever needed.

Two basic forms of consultation are most frequently provided: regular consultation with individual or groups of nurses in which case material is presented for discussion, and client-centered consultation, where the client is seen together with the nurse who has sought the consultation. In this case, the clinical nurse specialist becomes responsible for a full psychiatric assessment and offers recommendations for on-going management.

Consultation with nurses working with the elderly in residential institutions has resulted in the planning of programs to help maintain the residents' mental health or in the rehabilitation of the ill elderly. In addition, hundreds of practitioners, again mainly nurses, have participated in the weekly psychogeriatric seminars offered by the clinical specialists. Nurses learn, among other things, to regard lack of deterioration in a patient's condition as a sign of success. They learn to build upon patients' remaining strengths rather than focus on the deficiencies. "With the psychogeriatric population we consider the lack of deterioration as a satisfactory outcome and would encourage supportive visits by nurses in order to maintain this level of functioning. Although difficult to measure, a high degree of psychological support and actual lowering of stress has been noted through nursing visits to clients and families."[48]

Finally, nurses are impressed with the need to take a "team" approach to the care of the elderly client. "A knowledge of community resources is essential to facilitate a coordinated effort of both professional and lay persons. Family, neighbors, friendly visitors and phone calls are all examples of potential support that can be coordinated by the the the nurse."[49]

PROMOTING MENTAL HEALTH

Examples of measures with mental health implications are numerous, ranging from health screening to service coordination to assure thorough assessments and treatment. In addition, pre-retirement training, adequate income in retirement, and opportunities for employment and continuing activity can all be considered as contributing to good mental health and are thus preventive measures in the broadest sense.

A somewhat narrower focus brings us also to the importance of health education and advocacy for both professionals and the general public. In Britain, MIND has been conducting a campaign aimed at promoting assistance for the elderly mentally ill. Central to this campaign has been the development of a series of publications aimed at both the professional and the layman. Topics include mental changes in elderly people, depression and the elderly, reality orientation techniques, day care, day hospitals, and alternative living arrangements, as well as major reports on current policy, new approaches to service provision, and directions in service planning and research.[50] The campaign also produced an information kit for use by local "associations for mental health" in their efforts to develop special projects for their communities.

In this next section I will primarily consider those efforts at health promotion which increase the coping skills of individuals, enhance their self-esteem and alleviate those factors which may lead to mental illness. Such efforts are not yet very common.

Bereavement Counseling

One of the most profound experiences commonly accompanying old age is that of bereavement, whether of spouse, sibling or friend. The bereaved of all ages may experience feelings of shock, disbelief, anger and guilt, but for older people these feelings may be intensified as the recognition of their own mortality comes more sharply into focus. The bereaved need time to grieve, a period which for some can take up to two years. During this time, many practical as well as emotional problems may surface for which help is needed. Bereavement counseling programs have developed in some countries to deal with these problems.

In Britain, CRUSE, a non-profit organization founded in 1959, helps widows, who are primarily older women, and their children. CRUSE has a number of local branches throughout the country and offers many activities—professional and lay counseling (usually by widowed volunteers); information, social, educational, and recreational activities; and advice. Bereavement counseling is also offered through some local-authority social service departments and "citizens'" advice bureaus.[51] In the United States a similar program, the Widowed Persons Service, is operated in many areas of the country through the American Association of Retired Persons (AARP).

Creative Group Work

Elderly people suffering from functional mental illness are far more likely to receive pharmacological treatment than any form of psychotherapy. This is in part due to their lower socio-economic status, which for a number of reasons tends to reduce access to the "talking" therapies. Yet, for many older people, the losses and deprivations of old age may put them "at risk" in terms of maintaining their self-esteem and psychological well-being, often leading to increased dependency. It is at this point that they may benefit from a chance to share their feelings either in a one-to-one situation or within a group. Several interesting examples of the use of creative group work with the elderly are available from European countries.

One model program is being carried out in a senior club in Urdorf, Switzerland.[52] Here a psychologist has sought to increase the self-esteem of older members and break down negative stereotypes of old age through a variety of group activities. These include group discussions, painting and drawing, contemplation of pictures, movement to music, drama, and training the senses to greater physical awareness—including breathing exercises. In these group sessions, every new experience is seen as a learning exercise which encourages self-actualization and helps to overcome or compensate for role loss, inactivity, isolation and disengagement.

In the Netherlands, workers at the Department of Social Gerontology at the University of Nijmegen have developed a series of encounter groups, meeting on a weekly basis, for both elderly people and those who work with them.[53] In 1978, for example, they ran ten groups—three for "healthy" older people; five for older people in nursing homes; one for students taking a gerontology specialty at the university; and a group for directors of homes for the aged. An increase or reawakening in self-esteem and self-confidence was noted in both the older people and the students, while the group of directors succeeded in beginning to examine their feelings about what the future might hold after retirement. Researchers concluded that such sessions were beneficial to all age groups; that psychosocial training was possible with older people and that this is an important area of preventive health work. It was felt that the elderly should have equal access to psychotherapeutic services with those who are younger.

The use of psychotherapeutic techniques can also be of benefit to caregivers. At the Beaton Unit in St. James' Hospital in Portsmouth, England, for example, Pearl D. Hettiaratchy, a physician, runs an eight- to ten-member relatives' psychotherapy group which has been meeting an hour weekly since 1977. Relatives are referred to the group either by the consultant or by staff working in the unit; the majority are caring for a sufferer from dementia. The devastating effects of constant caring find expression within the group as members talk frankly about their feelings, giving vent to anger, resentment, bitterness and guilt. As Hettiaratchy states, "Though no solutions are found, members leave the group relieved that the problem has been aired, shared and discussed and go back fortified to continue caring."[54]

Reality Orientation

A treatment approach that has been used with some success in day hospitals, as well as residential facilities housing the elderly mentally ill, is "reality orientation." This technique, which is also used in the United States, is designed to stimulate and develop the senses and increase social contacts—especially among persons suffering from dementia. Interesting examples of its use are found in England. For example, Una P. Holden and Alex Sinebruchow, physicians at the St. James University Hospital in Leeds, England, have shown that promising results in slowing down the process of mental deterioration and relearning lost social skills can be achieved.[55]

Brian Lodge, a physician at the Carlton Hayes Hospital in Leicestershire, England, has incorporated a system of twenty-four-hour reality orientation into both his day hospital and his in-patient service.[56] The reality orientation involves staff and patients in a continuous process of information exchange. This includes information about names, the date, month, year, time, weather, next meal, and so on. Information is presented repetitively, but only in such a quantity as the patient can cope with comfortably. A more formal arrangement is the reality orientation classroom, with classes for three or four people; these are held daily and last about thirty minutes. In addition to the presentation of basic information, other cues to learning and memory are used, such as clocks, word games, menus, diaries and puzzles; a board with key words is a prominent feature of such a program.

POLICY IMPLICATIONS FOR THE UNITED STATES

The aging of the population necessitates planning adequate mental health services for the elderly. The basic issues demanding consideration in the United States are discussed in this section.

The Need for Training

Throughout this chapter the need for training all levels of staff, both professional and para-professional, has been a constant theme. Yet, although this need is recognized, widespread implementation of training programs still seems a long way off. A lack of interest and enthusiasm still surrounds the treatment of older people, coupled with the still too prevalent belief that little can be done for those over a certain age.

Nevertheless, the importance of training needs to be reiterated. In 1975, a national planning conference on training, held by the Center for Studies of the Mental Health of the Aging, outlined the need for programs aimed not only at professional workers, such as primary care physicians, psychiatrists, nurses and social workers, but also for homemakers, home health aides, workers in senior centers, and community mental health center staff.[57] While several good training programs can be pointed to, they are relatively few in number. However, a start has been made which must be built upon for the future.

A Specialty in Geriatric Medicine

Specialization of personnel, especially concerning the role of the geriatric psychiatrist, is the subject of debate in many countries. In the United States the general consensus appears to be that geriatric psychiatry, like geriatric medicine, should be a sub-specialty and that the overall care of the elderly should remain with the primary care physician. Some argue that too much specialization can be isolating. Ewald W. Busse and Dan G. Blazer state that "the strength of geriatric medicine and geriatric psychiatry has been the application of knowledge gained through scientific endeavors in the mainstream of science and practice. Isolation would seriously jeopardize this practice."[58]

In contrast, the role of the consultant geriatric psychiatrist in Britain is often viewed as a model of specialization. The consultant usually assumes the role of "key worker" within the health service, operating as facilitator, educator and advocate, while the general practitioner is still seen as the mainstay of primary health care in the community—the first port of call. In this way the two areas of practice—specialist and generalist—complement each other.

The strength of the consultant post lies in the importance such a specialization can bring to a very neglected area of practice. Many would argue that the problems of the elderly mentally ill are of sufficient complexity to warrant such special attention; however, even in Britain specialization is not the rule. In a national survey conducted by John Wattis, Libby Wattis and Thomas Arie (1980), of 106 consultant psychiatrists providing special psychiatric services for the elderly, only thirty-nine were full-time practitioners; another fifty-two devoted more than half their time to this function.[59]

Perhaps the most important issue is not one of specialization but of level of commitment. Given the multi-disciplinary nature of work with elderly people, the need for a key worker, or focal point, who will assume responsibility for coordination and collaboration in mental health care for the elderly, becomes vital. In the United States this role may or may not be assumed by the geriatric psychiatrist. In fact, many feel that the role of management and service coordination lies outside the medical profession. Nevertheless, few will deny the important influence which the development of a medical specialty or subspecialty can have in improving service provision. This should be encouraged.

Community Versus Institutional Care

The majority of the elderly mentally ill live within the community. Such individuals can be maintained reasonably well in their own homes, given adequate home health care services and medical expertise which will support both the patients and their carers. Maintenance of the elderly mentally ill in the community demands an adequate range of community services, including homemaker, home nursing and meals services, day hospitals and centers, and short-stay and respite care. Such services are important not only in maintaining the older person at home, but also in providing support to families, friends and neighbors.

Legislation such as Title XX of the Social Security Act (1975) in the United States has sought to provide the impetus needed to develop a wide range of community services for the elderly. However, in reality, variations in provision between states can be enormous.[60] In some of the industrialized countries where these services were first initiated for all people in need, some specialized services to meet the needs of the elderly mentally infirm are now being developed. Such countries are building on services already in place. In the United States by contrast, in many places the basic infrastructure remains to be created.

Having stressed community care, we must not neglect residential services, for which there is an increasing demand. Community care cannot totally replace residential care; rather, the two should complement each other. Indeed integration with the community has long been a major goal of residential services in their efforts to improve the well-being of older residents. Situating day care units and short-stay beds within homes for the aged and nursing homes is one step towards the development of a multi-function community home. In establishing these, problems may arise from trying to provide both a homelike setting for residents and a dynamic center for the community. However, recent research has shown that given the right kind of building design and the necessary staff training, such a scheme may benefit all concerned.[61] What is needed in residential care is a greater willingness to experiment in order to improve the quality of life for residents.

Segregation Versus Integration

One of the most controversial issues relating to elderly mentally ill people is whether they should be segregated or integrated with physically disabled but mentally alert older persons within residential and hospital facilities. Some countries, including the Netherlands, Sweden and Denmark, have developed segregated nursing homes for the mentally ill in the belief that the mentally ill elderly would be shunned by both staff and other patients in integrated homes.[62] Other countries have yet to develop a public nursing home level of care but are encountering increasing frailty among those living in their residential facilities. In Britain, the decision as to whether homes for the aged should be segregated or integrated is left to the local authority, whose policy can reflect local resources—residential places, staff members, hospital and community services. Research has shown that a mix of confused and mentally alert residents is manageable if the percentage of confused is no more than 30 percent.[63] However, this is one area where much additional research is required.

Needs of the Elderly Deinstitutionalized Mental Hospital Patient

The recent U.S. policy of "deinstitutionalizing" patients, many of whom were elderly, from mental hospitals did not result in their widespread reintegration into the community, as originally hoped. Many are now accommodated in other forms of custodial care, such as nursing homes. The goal should not be "more of the same" but alternative residential provision and individual programs of rehabilitation and care which offer the prospect of an improved lifestyle. In his important study concerning the needs of the elderly deinstitutionalized mental hospital patient, William E. Oriol considers housing needs within a package of after-care which can be managed by a number of agencies—the hospital, the community mental health center, or a private psychosocial agency.[64] Given the vulnerability of the ex-patient, appropriate support within the community is vital. The elderly person needs permanent accommodation and the opportunity to develop certain social skills, rather than a transitional setting and vocational training, which are more appropriate to young people. Meeting these needs requires an increase in resources, greater staff training and a commitment to seek alternative living arrangements for frail elderly people—arrangements which maintain as far as possible their independence, privacy, dignity and freedom of choice.

Coordination and Collaboration

In all of the developing services for the elderly mentally ill, one factor is of primary importance: mental health and aging agencies, services and disciplines must work together for the good of the client. How this is achieved depends very much on the structure of the society in which care is provided. In countries where public services dominate, the basic questions are whether or not the service should be medically or socially oriented, institutional or community-based; in countries with a mixture of private, public and voluntary services, the picture becomes more complex.

However, no matter what the form of organization, there is agreement on the importance of a clearly defined unit to assume responsibility—a so-called "focal point." In Britain this would be the specialist Department of Mental Health for the Elderly, which is hospital based but community oriented; in the U.S.S.R., it would be the community based psychoneurological dispensary. In the United States such a role is perhaps most easily assumed by community mental health centers (CMHC's). The Community Mental Health Centers Amedments of 1975 (Public Law 94–63) authorize the CMHC's to provide "a program of specialized services for the mental health of the elderly, including a full range of diagnostic, treatment, liaison, and follow-up services."[65] It was the lack of service provision for groups like the elderly within CMHC's which provided the impetus for these amendments. Indeed, in 1978, only 4 percent of patients seen at out-patient public and private mental health facilities were over age 65.[66]

The underutilization of CMHC's by the elderly has been explained in a number of ways—for example, the services they need are not available; the elderly are unaware of those services which are offered; there is a lack of outreach programs; the center may not be accessible; the center staff may have little interest in working with the elderly or lack the necessary skills; the elderly may have negative attitudes towards using a mental health service; and finally, the services needed may not be reimbursable through Medicare or Medicaid. These are *all* important problems which have to be tackled if the CMHC is to offer anything like a comprehensive service for the elderly mentally ill. Of course, some areas do not possess CMHC's and in these areas, other agencies—such as area agencies on aging or senior centers—may have to assume some of the roles outlined above.

The experience of other countries in attempting to develop a coordinated system of care provides a number of lessons. First, there must be flexibility which allows for variations in local resources and local needs. Second, someone must assume responsibility for the service. Third, because the needs of the elderly mentally ill are both medical and social, mental health workers should become more aware of the whole range of community and residential services available to support both patient and carer and put them in contact with the personnel involved. Fourth, those services which are hospital based, especially within the psychiatric hospital, should not become isolated backwaters, but a dynamic and integral part of the mental health system.

Innovation

Innovative services are vital to the development of a comprehensive service for the elderly mentally ill. In times of economic vulnerability, resources must be pooled. Innovations can spring from all sources—public, private and voluntary. However, each should guard against working in isolation. There is an urgent need to break through the red tape which often prevents or hinders true collaboration. A number of innovations in the financing and delivery of services are already underway in the United States. Some projects are experimenting with the provision of services such as homemaker services or day care, funded by Medicare. Project Triage in Connecticut, for example, has used Medicare funds to develop a coordinated system of service delivery for elderly people living in a selected geographical area. Here older people may apply for services at a central office, staffed by social workers and nurses. After an initial assessment, an individual package of care is planned which may include a range of services from meals-on-wheels to mental health counseling.[67] Such examples of what can be done must be supported so that they become common practice rather than exceptional projects. The needs of the elderly mentally ill are multiple and require multi-disciplinary solutions.

Accessibility

No service is useful unless it is accessible. In the United States, the present Medicare and Medicaid coverage actively discourages the development of widespread community home health care services and out-patient services for the elderly mentally ill. Medicare coverage for psychiatric disorders is extremely limited and appears almost as an afterthought. There is a 190-day lifetime limit on treatment in mental hospitals, and the patient must pay 50 percent of outpatient services from a physician. In fact, the maximum amount Medicare insurance will pay for outpatient services is $250 in a year, and social workers, psychologists and other mental health personnel are not appropriately covered on an outpatient basis. Because of these anomalies, mental health agencies are excluded from providing outreach or home health services. According to Butler and Lewis,

The system obviously affords inadequate coverage—and, contrary to sound psychiatric practice, it promotes hospitalization rather than care in the community. Some older people have themselves checked into a hospital just to get a physical examination (basing it on some physical complaint) because this will not be paid for on an outpatient basis.[68]

Only by providing coverage for mental health services to those with acute and chronic illnesses on an equal basis with coverage for physical health care services, will there be an improvement in the availability and accessibility of services to the elderly mentally ill.

An extension of coverage to the elderly mentally ill is also needed in other legislation which purports to serve the elderly. The national conference on Services and Service Delivery in Mental Health and Aging made two recommendations in this area which are relevant, that

1) Title XX of the Social Security Act be amended to require that social support services necessary for comprehensive mental health care be a component of the State social services plan.

2) Title III of the Older Americans Act be amended to provide that the State and area agencies on aging are responsible for the inclusion of mental health services in their State and area plans.[69]

Without such amendments, state and area planning programs in aging, health care and social services may continue to neglect the needs of the elderly who are mentally ill.

CONCLUSION

Many of the most urgent questions raised in this chapter center on those elderly people in need of long-term care, at the risk of forgetting that mental health is something which concerns all older people. Ageism and the negative stereotypes associated with old age only serve to decrease the self-esteem of the elderly, and in so doing affect their well-being and mental health. Our concern, therefore, must lie with both those older people already in need of support and care and those whose lives may become increasingly "at risk."

In this chapter we have seen that most industrial countries are becoming aware of the need to develop an adequate mental health service for older people. Yet certain inhibiting factors are common to all—a lack of outreach programs; a lack of coordination and collaboration between agencies; a lack of specialist knowledge; a lack of resources. There is a desperate need for greater recognition of the mental health needs of older people within the wider system of health and social services, before what is at present a pressing need turns into a major crisis.

NOTES

1. U.S. Department of Health, Education, and Welfare, National Institute of Mental Health, *Issues in Mental Health and Aging*, proceedings of the Conference on Research in Mental Health and Aging, Bethesda, Md., Vol. 1 (November 1975); proceedings of the Conference on Training Programs in Mental Health and Aging, Bethesda, Md., Vol. 2 (April 1976); proceedings of the Conference on Service Issues in Mental Health and Aging, Bethesda, Md., Vol. 3 (June 1976).

2. U.S., Department of Health, Education, and Welfare, Federal Council on Aging, *Mental Health and the Elderly: Recommendations for Action*, reports of the President's Commission on Mental Health; Task Panel on the Elderly, and the Secretary's Commission on the Mental Health and Illness of the Elderly (Washington, D.C.: Government Printing Office, 1979); and U.S., House of Representatives, 96th Congress, Select Committee on Aging, *National Conference on Mental Health and the Elderly* (Washington, D.C.: Government Printing Office, 1979).

3. WHO, *Psychogeriatric Care in the Community* (Copenhagen: WHO Regional Office for Europe, 1979), p. 106.

4. Brian Cooper and Ute Sosna, "The Epidemiology of Mental Disorders in Late Life: Report of a Psychogeriatric Field-Study" (paper presented at the 12th International Congress of Gerontology, Hamburg, Germany, July 12–17, 1981), p. 7.

5. D.W.K. Kay, K. Bergmann, E. M. Foster, A. A. McKechnie and M. Roth, "Mental Illness and Hospital Usage in the Elderly: A Random Sample Followed Up," *Comprehensive Psychiatry* 2, No. 1 (1970):26.

6. WHO, *Psychogeriatric Care in the Community*, p. 106.

7. Ibid.

8. Kazuo Hasegawa, "Aspects of Community Mental Health Care of the Elderly in Japan," *International Journal of Mental Health* (Fall/Winter 1979/1980):39.

9. Ibid.

10. Cooper and Sosna, "Epidemiology of Mental Disorders in Late Life," p. 9.

11. Ibid.

12. United Nations, *Introductory Document: Demographic Considerations, Report of the Secretary General*, World Assembly on Aging (A/Conf. 113/4, March 26, 1981), p. 29.

13. Ibid., p. 31.

14. Robert N. Butler and Myrna I. Lewis, *Aging and Mental Health*, 3rd ed. (St. Louis, Mo.: C.V. Mosby Co., 1982), p. 61.

15. Raymond Glasscote, Jon E. Gudeman and Donald Miles, *Creative Mental Health Services for the Elderly* (Washington, D.C.: Joint Information Service of the American Psychiatric Association and the Mental Health Association, 1977), p. 168.

16. Ibid., pp. 176–178.

17. R. J. van Zonneveld, "The Netherlands," in John C. Brocklehurst (ed.), *Geriatric Care in Advanced Societies* (Baltimore: University Park Press, 1975), p. 74.

18. Ibid., p. 59.

19. U.K., Department of Health and Social Security, "The Facilities and Services of Mental Illness and Mental Handicap Hospitals in England, 1976" (Statistical and Research Report Series No. 21, 1980), p. 14.

20. John Wattis, Libby Wattis and Thomas Arie, "Psychogeriatrics: A National Survey of a Branch of Psychiatry," *British Medical Journal* 282, No. 6275 (May 9, 1980):1532.

21. U.K., Department of Health and Social Security, "Psychogeriatric Assessment Units" (Circular HM [70] II, 1970).

22. "Mental Health of Elderly People" (London: National Association for Mental Health [MIND] 1979), p. 52.

23. Ibid.

24. Ibid.

25. M. G. Shchirina, "Services in the U.S.S.R.," in J. G. Howell (ed.), *Modern Perspectives in the Psychiatry of Old Age* (New York: Brunner/Mazel, 1975), p. 510.

26. Ibid.

27. Alison Norman, "Community Psychiatric Nurses," *Mental Illness in Old Age: Meeting the Challenge*, Policy Studies in Ageing No. 1 (London: Centre for Policy on Ageing, 1982), p. 64.

28. Ibid., p. 65.

29. K. Bergmann, E. M. Foster, A. W. Justice and V. Mathews, "Management of the Demented Elderly Patient in the Community," *British Journal of Psychiatry* 132 (1978):441.

30. Glasscote et al., *Creative Mental Health Services for the Elderly*, p. 139.

31. John C. Brocklehurst and J. S. Tucker, *Progress in Geriatric Day Care* (London: King Edward's Hospital Fund, 1980).

32. Sheila Peace, "Review of Day Hospital Provision in Psychogeriatrics," in *Health Trends*, No. 4 (November 1982):93.

33. Sheila Peace, *Caring from Day to Day* (Leeds: MIND, 1980) pp. 11–12.

34. Harriet Thieme, "Gerontopsychiatry in the City of Copenhagen," *Danish Medical Bulletin* 29, No. 3 (March 1982):163.

35. Ibid., pp. 163–164.

36. Glasscote et al., *Creative Mental Health Services for the Elderly*, p. 55.

37. Ibid., p. 56.

38. Ibid., p. 55.

39. *Catalogue of Developments in the Care of Old People*, report prepared for the group on Ageing and Later Life of the Personal Social Services Council (London: Personal Social Services Council, March 1980), p. 10.

40. Ibid., p. 7.

41. Alzheimer's Disease and Related Disorders Association, *Newsletter* (November 1980), p. 1.

42. P. Masters, "The Mentally Infirm and Their Carers: A Relative Support Group in Bristol," in Frank Glendenning (ed.), *Care in the Community: Recent Research and Current Projects* (Stoke-on-Trent, England: Beth Johnson Foundation Publications, 1982), p. 129.

43. WHO, *Psychogeriatric Care in the Community*, p. 4.

44. U.K., Department of Health and Social Security, *Growing Older* (London: Her Majesty's Stationery Office, Cmnd. 8173, March 1981), p. 55; and "Interim Guidelines for Regional Advisors on Consultant Posts in Psychiatry," 5, No. 6 (June 1981):110–111.

45. Cooper and Sosna, "Epidemiology of Mental Disorders in Late Life," p. 10.

46. WHO, *Psychogeriatric Care in the Community*, p. 97.

47. J. Britnell, "Community Mental Health Nursing with the Elderly" (paper presented at the annual meeting of the U.S. Gerontological Society, Toronto, Ontario, November 1981), p. 2.

48. Ibid., p. 5.

49. Ibid., p. 6.

50. "Positive Approaches to Mental Infirmity in Elderly People," (London: MIND, 1979).

51. *Age Concern Today*, special feature on bereavement and bereavement counseling (Autumn 1977):9–19.

52. Claus D. Eck and Annina Imboden-Henzi, *Erfülltes Alter durch reicheres Erleben* (Freiburg, West Germany: Lambertus-Verlag, 1972).

53. Nan Stevens and Michel Wimmers, "Encounter Groups from a Life Cycle Perspective" (paper presented at the 11th International Congress of Gerontology, Tokyo, August 20–25, 1978).

54. Pearl D. Hettiaratchy, "Hospital-based Initiatives in Caring for the Carers, Including a Relatives' Psychotherapy Group in Portsmouth," in Glendenning (ed.), *Care in the Community*, pp. 130–133.

55. Una P. Holden and Alex Sinebruchow, "Reality Orientation Therapy: A Study Investigating the Value of This Therapy in the Rehabilitation of Elderly People," *Age and Ageing* 7 (1978):83–90.

56. Brian Lodge, "Day Hospitals for Dementia," *Practitioner* 244 (October 1980): 1077–1082.

57. U.S., Department of Health, Education, and Welfare, proceedings of the Conference on Training Programs in Mental Health and Aging, Vol. 2 (April 1976).

58. E. W. Busse and D. Blazer (eds.), *Handbook of Geriatric Psychiatry* (New York: Van Nostrand Reinhold, 1980), p. 522.

59. Wattis, Wattis and Arie, "Psychogeriatrics, p. 1529.

60. U.S., Department of Health, Education, and Welfare, proceedings of the Conference on Service Issues in Mental Health and Aging, Vol. 3 (June 1976).

61. Diane Willcocks, Sheila Peace and Leonie Kellaher, with J. Ring, *The Residential Life of Old People: A Study in 100 Local Authority Old People's Homes*, Vols. 1 and 2, Research Reports 12 and 13 (London: Polytechnic of North London, Survey Research Unit, 1982).

62. See, for example, Thieme, "Gerontopsychiatry in the City of Copenhagen," p. 164.

63. G. Evans, B. Hughes and D. Wilkin, with D. Jolley, "The Management of Mental and Physical Impairment in Non-Specialist Residential Homes for the Elderly," Research Report No. 4 (Manchester, England: University Hospital of South Manchester, Research Section, Psychogeriatric Unit, January 1981), Chapter 9, p. 12.

64. William E. Oriol, *Housing the Elderly Deinstitutionalized Mental Hospital Patient in the Community* (Washington, D.C.: International Center for Social Gerontology, 1980).

65. Public Law 94–63 (Community Mental Health Centers Amendments, 1975); reiterated in Public Law 96–398 (Mental Health Systems Act, October 7, 1980).

66. H. Pardes, statement before the National Conference on Mental Health and the Elderly (Washington, D.C.: U.S., House of Representatives, Select Committee on Aging, Publication No. 96–186, April 23–24, 1978), p. 42.

67. J. H. Hodgson and J. L. Quinn, "The Impact of the Triage Health Care Delivery System on Client Morale, Independent Living and the Cost of Care," *Gerontologist* 20, No. 3, Part 1 (June 1980):364–371.

68. Butler and Lewis, Aging and Mental Health, 1st ed. (1977), p. 145.

69. U.S., Department of Health, Education and Welfare, proceedings of the Conference on Service Issues in Mental Health and Aging, Vol. 3 (June 1976), p. xii.

6

Community Services: Social Care

Charlotte Nusberg

All industrialized countries recognize the desirability of maintaining the elderly in their own homes in respect of the latter's own wishes; the hope or belief that "open care," as the Europeans call it, is more cost-effective than "closed" or institutional care; and a desire to promote age-integrated societies. Closely linked to this goal is the availability of a wide range of what sociologist Sheila Kamerman has called "the practical helping measures," such as home help, chore and escort services, laundry services, meals-on-wheels and congregate meals, adaptations to homes, senior centers and clubs, telephone reassurance programs, emergency alarm systems, night sitting, friendly visiting, transportation, counseling, information and referral, and so on.[1]

Unlike income and health services, the social care or personal social services outlined above are just beginning to come into their own as their importance both as preventive health measures, interpreted in their broadest sense, and as a means of maintaining individuals with chronic conditions at home is recognized.

While some countries have experimented with providing additional income in lieu of services, on the assumption that the private market would respond to the demand, the experience has not been encouraging—private market forces have not been able to provide services where and when needed. Increasingly, countries like Japan and the Federal Republic of Germany have found it necessary to supplement private market forces with publicly supported programs.[2]

In the countries thought of as "welfare states"—such as the United Kingdom, Denmark, Norway, Sweden and the Netherlands—national systems of service provision have emerged which, while unevenly funded (especially in the United Kingdom) and sometimes inadequately coordinated, do make many of the services mentioned above universally available. This means that any individual regardless of age or income may apply through multiple entry points for a particular social service or set of services on the basis of need. Individuals may be requested to contribute according to ability to pay, but the service itself is considered a citizen's right; no welfare stigma is attached. These policies reflect acceptance of public responsibility for the care of the elderly. At the same time, most of these countries also provide more supports to family members taking care of their older members than does the United States. Such policies are all part of a conscious effort to redress the balance between instutitional care and community-based services, which had been heavily tilted towards the former in the first few decades following World War II.

In the United Kingdom, Denmark and Sweden, certain social services, such as home help assistance, are mandated by law, although each local authority or municipality can still determine how and to what extent the service will be provided.[3] Under Britain's Chronically Sick and Disabled Persons Act (1970), a duty was placed on each local authority to locate disabled persons in its area, publicize the services available, and provide any additional services that might be needed, such as personal aids, telephones, adaptations to the home, meals, transportation and holidays.[4] Under earlier legislation, local authorities had already been given the power to provide other services, such as laundry, friendly visiting and counseling and referral, either on their own or in cooperation with voluntary organizations.

In Sweden no one, by law, may be forced into institutional care against his or her will, even if practically twenty-four-hour care is required.[5] The result has been the development of a very sophisticated array of in-home services.

In the Scandinavian countries, the social care services are provided mainly through the public sector. In the United Kingdom, Austria, the Federal Republic of Germany and the Netherlands, a strong partnership has emerged with voluntary agencies, many of which provide the actual services, for which they are partially or totally reimbursed by government. In the United Kingdom, for example, half the meals delivered at home or served in luncheon clubs are provided by voluntary organizations.[6] And in socialist Hungary, 14,600 of the 16,000 home help aides are volunteers. The social care services lend themselves particularly well to voluntary sector provision because of the flexibility and individual attention required by the clients.[7]

Regardless of the auspices under which the social care services are provided, their very nature requires their organization and administration at the local level—even in countries with unitary or centralized forms of government. Nevertheless, the social care services usually receive generous subsidies from the national government. For example, in Norway, Denmark and Australia, municipalities are reimbursed up to 50 percent of their costs for home help and other services.[8] Finland is currently developing legislative measures which will provide a similar level of subsidy to services provided by municipalities. The uneven level of funding provided heretofore for different services is thought to have served as a disincentive to providing community services over institutional forms of care.[9]

SOCIAL CARE SERVICES

In-Home Assistance

Home help assistance is without doubt the core service in enabling older people to remain at home and it is one of the most widely used. A Dutch study found that more than 15 percent of households in the 55–64 age group and 24 percent in the 65 + age group found themselves caught at least once a year in a situation where household chores could not be performed for a period of a week or more.[10] This translates into considerable home help assistance where such services are available. In Sweden, for example, about 25 percent of pensioners received some home help assistance in 1980;[11] some of this assistance was in the form of fees paid to family members providing home help services. In Hungary, 25 percent of pensioners 75 and older receive home help services; this figure increases to 60 percent for those over 80.[12] And the service is still considered far from adequate in meeting total need! In Manitoba, Canada, home help assistance accounted for 38 percent, home nursing 77 percent, of all the community services used by clients enrolled in the province's home care program.[13] While home help services were originally developed to assist families where the mothers are temporarily or permanently incapacitated, they now serve a predominantly elderly population. In most industrialized countries, the elderly account for the overwhelming majority of the home help services' clientele— for example, up to 90 percent in Belgium and in Sweden.[14]

Because the availability of the social care services is relatively new compared to other welfare provisions, such as health care, countries still show great variations in their level of service. Table 6.1, for example, indicates the great disparity in the provision of home help assistance, and even the countries with the greatest provisions, Sweden, Norway, and the Netherlands, do not believe they are meeting all the need.

In the United Kingdom, where official guidelines call for 1.5 full-time-equivalent home help aides per 1,000 population, the belief exists on the part of many that social services resources are not keeping up with the growth in the older population.[15] According to the critic D. J. Challis, while there have been substantial increases in the level of disability among the elderly continuing to live at home over the past two decades, "the home help service appears to have become more thinly spread over a larger number of cases. . . . It is generally rare that domiciliary support is sufficiently focused so as to prevent admission to long-term care."[16]

If this relatively generous level of provision is not meeting the need in the welfare states, what can one conclude about the United States which ranks along

Table 6.1
Home Helpers per 100,000 in Selected Countries,
December 1976

COUNTRY	TOTAL POPULATION (thousands)	NUMBER OF HOME HELPERS	NUMBER PER 100,000
Austria	7,525	340	4.5
Belgium	9,957	8,661	87.0
Canada	22,000	3,290	15.0
Germany (Federal Republic)	60,000	12,685	22.0
Finland	4,500	6,073	135.0
France	50,000	7,144	14.3
Great Britain	49,000	129,724	265.0
Israel	3,300	350	10.6
Italy	54,000	50	0.1
Japan	111,934	8,706	7.7
Netherlands	13,800	82,700	599.0
Norway	3,988	33,478	840.0
Sweden	8,220	74,900	923.0
Switzerland	6,000	2,505	41.7
U.S.	209,000	60,000	28.7

Source: Adapted from figures provided by the
    International   Council of Homehelp Services, February
    1978.

the low end of the spectrum? This can be explained only in part by the fact that the United States has a somewhat younger population than the above-mentioned countries.

Home help aides can perform a variety of functions, from housekeeping and heavy cleaning to personal care and emotional support. The particular functions differ from country to country. In some, they are empowered to perform tasks that elsewhere would fall within the jurisdiction of practical nurses. Geneva, Switzerland, for example, has developed the occupation of "extra-hospital aide," with duties that lie somewhere between those of the traditional home help aide and those of a practical nurse. These aides help with personal hygiene and supervise cleanliness and security in the client's home. In France, the occupation of *aide soignante* has been developed in recognition of the personal care needs of older persons. In Sweden, heavy cleaning is no longer performed by the the home help aides; instead, mobile vans equipped with heavy-duty cleaning tools and men capable of operating them perform this work. This specialization of in-home chores has also permitted Sweden to attract more men to the home help occupation.

Some countries have several levels of home help service according to the type of clientele served. Traditionally, those home help aides devoted to the care of a family while the mother, for example, is ill or incapacitated, have obtained the most training (up to two years), and this occupation has attracted young women as a career opportunity. Home help aides designated for service to the elderly, on the other hand, have traditionally been middle-aged housewives seeking part-time work, who obtained little or no training. The rate of turnover among these home help aides typically has been very high.

Concern about high turnover rates, the rapid increase in the number of elderly persons anticipated to require home help assistance, and the drying up of the manpower pool for home help work as more and more women seek full-time and better-paying employment elsewhere is leading a number of countries to upgrade the status of the occupation in order to obtain needed personnel. Increasingly, formal training is being provided to all home help aides and this training covers, among other subjects, the special needs of the elderly. Denmark, for example, requires all home help aides to undergo seven weeks of training within the first six months of their employment, to be followed by supplementary courses at later stages.[17]

In another attempt to upgrade the status of the occupation and to make better use of the knowledge acquired by the home help aides, some jurisdictions in the United Kingdom are experimenting with using the home help aide as a key liaison person with the health services. The aide, after all, probably knows more about the home conditions of the elderly client than anyone else, and her input can contribute much, for example, to the development of a coherent ''after-care'' plan following a hospital discharge.[18]

In Sweden, home help aides are now organized into teams of ten to fifteen persons, who meet every morning to discuss their common caseload and share responsibilities.[19] Each aide is given an opportunity to serve as leader during these meetings. Teamwork diminishes the isolation in which home help aides traditionally have worked and lessens the dependency that clients often develop upon one particular aide.

Other changes in the home help role include giving the aide responsibility for performing simple home nursing functions, for which the home help service is reimbursed by the health service. This is more cost-effective than sending out a district nurse to fill every health-related need. In addition, home help aides are being taught to help clients help themselves in order to attain maximum independence.

In Denmark, many towns have extended or plan to extend their home help provision to include evening, night and weekend services. One model that has been developed is establishment of home care centers staffed with both home help aides and nursing personnel.[20] People can simply call in any hour of the day or night in case of emergencies, and in some cases such centers may prevent unnecessary hospitalization.

Even in countries where home help services are highly developed, a shortage of personnel still exists, particularly in rural areas. To help overcome such deficiencies, countries such as Norway, Sweden and Denmark permit family members or neighbors to be reimbursed for home help (and home nursing) services.

Rural areas in Sweden also make extensive use of postmen to reach out to isolated older persons.[21] The postmen are specially trained by social service departments in the variety of benefits available to older people. They are then in a position to communicate this information to their clients while delivering the mail and at the same time check on their well-being. If something seems amiss, they then report back to the appropriate authorities. Postmen may also be used to deliver medications or foodstuffs and help in snow removal. This innovative use of public servants in duties beyond their traditional roles is being emulated in Germany and in several jurisdictions in the United States as well. The United Kingdom also utilizes milkmen, who still deliver dairy products on practically a daily basis, to perform similar early warning functions.[22]

Sweden's rural elderly are also reached by "service buses" which are specially equipped with cleaning materials, personal care supplies, library books and magazines, occupational therapy materials and containers for fresh and frozen foods and are accompanied by home help and cleaning personnel, to satisfy both some of the basic and leisure needs of the isolated aged.

Nutrition Programs

Lunch clubs or meals in a congregate setting and meals-on-wheels are another of the important social care programs. Meals-on-wheels are more common than meals in a congregate setting in other countries (the reverse is true in the United States), and volunteers are widely employed in their delivery in countries such as the United Kingdom and the Federal Republic of Germany. An interesting variation on the U.S. congregate meal site can be found in Stockholm, where meals are offered at mid-day in school cafeterias; the menus are printed every day in local newspapers so that participants can exercise some choice.[23] And the location of the meals program in the schools also holds promise for intergenerational contacts.

In the United Kingdom the number of persons receiving meals-on-wheels doubled between 1969 and 1979.[24] An estimated 6 percent of the elderly (compared to 1 percent in the United States) are meal recipients in the United Kingdom.[25] Yet, official guidelines at one point suggested that meals should reach about 20 percent of the aged. As in other countries, the recipients tend to be quite old—80 plus—and living alone. However, studies indicate that in both England and Canada, meals-on-wheels recipients are not notably impaired as far as their food preparation abilities are concerned.[26] In fact, many could probably profit more from assistance with shopping or delivery of raw food ingredients.

Such findings have led the Catering Research Unit at Leeds in England to experiment with providing other meal options to clients, including the delivery of long-life food, stored in pouches, and raw ingredient packages, which require some processing and cooking on the part of the recipient. The consumer reaction to these experiments has been good; users are happy to be able to prepare their food at a time of their choice.[27] In fact, when a group of meals-on-wheels recipients was transferred to one of the alternative meals options, 40 percent were content to have their food delivered in bulk.[28] According to British researcher Malcolm Johnson, such meal options ''proved to be a highly efficient adaptation of the desired compromise between prepared food and the flexibility of timing and sense of achievement in cooking.''[29]

The Federal Republic of Germany, where an estimated 10 percent of the elderly receive meals-on-wheels, was one of the first nations to experiment with the delivery of frozen meals that had to be warmed up by the recipient.[30] It found that frozen meal delivery not only cost one-fourth of hot meal delivery, but it permitted the delivery of meals on weekends as well—when hot meal delivery systems are usually shut down.[31] To the objection that frozen meal delivery cuts down on personal contacts with the recipients, the response is made that friendly visiting can compensate for whatever loss in socializing that might result. Agencies delivering meals at home seem to be moving towards the frozen meal alternative, even providing recipients with a small freezer if they don't already have one.

Senior Centers and Service Centers

Most countries also have large networks of senior clubs or centers which can provide an array of recreational, educational and social opportunities. Many also provide direct services, such as chiropody and bathing, or can arrange for in-home services to be delivered.

In many countries, senior centers, clubs, day centers, and the like are operated mainly by the voluntary sector, although generous government subsidies are often provided. With the exception of Japan, participation levels are around 25 percent of those eligible to join, and low-income single women join in disproportionate numbers.[32] Attracting men remains a difficult problem. In Japan, on the other hand, almost half of the elderly are organized into 90,000 clubs—70 percent in rural areas and 40 percent in urban areas.[33] It is also the middle- and upper-class elderly who are more likely to participate.[34] One of the clubs' strong attractions is the provision of communal baths—a popular Japanese tradition.

French gerontologists claim to have seen an evolution over time in their senior clubs, from provision of mainly passive entertainment to older people with little energy and few interests left in their retirement, to active engagement of the elderly, not only in the clubs' activities but in their administration.[35] The most advanced centers are considered to be those which are fully autonomous in terms of elder self-rule, the activities of which encompass the broader community, in terms of both social activism and involvement of other age groups in club activities.

Senior centers by their very nature offer group services to their clients, and given the higher costs of individualized service, it is likely that the role of centers in service to the elderly will increase. The Finns have found not only that it is more cost effective to bring people to service centers than to provide them

with care in their own home—even if they require transportation to the center—
but that it has a valuable activating effect by increasing opportunities for socializing.[36] In South Africa, a number of social workers specializing in service
to the elderly are already working from senior centers. It seems probable that,
in the future, individual casework in that country will be reserved primarily for
crisis intervention situations.[37]

Centers are becoming increasingly important as coordinating bodies for the
wide range of community services available. The Dutch especially have placed
heavy emphasis on the development of ''service centers,'' of which there are
now several hundred, each of which is capable of serving a catchment area including 1,000 older persons.[38] These combine many of the social and recreational activities of the traditional senior center, but also function as important
coordinating bodies for a wide range of health and social services. A number
of health care functions, such as medical checkups, physical therapy and foot
care, may, in fact, be provided on site. Service centers may be located in a
variety of settings—for instance, they may be attached to a community facility
or a home for the aged, or free-standing. The Dutch government considers the
service centers as the linchpin of its policy to maintain the elderly in the community.[39]

Norway and South Africa too seek to provide comprehensive activities and
service to the elderly through networks of service centers. According to the South
African National Council for the Aged, the ideal center should provide social
work services, recreational and cultural activities, a health clinic, mid-day meals
and meals-on-wheels, home help assistance, visiting service, and laundry, chiropody, transportation and hairdressing services.[40] However, in both countries,
significant gaps still exist in the provision and quality of services. Researchers
in both Norway and South Africa have concluded that the service centers should
improve their methods of finding older persons in need of care and obtain more
highly trained personnel, especially social workers, to help staff the centers.[41]

Transportation

Despite the excellent public transportation systems of many industrialized
countries, mobility among the elderly remains a major concern. In most countries, the old account for a disproportionate share of the mobility-disabled, a
situation which jeopardizes their opportunities to participate in the life of the
community.[42]

By far the most common strategy adopted to increase mobility among the
elderly is to provide reduced fares on some or all forms of public transportation. Since many of the railroads and airlines are also publicly owned in other
industrialized countries, concessionary fares often provide broader travel opportunities to the elderly than is the case in the United States. While some studies, such as one done in Newcastle, England, show that fare reductions do lead
to substantial increases in the use of public transport by the elderly, there is
some question as to what proportion of the elderly really need this kind of fi-

nancial assistance and whether their needs might not be better served by improved routing or increased frequency of service.[43]

Many countries have enacted legislation requiring that public facilities be made readily accessible to the physically handicapped. The United Kingdom's Chronically Sick and Disabled Persons Act, for example, has served as a strong stimulus to municipalities to improve accessibility for the disabled.[44] The act also established the position of a minister with special responsibility for the disabled; his functions are to promote interministerial coordination and to examine the totality of assistance available to the handicapped.

The most sophisticated array of service provision for the mobility-disabled exists in the County of Stockholm, where 26 percent of all pensioners are eligible for special transport services. (The elderly constitute some 80 percent of the mobility-disabled.)[45] For the severely disabled there are special service buses which must be booked one day in advance. Most trips are for medical or educational purposes. Persons suffering from lesser disabilities are entitled to up to seventy-two subsidized taxi journeys a year for leisure purposes and as many as needed for work, school or medical treatment.[46] Of the fares for taxi journeys, 95 percent are subsidized by government; journeys by the mobility-disabled, in fact, account for 40 percent of all taxi services.[47] Clients average about seventy rides a year.[48] The county has practically completed elevator installations in all subway stations so that the mobility-disabled can better use existing public transportation.

Providing special transportation services for the mobility-disabled is expensive but is still considerably less expensive than converting existing transport so that the handicapped can take advantage of it. Belgium is a country that has purposely chosen special transportation in preference to radically adapting existing public transportation.[49] And planners in a number of countries have pointed out that improved transportation is not necessarily the most appropriate solution for a mobility problem; conveniently based community services, in-home services or subsidized telephone services can all substitute to some extent for the need to use extensive, and expensive, transportation.[50]

Other Forms of Social Care

There are numerous additional services, some or all of which are provided in many different countries, which further assist the elderly to remain in their own homes. Among them are laundry pick-up and delivery, snow removal, gardening, deliveries of groceries and other goods, installation and subsidy of telephones and emergency alarm systems, friendly visiting, and telephone reassurance chains.

None of these services is as common as those described in previous sections, and they are almost all characterized by heavy volunteer participation. The United Kingdom, in fact, has emphasized "good neighbor schemes" in recent years, through which neighbors are encouraged to provide unobtrusive services such as watching over older people living alone in their block. This, in turn, sometimes leads to the provision of more direct services, such as friendly visiting. Most important, such schemes provide "a safety net of information and contact for those who have fallen through the web of social services provided by statutory and voluntary services."[51] The hope is that good neighbor schemes will take some pressure off the public social services and provide needed early warning systems.

The experience with the some 3,000 good neighbor schemes that exist in the United Kingdom has been a mixed one. They often reflect the availability of helpers and organizers rather than the degree of need, and good neighbor schemes, not surprisingly, are more likely to be found in neighborhoods where many women do not work full-time outside the home.[52]

The richest array of social services will be of no use unless people know about them. In the United Kingdom, "good neighbors" perform an important outreach function. In Vienna, Austria, older persons are visited every three years, following a written communication, to determine whether they have needs to which the health and social service system can be responsive. In a number of cities in the Federal Republic of Germany, all persons reaching the pensionable age receive a packet of information from their liocial government regarding the benefits they are now entitled to. In Norway, neighborhood service centers systematically register all older persons living in their jurisdiction in order to be able to monitor their status over time. And in Sweden, all municipalities are required by law to actively seek out older persons who may be in need of services.

Coordination of Services, Case Management and Information and Referral

Most industrialized countries are still experimenting with the best means of coordinating the social services, not only for the elderly but for all age groups. Many models exist but none has proven itself clearly successful. And ignorance about services and benefit entitlements is still a common problem in many places.

In the absence of a statutory base assuring a particular agency the necessary coordination role, key individuals within the care services often take this function upon themselves. For example, in many countries the general practitioner must assume the coordinating responsibility with the social services, since he or she is usually an ailing person's first point of contact. The physician may be helped in this task, as in the United Kingdom, by the district nurse or health visitor, who maintains close liaison with the relevant social services. In the United Kingdom the hospital based medical social worker is another essential link between the health and social services. He or she is an employee of the local social services department and so can best assure on-going care upon a patient's discharge home.

In the Scandinavian countries, "one-stop" service centers for meeting the social care needs of the population are common, but coordination with the separately administered health services remains difficult. In addition, older people may be more hesitant about availing themselves of social services than younger people are. To help deal with this situation, Denmark has introduced the occupation of "social health counselor" to help identify the social and economic needs of older people and put them in touch with the relevant services.[53] The intent is to take preventive action before crises with expensive cost implications arise. The counselors obtain broad-based training in order to be able to deal with the panoply of human needs. Norway is expected to enact legislation shortly which will strengthen the legal basis for health and social services in local communities—all services will function as a coordinated unit.[54] Under the legislation, health services, involving physicians', nurses' and physiotherapists' services, will join the social services as the responsibility of municipalities. The national government will provide block grant funding, taking into account such factors as the age structure of the population.

In the United Kingdom, social care services for all age groups are centralized in local social services departments, but tensions continue in coordinating the social services with housing and health care, which continue to be separately administered. Even within the social services departments "the picture of resource provision for the frail elderly is one of a series of piecemeal interventions by a range of actors," according to Challis.[55] To overcome this fragmentation, he and colleagues at the University of Kent are experimenting with various mechanisms to bring about more effective case management.

One promising step towards greater coordination in the United Kingdom has been the establishment of joint care planning teams between local health authorities and social service departments to plan and coordinate services for their common clientele. Their work has been given a boost in recent years through "joint financing," a special allocation of monies which can be used by health authorities to share costs with social service and housing departments for programs that benefit them all, such as various in-home services that facilitate early hospital discharges.

The Netherlands and Austria are emphasizing neighborhood service centers for the elderly, which offer a wide range of services at one site, including the organization of home care. In a parallel development, the Federal Republic of Germany is attempting to reorganize its home care delivery system through the development of *Sozialstationen* (social service centers).

In Germany, where the bulk of community services is provided by religious and voluntary organizations, although publicly subsidized, *Sozialstationen* have also been created through the initiative of the private sector. Once a plan is approved, it is eligible for public funding, ranging from 40 to 80 percent of costs.[56] Given the federal nature of the German governmental structure, there is no one model for a *Sozialstation*. Each state has its own concept of what coordinated service delivery should involve. Generally speaking, however, *Sozialstationen* are run under the auspices of one or more private service-provider agencies, and all offer home help services, home nursing and various forms of personal care to clients of all ages. In practice, however, the elderly constitute

70–90 percent of the clientele.[57] Some of the more sophisticated *Sozialstationen* also offer social and psychological counseling requiring the expertise of trained professionals. Some reach out into the community to encourage individual and neighborhood self-help. "In this sense, *Sozialstationen* are boundary systems between the system of organized social and medical helps and the important system of self-help."[58]

While *Sozialstationen* are too new to objectively assess their impact on the well-being of older persons, German researcher Dieter Grunow believes that about two-thirds of the persons served by *Sozialstationen* would have to move to an institutional setting if the ambulatory care they are receiving were stopped.[59]

Manitoba, Canada, probably has one of the most comprehensive service coordinating and case management systems available, through its Home Care program.[60] Home Care is centrally administered through Manitoba's Department of Health and Community Services, but case management and service delivery is decentralized, largely through local and regional department staff.

While there are multiple entry points into the system, clients are all served by one case coordinator, responsible for assessing needs, coordinating a program of care, and organizing the delivery of services using whatever local resources are available—from family and friends to volunteers and trained service providers. The persons chosen to provide services are those with at least the minimum skill level required to perform the identified task. The goal is "to minimize dependence and to foster the maximum degree of independent functioning."[61] Any one or several of the following services can be provided through Home Care: household maintenance; personal care and hygiene; health maintenance; health treatment, including therapy; information, referral and counseling; personal and family social services; facility services, such as day care and clinics; volunteer services, such as friendly visiting, meals-on-wheels, handyman, transportation and shopping; and special equipment and household aids.

Since Manitoba's health and social services are funded through the same source, that is, the Department of Health and Community Services, an incentive is created to prescribe the least expensive level of care to accomplish treatment goals.

Financing the Social Care Services

While a number of industrialized countries do commonly impose means tests to determine service eligibility—including the Federal Republic of Germany, Israel and Japan—there is a general consensus that means tests should be abolished wherever possible because of their detrimental effect on service utilization.[62] In the Federal Republic of Germany, as many as 50 percent of those older persons entitled to benefits, according to one estimate, may not be applying for them.[63] A national conference on the subject of means tests in the United Kingdom (1978) concluded that "non-take-up" was "a major symptom of the inefficiency of means tests, and the ignorance of [the extent of non-take-up was] a serious error in social services administration."[64] An examination of one local authority that had abolished means tests found an improvement in the relationship between client and service provider, who could now focus entirely on assessing need rather than determining income or collecting bills.[65] In addition, the time of staff persons who had been administering the means tests was now freed for other purposes. The cost of eliminating means tests, according to the British National Consumer Council, would come to about $18 million, a small amount compared to the total personal social services budget of more than $1.7 billion in 1975/1976.[66]

In fact, the older the welfare system, the greater the likelihood that services are universally available regardless of income level. The major eligibility criterion then becomes need. In most systems, clients are asked to contribute to the cost of the service, although individuals whose income falls below a certain level are exempt from paying any fees. Usually the fee is based on the ability to pay, but in almost all cases, there is a ceiling, which rarely covers the entire cost of the service. In Denmark, for example, the most a client receiving home help services might pay—no matter how many hours of service actually obtained—is the equivalent of six hours per week of the aide's minimum wage.[67] In Stockholm, no one is obligated to spend more than 832 krona (about $180) a month for home help services.[68]

Everywhere, fees paid by clients cover a relatively small although not insignificant portion of the actual costs. While some jurisdictions have abolished all fees because the costs of administering them were found to outweigh the income received, policy-makers elsewhere consider it important to permit the elderly to pay something towards the services they obtain in order to enhance feelings of self-respect and maximize service utilization.[69] There is little known about any adverse consequences on service utilization of charging user fees.

Eligibility for services may also be limited in other ways than by need or income. For example, Oslo, Norway, limits the amount of home help assistance to eighteen hours per week. (Individuals requiring more assistance than that find themselves on a three-year waiting list for admission into an old age or nursing home.) The province of Manitoba, Canada, only accepts clients into its Home Care program who are at risk of being institutionalized, and individuals will be recommended for institutionalization at the point that home care becomes more expensive than institutional care. On the other hand, services in Sweden are truly open-ended; legally, individuals may obtain as much assistance as they require to avert institutionalization. In one case, where the home help service refused to provide further services to a particularly demanding client, she was given the money necessary to purchase her services on the open market.[70] The Swedish government reimburses municipalities for 35 percent of the costs of all home help services rendered.[71]

Universally available services with relatively low user charges result in heavy central and local government subsidization. Denmark, which along with Sweden probably spends the most on the whole range of services for the elderly, in 1980 expended 10.4 percent of its GDP for pensions, medical care and social services for the old.[72] This amounted to 50 percent of Danish social expenditure.[73] While public sentiment for cutting back government expenditures is increasing in the "welfare" states of Scandinavia, so far it has not been directed at services for the elderly.[74] A consensus seems to exist about the desirability of maintaining the elderly in their own homes for as long as possible.

In the United Kingdom, on the other hand, the Conservative government now in power has introduced budget and personnel cuts which directly and indirectly impact on the well-being of the elderly. Not surprisingly, some of the more recently introduced "public services," such as subsidized vacations, have been among the first to be cut back. But with potentially more serious impact, local authorities have had to either cut back on their levels of home help services or impose additional fees, or both.[75] In addition, the government's policy not to replace most departing public employees has disproportionately affected the availability of personnel in the home help services, which have always been characterized by high turnover rates.[76]

Finland is taking a different approach to keeping costs under control. Some localities have found it more economical to bring the elderly once a week or every two weeks to a service center where many of their personal care needs can be addressed at one time—including use of a sauna.[77] Japan, similarly, has several hundred large multi-purpose centers, complete with bathing facilities, in recognition of the inadequacies of much of the private housing. Group services also have the advantage of providing opportunities for socializing. The policy debate over the merits of group services versus individualized in-home services will undoubtedly continue and perhaps intensify in the future as budget constraints increase.

Finally, one municipality in the Tokyo metropolitan area in Japan has taken the unique approach of permitting individuals owning real estate to obtain a loan from a "public welfare corporation" for the purchase of needed services, using their property as security.[78] The loan can be used to buy a wide variety of personal social services, such as home help assistance and medical care. Upon the termination of the contract or the subscriber's death, the property is then sold and the public corporation is paid back with interest. Heretofore, public social services had only been available to the low-income elderly.

Effectiveness of the Social Care Services

Expensive as in-home services are, the belief exists that in the long run they are less costly than institutionalization. Manitoba, Canada, is one of the few jurisdictions that may actually have proven this to be the case. In Manitoba, the waiting lists for entry into institutional care were greatly reduced as a result of the introduction of Home Care, and one significant research study found that in the absence of Home Care, 70 percent of the program's clientele would have been institutionalized, at a much higher cost.[79] It should be emphasized, however, that Manitoba restricts admission into Home Care to those persons deemed at risk of institutionalization.

Other countries have only recently begun to undertake serious studies of the effectiveness of their social care programs; the results are not yet in. However, some of the data that are available raise serious questions about the relationship between in-home services and rates of institutionalization. Sweden, for example, which has one of the most sophisticated arrays of community services available anywhere, also has unusually high institutionalization rates, between 8 and 10 percent.[80] The reasons for this are not clear. A comparative study done between the cities of Bristol, England, which has a relatively low rate of institutionalization among the elderly, and Stockholm suggests that some of the difference might lie in the greater access had by the British to general practitioners and geriatric services and in the fact that many more of the women work in Stockholm than in Bristol, and thus are not available to provide support to older family members.[81] Bristol also had a more extensive network of voluntary services to the elderly.

The extent and nature of service utilization will also bear to some extent on the need for institutionalization. The United Kingdom, while it has a coherent system of service delivery, does not have the resources to fund the services adequately. According to researcher Anthea Tinker, while those with the greatest needs are likely to obtain some services, they are unlikely to obtain all they require. And many older persons, even where services are freely available, are reluctant to take advantage of them because they view them as still tantamount to accepting charity. It is those persons who are already in touch with one service who are the most likely to apply for others.[82]

How one determines adequacy with regard to service provision is an issue likely to remain full of thorns. A study conducted in the early 1970's by the Danish Institute of Social Research found that no matter how high or low the level of provision, the degree of need for additional services was about the same.[83] The conclusion drawn was that policy-makers must reconcile themselves to the fact that there will always be waiting lists and that firm decisions with regard to priorities are necessary.

Thus, while the evidence is not yet in on the extent to which home and community care substitute for institutionalization in a cost-effective manner, it should be borne in mind that cost considerations have only been one, albeit a major, factor in establishing a range of social care options. Equally important have been a desire to promote an age-integrated society by permitting older people to remain in their own homes and a respect for the overwhelming desire of the elderly everywhere to remain in their own homes for as long as possible.

Other Problem Areas

One of the strongest critiques made against the welfare state as it is practiced in the Scandinavian countries is the rigidity and inflexibility of response to new problems on the part of government, which prefers relying on traditional approaches to experimenting with innovations.[84] Social analyst Bent Rold Andersen of Denmark, as well as others, has called for a greater openness to private sector innovation and encouragement of self-help measures at the individual and neighborhood levels to restore a sense of spontaneity in civic life.[85] A new approach also requires greater consultation with the consumers of services, whose interests and concerns have not always been reflected in public policy.

Other problem areas relate to access to community services. On the one hand, many older people who need services are not taking advantage of them, for a variety of reasons; on the other hand, the demand for services seems practically open-ended, no matter how generous the level of provision. And judging eligibility on the basis of need can also lead to some pretty arbitrary decision-making. Few jurisdictions have thought through as carefully as Manitoba has, the point at which home care should no longer substitute for some form of institutional care, but clearly there is a point at which home care becomes not only more expensive than institutional care, but when clients' homes become mini-institutions and their needs might better be met in a group setting, offering greater opportunities for socializing. In fact, most countries still face a shortage of institutional beds, despite the rapid expansion of community services.

A shortage of personnel also plagues the social care services, where the nature of the work has not so far been competitive with the higher-status, better-paying jobs offered elsewhere. Sources of volunteers are also drying up as women enter the labor force in larger numbers.

However, the challenge of meeting the needs of an increasingly dependent older population is leading several countries to take imaginative steps to upgrade the status and functions of the helping occupations in order to attract the personnel required and to broaden the scope of other occupations not traditionally associated with the caring professions, such as those of postmen and milkmen, in order to make the most efficient use of resources.

POLICY IMPLICATIONS FOR THE UNITED STATES

Despite these problems, the welfare states have chalked up some remarkable achievements. Most already have 14 percent or more of their populations in the 65+ age group, a situation the United States will not approach for many years yet, and are coping with the situation in a reasonable and humane fashion. Sharp misery among the elderly for lack of resources is rarely found. The universal availability of benefits in many cases permits needs to be met on the basis of functional criteria, and the fact that such benefits are usually available to all age groups regardless of income level increases the political support available for social services. Access to the social care services is viewed by everyone as a right; they are not simply regarded as programs "for the poor alone." Perhaps a reason the social care services have never obtained adequate political support in this country is that they have never been perceived as services required by potentially everyone at some point during his or her lifetime.

In the United Kingdom, an underlying social philosophy created the base for the "welfare" state. In the Scandinavian countries, the "welfare" state emerged more gradually as a result of many pragmatic considerations. It just seemed simpler—and more cost-effective—to provide for the needs of everyone through one bureaucratic structure—the government—than to create numerous bureaucracies, public and private, catering to clients eligible for benefits on the basis of differing criteria. The private, for-profit sector is hardly at all involved in the social care system, for both historical and ideological reasons. Profit motives are not thought to mix well with social care needs.

There is little question but that other countries have been willing to fund the social care services at a more generous level than has been the case so far in the United States. This is reflected, for example, in the much higher availability elsewhere of home help services. A higher value set on public responsibility for the welfare of others and feelings of greater solidarity with one's fellow citizens explain much in the greater willingness to be taxed in other industrialized countries. These differences are highlighted by the fact that cost-effectiveness has not been at the forefront of European policy discussions regarding the extension of community-based services, as they have been in the United States. The possibility that home care might end up costing more than institutional care was considered a risk worth taking in favor of permitting the elderly to stay in their own homes and preserving age-integrated societies. It is only relatively recently, as other countries have begun to experience hard times economically, that serious research into the cost-effectiveness of ''open'' versus ''closed'' forms of care have been undertaken.

While the U.S. taxpayers may not wish to fund the social care services to the same extent that they are supported in some other countries, there is still much this country can do to streamline and improve existing efforts. The fragmentation in the service delivery system so common in the United States does not exist to the same degree in most other industrialized countries. Systems have been put into place which, funding permitting, can provide a readily accessible continuum of care. This has been achieved in almost all cases by the public sector's taking the lead in both providing services itself and coordinating the efforts of voluntary agencies along with its own, to assure that a full range of services is provided. Responsibility for the provision of services usually rests with local government. The national governments set policy guidelines, provide much-needed financial aid, and monitor program implementation. In several countries with an interest in preserving a strong voluntary sector, non-profit agencies obtain large public subsidies to perform functions that government would otherwise have to provide.

Various institutional mechanisms have been developed to assure easy access to the social care system, such as unified social service departments in the United Kingdom and service centers in the Netherlands. Manitoba has carried its service coordination function one step further by unifying its health and social services in one Home Care program. These institutional mechanisms provide simple access in one location to a fairly comprehensive range of services. At the same time, there are multiple entry points into the system.

Income tests are widely used to help defray the cost of the social care services. While services may be free to the poor, others pay according to their ability; the fees are nominal in most countries, but they certainly hold the potential for providing a fair way of sharing costs between consumers of services and taxpayers. In many areas of the United States where older persons cannot obtain services even though they can pay or contribute towards them, consideration could be given to providing public or publicly-supported services on a sliding fee scale basis, which can be adjusted according to a community's financial circumstances.

If cost factors remain the primary consideration, another approach would be to limit eligibility for the range of home care service to those at risk of institutionalization. The province of Manitoba believes it can identify such individuals with reasonable precision and that home care for such people is less costly than the institutional alternatives. On-going case management assures that home care functions are appropriately allocated and coordinated among family and neighbors (if available) and volunteers and the public social (and health) services.

Finally, the United States might consider experimenting more widely with the use of non-traditional personnel, such as postmen, in reaching out to the elderly. Neighborhoods could be mobilized successfully, as has been the case in some areas in the United Kingdom, to watch over their vulnerable elderly and provide a needed early warning system.

The United States has been accused by some of "throwing money at problems." Perhaps a more systematically thought through use of the money already being spent might take us a major step forward toward a comprehensive social care system.

NOTES

1. Sheila B. Kamerman, "Community Services for the Aged," *Gerontologist* 16, No. 6 (December 1976):536.

2. Alfred J. Kahn and Sheila B. Kamerman, *Social Services in International Perspective* (Washington, D.C.: U.S. Department of Health, Education, and Welfare, Social and Rehabilitation Service, Office of Planning, Research and Evaluation, 1976), p. 308.

3. Kamerman, "Community Services for the Aged," p. 534; Inger Erdal, "Social Services for the Elderly," *Danish Medical Bulletin* 29, No. 3 (March 1982):124.

4. Anthea Tinker, *The Elderly in Modern Society* (New York: Longman, 1981), p. 102.

5. Tullia von Sydow, First Secretary, National Swedish Board of Health and Welfare, personal communication with author, October 1980.

6. *Ageing in the United Kingdom*, report prepared for the World Assembly on Aging (London: Department of Health and Social Security, 1982), p. 12.

7. *Hungarian National Report on Aging and the Situation of the Aged Population*, report prepared for the World Assembly on Aging (Budapest: Hungarian Academy of Sciences, 1982), p. 14.

8. Erdal, "Social Services for the Elderly," p. 124; *Aging in Norway*, report prepared for the World Assembly on Aging (Oslo: Ministry of Health and Social Affairs, 1982), p. 29.; *Ageing in Australia*, report prepared for the World Assembly on Aging (Canberra: Australian Department of Social Security, 1982), p. 54.

9. *Aging in Finland*, report prepared for the World Assembly on Aging (Helsinki: Ministry of Social Affairs and Health, 1982), p. 73.

10. *Netherlands National Report on Aging Policy*, report prepared for the World Assembly on Aging (Rijswijk: Ministry of Cultural Affairs, Recreation and Social Welfare, 1982), pp. 7–8.

11. *Just Another Age*, report prepared for the World Assembly on Aging (Stockholm: Ministry of Health and Social Affairs, 1982), p. 31.

12. *Hungarian National Report on Aging*, p. 14.

13. E. Thompson and C. Motuz, "The Manitoba/Canada Home Care Study: Some Preliminary Findings" (paper presented at the annual meeting of the Canadian Association on Gerontology, Halifax, Nova Scotia, November 1979), p. 10.

14. Report from the Congress of the International Council of Homehelp Services (Stockholm, 1981); *Just Another Age*, p. 31.

15. Shena M. Latto, "Managing the Care System," in Frank Glendenning (ed.), *Care in the Community: Recent Research and Current Projects* (Stoke-on-Trent, England: Beth Johnson Foundation Publications, 1982), p. 65.

16. D. J. Challis, "Towards More Creative Social Work with the Elderly: The Community Care Project," in Glendenning, *Care in the Community*, p. 44.

17. Erdal, "Social Services for the Elderly," pp. 124–125.

18. *Organising Aftercare* (London: National Corporation for the Care of Old People, 1979), p. 19.

19. Courtesy of Tullia Von Sydow.

20. Erdal, "Social Services for the Elderly," p. 125.

21. *Just Another Age*, p. 33.

22. Age Concern England, *Information Circular* (December 1975).

23. Courtesy of Jennifer Ruddick, report of a study tour, December 1975.

24. Malcolm Johnson, Silvana di Gregorio, and Beverly Harrison, *Ageing, Needs, and Nutrition: A Study of Voluntary and Statutory Collaboration in Community Care for Elderly People* (London: Policy Studies Institute, 1982), p. 13.

25. Kahn and Kamerman, *Social Services in International Perspective*, p. 290.

26. Johnson et al., *Ageing, Needs, and Nutrition*, pp. 79–81; Community Care Services, Inc., and Ilsa Blidner, "Client Satisfaction Report 1: Meals on Wheels of Metroplitan Toronto" (June 1979), p. 12.

27. Johnson et al., *Ageing, Needs, and Nutrition*, p. 124.

28. Ibid., p. 122.

29. Ibid., p. 124.

30. Dieter Grunow, "Sozialstationen: A New Model for Home Delivery of Care and Service," *Gerontologist* 20, No. 3 (June 1980):311.

31. *Urban Innovation Abroad*, May 1979.

32. See, for example, Colette Douriez, "Le Club d'Hier, d'Aujourd'hui et de Demain," *Années, Documents CLEIRPPA* (June 1978):7; Henning Friis, "The Aged in Denmark: Social Programmes," in Morton Teicher et al. (eds.) *Reaching the Aged: Social Services in Forty-four Countries* (Beverly Hills, Calif.: Sage Publications, 1979), p. 207.

33. Daisaku Maeda, "Self-Defense of the Aged Through Old People's Clubs," in *On Defense of the Ageing and Ageing, Mankind's World Problem* (Washington, D.C.: International Federation on Ageing, 1974), pp. 8–9.

34. Ibid., p. 9.

35. Colette Douriez, "Le Club d'Hier, d'Aujourd'hui et de Demain," pp. 5–6.

36. *Aging in Finland*, p. 31.

37. South African National Council for the Aged, Annual Report (1979).

38. R. J. van Zonneveld, "Les Centres de Services aux Pays-Bas," *Gérontologie et Societé* (December 1978):90, 92.

39. Ibid., pp. 90–91.

40. Margaret Bromberger, *An Evaluation of Service Centers for the Aged in South Africa* (Johannesburg: South African National Council for the Aged, 1981), pp. 30–31.

41. Ibid., pp. 24, 27; *Service Centers for the Elderly in Norway, 1974–1977* (Oslo: Norwegian Institute of Gerontology, 1980), p. 31.

42. Charlotte Nusberg, "Report on an International Conference on Mobility for the Elderly and Handicapped," *Ageing International* 6, No. 1 (Spring 1979):16.

43. Ibid., p. 19.

44. Ibid., p. 17.

45. Ibid., p. 16.

46. Ibid., p. 18.

47. Ibid.

48. Ibid.

49. Courtesy of the Council of International Urban Liaison, Washington, D.C. 1979.

50. Nusberg, "Report on an International Conference on Mobility for the Elderly and Handicapped," p. 20.

51. Philip Abrams et al., *Action for Care: A Review of Good Neighbour Schemes in England* (Berkhamsted, Volunteer Centre, 1981), p. 17.

52. Ibid., p. 37.

53. Inger-Lise Dyrholm and Larry Coppard, "Social Gerontology in Denmark: Improving Services in a Time of Recession" (paper presented at the annual meeting of the U.S. Gerontological Society, San Diego, Calif., November 1980), p. 16.

54. *Aging in Norway*, pp. 54–55.

55. Challis, "Towards More Creative Social Work with the Elderly," p. 45.

56. Grunow, "Sozialstationen: A New Model for Home Delivery of Care and Service," p. 312.

57. Ibid.

58. Ibid., p. 314.

59. Ibid., p. 316.

60. Thompson and Motuz, "Manitoba/Canada Home Care Study," p. 2.

61. Kahn and Kamerman, *Social Services in International Perspective*, pp. 396–397; *Means-Tested Benefits: A Discussion Paper* (London: National Consumer Council, 1976), p. 80.

62. Kahn and Kamerman, *Social Services in International Perspective*, pp. 396–397; *Means-Tested Benefits: A Discussion Paper* (London: National Consumer Council, 1976), p. 80.

63. Maria Kroger, "Barriere bei Inanspruchnahme von Sozialhilfe bei Alten Menschen," *Altenpflege* (January 1980).

64. "Means Tests in Local Authority Social Services—Who Needs Them?" (discussion paper, London: National Consumer Council, July 1978), p. 12.

65. Ibid., p. 11.

66. Ibid., pp. 13–14.

67. Erdal, "Social Services for the Elderly," p. 125.

68. *EURAG Newsletter* (March 1978).

69. *Means-Tested Benefits*, p. 5.

70. Courtesy of Tullia von Sydow.

71. *Just Another Age*, p. 32.

72. Peter Uldall, "The Elderly's Consumption of and Contribution to the Gross Domestic Product in Denmark," *Danish Medical Bulletin* 29, No. 3 (March 1982):98.

73. Ibid., p. 97.

74. Dyrholm and Coppard, "Social Gerontology in Denmark," p. 9.

75. Rodney Hedley and Alison Norman, "Homes Help—Key Issues in Services Provision" (London: Centre for Policy on Ageing, 1982), p. 11.

76. Courtesy of David Hobman, 1980.

77. International Council of Homehelp Services, *Information Bulletin* (April 1979).

78. *Rojin no fukushi to hoken* (April 1981).

79. Thompson and Motuz, "The Manitoba/Canada Home Care Study," p. 10.

80. "Old-Age Care in Sweden" (Stockholm: Swedish Institute, May 1981), pp. 3–4.

81. R.B.K. MacGregor and S. Sjolund, "Why Does Stockholm Have Eight Times As Many Hospital Beds for the Elderly As Bristol?" *World Hospitals* 16 (May 1980):13–14.

82. Tinker, *The Elderly in Modern Society*, p. 179.

83. Friis, "The Aged in Denmark," pp. 209–210.

84. Bent Rold Andersen, "Commentary on the Basic Document," *New Directions in Social Policy—A Critical Examination of the Scandinavian Experience and Its Lessons for the Region* (Paris: Regional Office for Europe, International Council on Social Welfare, 1979), p. 65.

85. Ibid., p. 68.

7

Housing Provision

Charlotte Nusberg

The broad picture of housing for the elderly in other industrialized countries is similar to that in the United States. In disproportionate numbers the elderly live in older and more dilapidated housing, often without adequate sanitation, or must spend a larger percentage of their income for good quality housing.[1] Almost everywhere the rural elderly fare worse in their housing conditions than do their urban counterparts.[2] However, even in urban areas, the elderly tend to be concentrated in the inner city where conditions of blight are common.

In the United States and in some other countries, the elderly are also disproportionately represented among homeowners; many of them have finished paying off their mortgages. Despite this wealth in assets, a good number of older persons find themselves caught in an income squeeze because of high property taxes and the need for continuous maintenance and repairs. And once their families have gone or their spouses have died, many older persons find themselves inhabiting homes that are too large, with few viable alternatives open to them.

Despite such problems, these countries are practically unanimous in reporting that the overwhelming majority of the elderly wish to continue living in their own homes as long as possible—even to the point where it may become impractical for them to do so.[3] Many kinds of measures have been adopted to permit the elderly to remain in their homes, not only in respect of their wishes, but also in the belief that encouraging continued residence in the community is less costly than institutionalization and promotes integration in the community. It is in the measures that have been adopted to meet the elderly's housing needs that other countries differ from the United States—not so much in the kinds of initiatives, but in the degree of effort. Few, if any, countries have solved all the housing needs of their older populations, but a number have taken large steps in this direction.

MEASURES FACILITATING CONTINUED COMMUNITY LIVING

Increasing the Housing Stock

Although some people believe that putting enough money into consumers' hands will stimulate the private housing industry to build a large enough variety of housing to meet a wide range of needs, that money has either not been available or the housing industry has not risen to the challenge in most countries. The result has been the introduction of a number of production subsidies in the form of grants, low-interest or subsidized loans, and loan guarantees by either national or local governments to stimulate housing construction, including dwellings for the elderly.

The extent of public sector participation in the construction of housing varies considerably. In the socialist countries of eastern Europe, for example, practically all housing is constructed through public agencies. By contrast, in most industrialized countries of the West, the national government only sets housing policy and provides some financial assistance. The construction and management of much of the housing stock is left to local governments and non-profit and for-profit developers. Building societies and cooperatives are especially active in countries outside the United States.

In the United Kingdom about one-third of all housing is "local authority" housing—that is, built by local government—and about one-third of the elderly live in such housing.[4] (Local government in the United Kingdom has a legal duty to house older people who find themselves homeless.) In the United States, only about 3 percent of the housing stock is "public" housing, and 3 percent of the elderly inhabit it.[5] (However, about 40 percent of the public housing is occupied by older persons.)[6] In France almost all housing is built by non-profit or limited profit developers, but about 50 percent of all housing starts obtain some form of governmental financial assistance.[7]

In addition, most governments have supported the construction of specially designed housing for the elderly. In Ireland, local governments have largely complied with a national government directive that not less than 10 percent of overall housing output by local housing authorities be devoted to special housing for the elderly.[8] In the United Kingdom, a considerable proportion of local authority housing construction has been dedicated to housing the elderly. Under the Thatcher government's spending cuts, however, the amount of new construction has declined considerably. Instead, partnerships between the private sector and local government are being encouraged. One manifestation of this policy is the increasingly privately financed construction on land made available by the local authorities.[9] In some cases, older persons wishing to buy into such a housing development may then be eligible for a discount on the purchase price.

Many western European programs make extensive use of low-interest loans and loan guarantees to stimulate the construction of low- and moderate-income housing for their populations. In France and the Netherlands, for example, one-half to three-quarters of new housing starts receive some sort of governmental assistance, in exchange for which rents are kept reasonably low.[10]

In France the Habitation Loyer Moderée (HLM) is the main sponsor of low- and moderate-rental housing; for a number of years it has made mortgage loans available covering 85 percent of project costs at 1 percent interest for forty-five years.[11] Rents in HLM projects are set at the amount needed to repay the loan and cover maintenance costs without profit to the developer. Other low-cost loans are also available to private developers if they agree to devote a portion of a large project to non-profit housing. France, in fact, has had a law on its books since 1973 requiring builders of projects with more than 300 units to allocate at least 20 percent of these to the elderly in exchange for low-interest loans.[12] Under this requirement, about forty thousand new dwellings have thus far been set aside for the elderly.[13] Finally, low-interest loans and loan guarantees are available from the Crédit Foncier to private developers who agree to limit profits to not more than 6 to 7 percent.[14] A considerable amount of middle-income housing is financed in this way. The financial institutions providing these funds in France are controlled by the government but draw their revenues from a variety of sources, including individual depositors and payroll tax contributions—that is, employers with more than ten employees contribute 1 percent of their payroll to a national housing fund.[15]

In the Netherlands, one-fourth of new housing starts have been made possible by fifty-year loans at below-market interest rates, mainly to non-profit associations—but again with the requirement that rent limits be set.[16] In addition these associations are reimbursed the difference between rent receipts and increases in operating expenses attributable to inflation. Loan guarantees up to 100 percent are the second major source of funding for low-income housing in the Netherlands.[17]

The result of such financial incentives has been a rapid expansion in new construction in countries such as France and the Netherlands since World War II. American researcher James M. Rubenstein observes that in the late 1970s about 525,000 new housing units were added each year in France, which then had a total population of about 52 million; in the Netherlands there were 115,000 annual housing starts for a population of 13 million.[18] "In contrast, the United States, with 215 million people, has averaged 1.5 million new houses in recent years and has rarely seen more than 2 million per year."[19] This burst of construction can be partly explained, perhaps, by the more serious housing needs in other countries, but, no doubt, the greater willingness by government to play an active role in housing policy has also played an important role.

Housing Subsidies

Consumer subsidies in the form of housing allowances or rent rebates are quite common in many European countries. These are usually available to all age groups who pass an income and/or means test, but older persons, because of their usually lower economic status, tend to be the chief beneficiaries, perhaps accounting for as much as three-fourths of the subsidies in countries such as the United Kingdom, Denmark and the Federal Republic of Germany.[20] (In the United States, an estimated 50 percent of beneficiaries of rent subsidies are elderly.[21]) The proportion of pensioners receiving housing allowances can be quite high. In Denmark, approximately 20 percent of pensioners receive a housing allowance.[22]

Housing allowances were commonly introduced following World War II to help cope with high housing costs resulting from severe housing shortages. They can be provided by both national and local governments. Unlike in the United States, such allowances are paid directly to individuals rather than to landlords, increasing the potential impact of this benefit on the housing market. These allowances are often available to homeowners as well as to renters, in order to help defray the costs of home repairs and property taxes. (A Reagan administration proposal would modify the existing United States rental allowance program so that, as in many European countries, individual tenants and homeowners would be eligible for benefits. However, the annual subsidy would be reduced from an average of $2,800 a year to a maximum of $1,800.)[23]

Housing allowances permit older persons to live in quality housing they would otherwise not be able to afford. Under Denmark's Act on Housing Allowances for Pensioners (1978), it is expected that, eventually, the majority of pensioners will move to improved housing in their old age, although it will be some time before the supply of adequate housing will be sufficient to meet the demand.[24] In many cases, housing allowances simply permit individuals to continue living where they have always lived despite rapidly increasing rents or property taxes.

Housing allowances typically are means-tested and/or income tested, and eligibility requirements can vary greatly. These may relate to the size of the dwelling and the number of rooms per inhabitant, the proportion of one's income spent on rent, and so on. The proportion of the rent paid above what is considered a fair contribution by the tenant—such as 15 percent of taxable income—can range between one-third to three-quarters or more and is frequently on a sliding scale, with higher allowances for persons with lowest incomes.[25] In Denmark, the maximum annual housing allowance could not exceed 14,604 kroner (approximately $1,622) in 1981, nor was this payable on rents exceeding 27,600 kroner (approximately $3,066).[26] (These amounts could, however, be raised by 50 percent for dwellings designed for the disabled.)

There are few studies available indicating the extent to which the existence of housing allowances actually encourages new housing or the improvement of existing stock, as opposed to landlord profiteering. Debate also continues on whether it would not make more sense to assure the adequacy of pensions rather than provide special housing allowances. Despite these uncertainties and disagreements, there is a widespread belief that consumer subsidies in the form of housing allowances are still a necessary complement to production subsidies to assure quality housing for the elderly.[27]

Rehabilitation, Renovation and Adaptation of Homes

Because older people tend to be found more frequently in older, delapidated housing, loans and grants for home repairs, rehabilitation and adaptations can play an important role in their ability to continue living in their own homes. The one U.S. program established to assist homeowners with rehabilitation is no longer being funded. By contrast, other industrialized countries are still making such funds available on relatively generous terms.

France, for example, several years ago set for itself the goal of rehabilitating some 200,000 sub-standard housing units a year, of which some 60,000 were estimated to be occupied by elderly households.[28] (An estimated 2 million French elderly live in sub-standard housing.[29]) This program has been accelerated under the Mitterrand administration, which is now making available up to Fr 6,000 (approximately $857) per unit for rehabilitation purposes—double this amount where a disability exists in the household.[30] Applicants eligible for rehabilitation loans and grants include the owner occupant, landlord or tenant. Housing allowances prevent displacement of low-income tenants, many of whom are elderly, when the landlord passes on the costs of rehabilitation to the tenant in the form of higher rents.

Similarly, in the United Kingdom, owners, landlords or tenants can apply to their local governments for small grants to cover the costs of adaptations, improvements or repairs to their homes. Individuals wishing to improve the home of a close relative are also eligible. The grants can cover from 75 to 90 percent of eligible costs for the renovation of sub-standard dwellings or for the adaptation of housing specially for the benefit of disabled persons.[31] Qualified homeowners can seek, in addition, a "maturity loan" from their local government to help cover their share of the costs of improvements.[32] Only interest must be paid on such loans; the principal can be deferred until the death of the owner. These benefits, however, have all been seriously threatened by cutbacks in expenditures for housing by the Thatcher government.[33]

Means-tested home improvement or repair loans are available in Norway with no repayment required the first six years. Thereafter, interest is charged starting at the subsidized rate of 5 percent a year; this is increased by 1 percent a year until a ceiling of 10.5 percent is reached.[34]

New Zealand provides interest-free loans to the seriously disabled for essential alterations—no repayment is required until the home is sold.[35]

The Netherlands provides a grant of G2,000 (approximately $666) towards the cost of adapting small rented houses to meet the needs of the elderly.[36]

And Sweden deliberately favors low or no interest loans to the elderly over other age groups for home improvements or modernization in order to prolong older people's independence. Loans made to the elderly for modernization are forgiven after five years. The result is that Sweden may have one of the highest quality housing stocks for the elderly in the world.

Housing to Scale

The problem of elderly homeowners living in oversized houses at a time when there are severe housing shortages for others is being approached imaginatively in some countries. France provides moving and resettlement subsidies to low-income persons moving from overpopulated areas and underutilized homes.[37] The home to which one is moving must be one's principal residence and, as a rule, one must move into a community of less than 10,000 population. This latter requirement can be waived, however, if the applicant is leaving an underoccupied building or moving into a home for which the applicant has financed the construction. The subsidies are paid by the community the person is leaving. Persons who were receiving housing subsidies in their old homes remain eligible to receive them in their new locations.

In Munich, West Germany, the city government has set aside $600,000 to stimulate the voluntary release of underoccupied housing, much of which is inhabited by older persons. Individuals can receive over $3,000 in moving assistance plus a smaller subsidized apartment if they give up their homes. In 1980, 250 housing exchanges had been completed, saving city officials an estimated $13 million—the estimated cost of constructing 250 new units to house the larger families who ended up moving into the underoccupied housing.[38]

In New Zealand, the national housing corporation provides bridging financing to local authorities and non-profit housing groups for the construction of apartments for sale to owners of over-sized housing. The purchaser must contribute at least 90 percent of the equity from the sale of his or her home, minus expenses for moving and new furnishings. Since 1969, more than 560 apartments have been constructed under this scheme.[39]

And in the United Kingdom, Help the Aged, a charity organization, developed the concept of "gifted housing" to deal with the situation of large, underinhabited homes and the need for additional housing by the elderly. Through this program, older people owning large homes donate them to Help the Aged, which, in turn, converts them into rental apartments for other elderly persons. In exchange, donors and their spouses can live in one of the renovated apartments rent-free for the rest of their lives. It also frees them of the burden of property taxes and the costs of keeping up large homes, while providing them with companionship and emergency assistance. Finally, it allows homeowners to continue living in a familiar neighborhood.

Special Safeguards

Some countries have adopted measures which have the effect of providing the elderly with special safeguards to their continued living in the community. The Federal Republic of Germany's Social Tenancy Law, for example, regulates the length of notice required before a landlord can evict a tenant; the period of notice increases with the length of tenancy. This provision favors older tenants, who are less mobile and more likely to have lived in the same place for many years.[40] In addition, a tenant can demand the continuation of his or her tenancy if the hardship imposed by an eviction cannot be justified. Other provisions forbid individuals who have bought rental property for their own use to give tenants notice before three years have expired. The law also protects tenants against inordinate rent increases.

Several local jurisdictions in Germany have gone even further. In Düsseldorf, for example, a landlord who gives notice to old or sick tenants must suggest places to which they can move, and investigate the suitability of new locations from both a physical and financial viewpoint.[41]

A very different kind of safeguard is extended to rural elderly persons in France, where survival during harsh winters is problematic in isolated homes having inadequate heating and sanitary facilities. The Home du Cameroun, in the Vosges, is one example of a winter residence for the rural elderly.[42] This publicly subsidized facility charges its winter residents about Fr 25 ($3.50) per day for food, lodging and a variety of therapeutic and recreational activities.

Housing to Encourage Family Support

While only a minority of older persons live with adult children in western industrialized countries, even if they wished to they might experience difficulty in living with them because housing today is not constructed to accommodate the extended family. Japan is an exception in this pattern among industrialized countries; approximately 74 percent of the elderly do still live with an adult child, despite cramped housing conditions.[43] The government there attempts to facilitate co-residence by providing low-interest loans to people who wish to add a room to their home in order to accommodate an older parent.

Examples of housing measures to facilitate support between generations are few in other countries, although there are some interesting exceptions. In the United Kingdom, where a large proportion of the population lives in public housing, a number of local governments have abolished residential qualifications as a basis for admission to such housing, so that older persons living in other jurisdictions may move closer to their families. And the new Tenants Exchange Scheme has set up a computerized information service to help tenants in public housing locate similar units elsewhere in the country, as a first step in organizing a housing exchange.[44] In Sweden, families can receive an allowance of up to $5,000 to adapt their home and buy special equipment to meet the needs of a disabled elderly relative who lives with them on a permanent basis.[45]

One of the most interesting solutions to facilitate intergenerational living is the "granny annex," as it has come to be called in the United Kingdom and Australia. Modeled perhaps on what is a common private practice in many rural areas around the world, granny annexes in the United Kingdom take the form of bungalows or apartments built to adjoin a family home. They are constructed by local government as a form of public housing and permit older persons to live independently, but still close enough to their families so that the two households can exchange services. The experience to date has been encouraging. For those choosing this housing option, it permits a rich and supportive environment. Interestingly, even where the family or older persons moved away or died and were replaced by a non-relative, the pattern of support between generations continued, although not as intensively as between close relations. The first evaluation of granny annexes in the United Kingdom concluded that such linked units were indeed a viable housing alternative for frail older persons and were less expensive than sheltered or congregate housing.[46]

In the state of Victoria in Australia, where land congestion is not a problem, housing authorities have developed pre-fabricated units which can be erected on the property of an established home and connected to the sewer, water and electrical supplies of the main house. When the granny housing is no longer needed, it can be dismantled and removed, a flexible feature of the program which is not available in the United Kingdom. The cost to the government is about $5,000 for its removal.[47] The ''life expectancy'' of these granny annexes is about twenty-five years.[48] Australian granny annexes are a self-amortizing housing assistance program; the costs, including administrative charges, are covered through rents. Because there are no land costs involved and few maintenance problems, rent can still be kept low, yet pay for the granny annex over its lifetime. In the interim, financing is made available through tax-exempt bonds.

Granny annexes are rented as a form of public housing for about $14 and $21 a week for a single person and couple respectively.[49] Family lots eligible for granny housing must be at least 6,000 square feet in size.[50] While the occupants of granny annexes were originally limited to the parents or parents-in-law of the homeowner, consideration is now being given to liberalizing this requirement so that more distant older relatives or friends may also apply.

The public response to Victoria's housing program has been overwhelming, and a long waiting list exists for additional units. Granny annexes have proven themselves to be an attractive and cost-effective living arrangement for older persons that helps to free up underoccupied housing in a tight housing market. No detrimental effects are expected on the marketability of the main residence, and since the granny annex is a form of public housing, no increased real estate taxes result. In order to meet the demand, housing officials are now considering allowing individuals to purchase units directly from private builders, provided the annexes meet all the specifications. These units would then be sold to the housing authority when they are no longer required in order to maintain their temporary nature.

Granny annexes have aroused considerable interest in the United States, as well, but have run into opposition from zoning officials. California has become the first state to enact legislation to facilitate the construction of such units. Two private builders, Flair House in California and Coastal Colony in Pennsylvania, have developed prototype models costing under $20,000, to tap what they hope will be a growing demand for such units in the United States.[51]

Small Group Housing

For those single older persons who have no family support available to them and who, for a variety of reasons, no longer wish to live alone, an innovative option that is beginning to become more commonly available is the shared or small group home. These permit a small number of unrelated older adults to live together as a supportive family group in an ordinary residential setting. The programs discussed here are usually organized by social service departments or voluntary agencies, although undoubtedly many older homeowners can also be found who have opened their doors to age peers in the search for companionship and support. There are many variations on small group housing around the world. Groups can range in size from three to thirty residents, although most average from eight to twelve.[52] In most homes, residents have their own bedroom, may share a bathroom, and usually share all other common spaces, such as kitchen, living and dining rooms. The type of support provided also varies, from homes where a manager and staff are responsible for the major meals and day-to-day operation of the home, to homes where the tenants assume most of these responsibilities. Services may also be brought in from the outside in order to help the group maintain a semi-independent living arrangement.

The oldest experiment in small group housing is probably that of Abbeyfield Society in the United Kingdom, a national voluntary organization formed in 1959, which serves as the parent group for over 400 autonomous local societies throughout the country. The society runs about 760 group homes housing some 6,000 older persons.[53] Although a few of the homes have been specifically designed for group living, the majority are simply large family houses in well-established residential neighborhoods. The average house accommodates six to eight residents, plus a housekeeper who prepares the two main meals for the day and does all the household shopping. The residents have their own rooms, which they can furnish as they wish, and responsibility for taking care of their rooms.

Charges vary from house to house, but most tenants pay their own way. If necessary, residents can apply for a "supplementary benefit" to cover the charges, under an agreement negotiated for Abbeyfield residents with the United Kingdom Supplementary Benefits Commission. Each local Abbeyfield society is responsible for determining the need for a group home, purchasing a property, and deciding who should live in it. Residents are expected to be reasonably fit and active for their age, since no nursing services are provided.

Since Abbeyfield is one of the oldest experiments of its kind, it is already having to face the problem of what to do as residents become more frail and require medical assistance. A few of the local societies have set up "extra care" houses; however, most cannot afford the additional resources such care requires.

The limited research that has been done on small group homes, including the Abbeyfield ones, indicates a high level of satisfaction among residents with this kind of living arrangement.[54] A very important contributing factor to their success is the compatibility of the residents, and project organizers must spend considerable time to assure the best possible "matches." In a group home project run by the Jewish Council on Aging in Washington, D.C., applicants are sought who not only suffer from some disability which might be alleviated by group living, but who are seeking companionship, have a positive attitude towards sharing and will not become too dependent on their roommates for assistance.[55]

According to researcher Sheila Peace,

it would probably be advisable, if at all possible, to permit new residents of shared housing to undergo a trial period during which time their former residence is kept open for them should they need to return to it if group living does not work out. The move to shared housing also appears to be most successful where there is adequate social work support, especially through the admissions process.[56]

Most small group home experiments are still too new to determine how they will cope with increasing frailty among their residents. Forcing residents to move to an institution offering a more intensive level of care may break up what has become a surrogate family. On the other hand, the majority of small group homes are run by voluntary organizations, whose own resources rarely permit the laying on of additional services.

Nevertheless, according to Peace,

While it is premature to draw any final conclusions about small group living, it does seem evident that most residents are satisfied with what they see as a safer, more supportive environment, which offers them a degree of companionship. Their only alternative is often a nursing home, home for the aged, or the loneliness and isolation of a hostile environment which no longer meets their needs. Group living may not be their first choice of alternative accommodations, and is not the most appropriate choice for everyone, but for those who can adapt to the communal way of life, it certainly broadens the housing options for older people and holds the potential for becoming a personally enriching experience for them.[57]

Shelter with Services

Purpose-built housing that includes services has become a popular arrangement for the elderly in many countries and is certainly considered an improvement by most over the traditional, more regimented existence of a home for the aged. In some countries, housing plus services is called congregate housing; in others it may be called sheltered, warden or adapted housing. Whatever the terminology, the concept is the same—to provide certain services, such as meals, alarm systems, laundry, cleaning and home help assistance, recreational opportunities and so forth as needed, along with shelter. Usually, such services are provided as an additional option to residents, unlike the home for the aged, where everyone must take advantage of common services, whether or not they are really needed. At best, the availability of such services allows older people to build upon their remaining capacities in order to maximize possibilities for independent living. The housing discussed here is distinguished from some forms of small group housing mainly by size and the greater degree of privacy thereby afforded. Unlike small group housing, sheltered housing may result in less control over day-to-day decisions governing the management and operation of the home.

Residents of sheltered housing are usually older than those remaining in their own homes in the community and have experienced some difficulty in living on their own. However, they do not yet require the full range of personal care and health services that are available in a more institutionalized setting. In a number of cases, older persons who are quite fit seek admission to sheltered housing in anticipation of future need.

According to Leonard F. Heumann, both British and American studies suggest that 3–5 percent of the population aged 65 and older living in the community share characteristics which make them appropriate candidates for sheltered housing.[58] These include living alone, having less than one visit a week from family or friends, and having a significant impairment in the ability to perform activities of daily living. Another 1–2 percent could benefit from sheltered housing if one takes into account the estimated 20–30 percent of the elderly who are considered to be inappropriately institutionalized in both the United States and the United Kingdom.[59] Finally, Heumann would add another 3–10 percent of the elderly population who suffer from "social deprivations" and have no other support—for instance, the low-income elderly, and those living in substandard housing or unsafe neighborhoods.[60]

The average northern European country has three to five times the amount of sheltered housing available in the United States—which is .15 percent for the total U.S. elderly population.[61] The Netherlands probably has the highest proportion, with some 15 percent of its elderly population living in what is called "adapted" housing.[62] The Netherlands hopes to make such housing available to 25 percent of the population by 1985 as it phases out its homes for the aged.[63] The United Kingdom is probably next in line, with about 5 percent of its older population living in "warden" or other forms of sheltered housing.[64]

Sheltered housing can take many different forms, ranging from the *béguinage* in France—one- or two-story houses integrated into predominantly single-family neighborhoods—to blocks of "service flats" in Sweden which can house up to several hundred persons. Efforts are usually made to place sheltered housing, whatever the size, in areas with good access to transportation and other community services. The larger the housing complex, however, the less likely it is to be located near one's former neighborhood and the greater the risks of age segregation. The United Kingdom's Department of the Environment has concluded, however, that the size of the complex is not as important as the choice of a good warden (manager), a good building design, a location with easy access to transportation and shops, congenial neighbors and freedom from noise and children.[65] Large buildings can always be broken down into a number of smaller units, if designed correctly, to encourage personal interactions and greater feelings of intimacy. This has been done in a number of the residential complexes for older people in Sweden.

In the Federal Republic of Germany, the "two-stage home," combining service or pensioners' flats with a nursing home have become quite popular.[66] Through this arrangement it is hoped to minimize the traumas that can be associated with moving far away from one's home if one's health deteriorates to the point where institutionalization is required. However, there is as yet little research available as to the degree of interaction between the relatively well elderly still living independently in their service flats and the more impaired elderly living in the adjacent nursing home.

Sweden, too, has combined some of its sheltered housing with more traditional homes for the aged. In addition, such complexes may also incorporate day care centers and other amenities, which are open to all pensioners in the community in order to ward off isolation among its residents. Sometimes, too, a library, bowling alley or cafeteria is located on these premises to bring in younger people in an attempt to overcome age segregation.

In one of its housing programs, Denmark has attempted to reduce the distinction between housing with services for the elderly and that for other age groups. Through its "collective housing," Denmark provides to all age groups services such as restaurants, cleaning, baby-sitting, laundry and hobby rooms under one roof.[67] Some apartments have been specially adapted for the elderly and disabled, but collective housing is also considered suitable for families with two working parents, as well as single persons. Shelter, services and intergenerational contacts are all made possible through this kind of living arrangement.

However, the more typical sheltered housing project is designed exclusively for the elderly and houses from thirty to eighty persons.[68] In Sweden, some municipalities have built residences with no more than ten to fifteen units in order to facilitate the integration of the elderly into the larger community.[69] Until recently, the typical standard of provisions in many countries was an efficiency or one-room apartment for a single person, two rooms for a couple. Planners are now beginning to recommend a more generous standard, starting with a one-bedroom for single persons, in recognition of the difficulties experienced when someone who formerly lived in a large home makes the transition to sheltered housing.

The range of services that can be provided in sheltered housing varies considerably. For example, "adapted" housing in the Netherlands is simply ordinary apartment units which, however, are linked up by an alarm system to a central location. Similarly, "warden" housing in the United Kingdom provides only an alarm system, some communal rooms and a resident warden to handle emergencies. Residents are thus forced to interact more with the community at large to meet many of their needs.

At the other end of the scale are Sweden's service flats and France's *logements-foyers*. These usually have a full array of services available on the premises for residents' use. In many cases, these services may also be available to older persons living nearby. While this alternative is very attractive to many, the very generosity of service provision may result in minimal interaction by older residents with the world outside.

On the other hand, as many of the residents of Britain's warden housing have become older and more frail, the need for additional services and skills on the part of the warden has also become apparent. Interestingly, the British have not recommended that the warden be replaced by someone more highly credentialed, but rather that present wardens be provided with additional training. (Wardens are typically housewives who may have had some nursing or social service experience.) Additional options being considered by British planners are the desirability of locating future warden housing near residential homes so that tenants can share in the services, or building larger complexes that can make services available on a more efficient basis—even at the risk of promoting greater age segregation.

American researcher Heumann finds the minimal service level provided in Britain's "warden" housing attractive not only for cost reasons, but because it stimulates residents to be more independent and to interact with the local community. Prerequisites for its success, however, are the availability of adequate community services, which can be brought in as required, and continued family involvement with tenants. Heumann likes the friendly and unbureaucratic style of the typical warden, who often comes from the same socio-economic background as the tenants. More professionally trained wardens might be prone "to create an overly supportive environment encouraging dependence on their skills and training."[70] The ideal warden is considered to be "someone who keeps residents independent and actively engaged in society."[71] Since "the needs of residents usually grow slowly over many months, . . . the lay warden is able to grow and learn with the changing demands of the job."[72]

The financing of sheltered housing is usually made possible through low-interest loans to non-profit associations. In Sweden, for example, non-profit housing corporations can receive 100 percent of their loans from the National Housing Board.[73] In the Netherlands, special housing for the elderly is constructed by a national corporation, the Nederlandse Centrale voor Huisvesting van Bejaarden, on behalf of non-profit organizations or local government. Usually the management of the housing project is turned over to the originating sponsor. "Adapted" housing is also entitled to a subsidy of G2,000 (about $666) per unit if various architectural barriers are removed and additional special features are added.[74] In France, a developer may earn limited profits on the *logements-foyers* and still be eligible for a low-interest loan if a non-profit operator runs the project.[75]

There is no question but that sheltered housing is more expensive to the consumer than ordinary housing. In France, for example, local government has to subsidize about one-third of the rent of tenants in *logements-foyers*.[76] Typically, residents in sheltered housing in many industrialized countries are charged according to ability to pay; the deficit is then made up either through public or voluntary sources.

While sheltered housing is an expensive option, it certainly costs less than skilled nursing care environments, and even service-rich housing in the United States is approximately 40 percent cheaper than intermediate nursing home care.[77] The research done to date on the well-being of residents of sheltered housing, most of which has been done in the United States, shows "a relative improvement in morale and satisfaction over time when compared to control groups in conventional housing residents."[78]

To some extent, the availability of sheltered housing will reduce the need for future institutionalization and decrease overall public costs. The experience in the state of North-Rhine Westphalia in Germany, for example, has shown "that where appropriate and opportunately [*sic*] located senior citizens' housing is available, the demand for space in old age homes decreases."[79] In the state of Baden-Württemberg, an estimated 30 percent of residents of homes for the aged are inappropriately placed and belong either in sheltered housing or a nursing home.[80] In the United States, estimates of inappropriately institutionalized older persons range from 12 percent to 60 percent.[81]

The degree to which sheltered housing can substitute for institutional care may hinge on the extent to which some medical care is available. This, of course, may increase the costs of sheltered housing yet further and turn it into a mini-institution. For example, Swedish policy-makers thought their blocks of service flats would eliminate the need for homes for the aged altogether, but events have not turned out quite as expected. Elderly Swedes have proven reluctant to move into service flats until some serious handicap or disability arises. Service flats, however, were designed primarily with a relatively less disabled population in mind, and the question of the extent to which one "medicalizes" blocks of service flats is becoming a critical one. The fear is that "overmedicalization" will detract from the quality of the living environment. It already seems clear that sheltered forms of housing cannot eliminate the need for institutions providing more intensive forms of care, although they can certainly diminish the number of persons entering such care for inappropriate reasons, such as the lack of any alternative. It is when sheltered housing is viewed as one more option along the continuum of housing provision that its place can be assessed most objectively.

HOMES FOR THE AGED

Most countries have homes for the aged, usually for the very old, that is, persons over 80 years of age who need more extensive supports and supervision. Homes are usually run under the auspices of voluntary, religious or governmental bodies.

The standard of provision can vary considerably, from providing all the residents with their own apartments, which they can furnish as they will, to a more dormitory-like facility offering little privacy or personal choice. The consumption of common services, such as meals, is usually mandatory, unlike the more flexible arrangements in sheltered housing.

Homes for the aged differ from other long-term care institutions in that they provide some forms of personal care but usually little medical care. Sometimes, however, there is little to distinguish a home for the aged from a nursing home or long-term care ward other than that they are run under different administrative auspices. More typically, though, residents must move to institutions such as a nursing home or long-term care hospital ward if their physical or mental condition seriously deteriorates. France has recently begun to move away from this policy by permitting homes for the aged and other retirement residences to establish medical departments, as long as their capacity does not exceed 25 percent of the total beds; social insurance funds reimburse the homes for the health care provided.[82] This measure was adopted to lessen the traumas associated with moving.

Residents of homes usually contribute a significant part of their pensions toward the costs of their stay, but in almost all cases, public or private subsidies are required to cover the full cost. In no case are residents left without any allowance. And the residents are usually allowed to keep some portion of their personal assets and other sources of income. For example, in Norway, residents must contribute that part of their assets or income which exceeds 50,000 kroner ($7,143) or 9,800 kroner ($1,400) respectively.[83]

Countries with a pluralistic population, such as Israel, have found that homogeneity in the cultural and class background of residents of homes is positively related to life satisfaction, even if it does foster what some may consider undesirable segregation.[84] A central referral agency in Glasgow goes even one step further in facilitating a new resident's admission to a home by trying to match the personality of the applicant with that of the matron in charge of the home.[85]

There is little agreement among countries on the number of places required in homes for the aged per a given population. Each uses a different standard, which is somewhat related to the provision of housing and other community services. New Zealand, for example, has adopted a standard of 30 beds for every 1,000 persons over age 65; the state of North-Rhine Westphalia in the Federal Republic of Germany has targeted 23 beds for every 1,000.[86]

A number of countries, such as Sweden, the Netherlands and the Federal Republic of Germany, have decided to phase out homes for the aged in favor of more sheltered housing projects, community services and nursing homes. According to German gerontologist Margret Dieck,

Old age homes are designed to care for a small target group: older people who can no longer manage their own household but who are not in need of nursing care. In reality, residents are almost always too vigorous and able to live in a senior citizens' housing project or at home if they had supportive services. At the other extreme, some are in urgent need of nursing care and must transfer to a nursing home anyway. The tragedy is that old age homes are built and staffed according to the small theoretical target group and not the real one. Misplacement is the inevitable result.[87]

However, serious doubts exist whether homes for the aged are completely replaceable. Despite Sweden's rapid expansion of service flats, its homes still fill a great need, providing some 58,000 places, compared to only 20,000 service flats.[88] And despite the Dutch goal of having no more than 7 percent of the elderly population residing in homes, 10 percent are currently living in such facilities and waiting lists remain long.[89] Dutch policy-makers claim that homes for the aged encourage social isolation and dependency, and do not have the necessary flexibility to deal with increased frailty among their residents. They also cite the greater costs of homes over community services, such as home help assistance. However, according to researcher Rubenstein, the Dutch government has not carefully considered the proper mix of services required by the elderly—its cost comparison of homes for the aged with home help services overlooks what may be differing needs on the part of the two populations being served.[90]

Increasingly, applicants for admission to homes for the aged must undergo careful screening to determine whether they really require this intensive level of care. In the Netherlands since 1977, every municipality has been required to set up a "selection committee" which judges need for admission into the home by a uniform set of criteria.[91] Planners everywhere are concerned with the high costs associated with inappropriate institutionalization.

INTEGRATION INTO THE COMMUNITY

The research done on the living patterns desired by the elderly in industrialized countries shows overwhelmingly that most wish to remain integrated in the community and with other age groups.[92] The preference for age-segregated housing indicated by some older people in the United States, partly because of fear of crime, has not yet materialized to any visible extent elsewhere, although with crime against the elderly also on the rise in other countries, this pattern may change in the future.[93] Nor does one find the pattern of retirement communities in other countries that can be found in the United States.

One Dutch study, however, does point to the desirability of age-segregated housing under some circumstances.[94] In one project where older people lived in close proximity with younger people (mostly university students), the relationship between them was marked by irritation; few older residents received any help from their younger neighbors. An examination of an age-segregated project, however, showed that a pattern of reciprocal commitments and sharing had clearly developed. Researchers from the University of Groningen concluded that a system of stable relationships among neighbors in the same age group is of great importance for optimal integration. In terms of size, they believe projects housing seventy to eighty units would more easily facilitate neighborly contacts than smaller units where pressures for social control might be stronger. The goal of age integration, in turn, could be promoted by locating housing for the elderly in the hub of the community.

A number of countries avoid concentrating large numbers of older people in one place. Instead, they seek to adopt housing policies which facilitate the elderly's integration into the community. For example, France, through its requirement that 20 percent of all new large housing projects be set aside for the elderly if the housing is to be eligible for low-interest loans, assures the dispersal of older people throughout the community. This policy has, however, been criticized by some for its inflexibility. For example, a particular building may not be suitably located for elderly tenants in terms of community facilities or proximity to friends and relatives. What might be more desirable is that a fixed percentage of units be set aside for the elderly within a geographic area rather than in a particular building.

Even though the motivation behind French policy is to encourage age integration, some age segregation has nevertheless resulted. In the desire to reduce construction costs, encourage mutual help and reduce noise from children, apartments for older people may be built in separate wings or limited to sheltered areas on the ground floor.

Denmark and the Netherlands, like France, earmark small sections of housing projects for the elderly.[95] These units are usually located in one-story buildings and with easy access to community facilities. In addition, Denmark stimulates intergenerational contacts through its "collective" housing for all age groups. Apartments for the elderly and disabled are purpose-built, but effort is taken to limit them to not more than 30 percent of the total number of apartments in order to avoid an institutional feel to the building.[96]

In Montreal, the charity Les Petits Frères des Pauvres has developed a residential community in the heart of the city housing approximately 400 people of all ages.[97] The administration of this "village within a city" will explicitly foster intergenerational solidarity and make every effort to ensure frequent contact among all the generations in the village and those of the surrounding neighborhood. This village, which opened in 1983, is located within minutes of many public conveniences, including a school and a retirement home.

So far, both the United Kingdom and France have limited the size of their sheltered housing projects so that they can easily fit into the neighboring community. Warden housing in the United Kingdom usually provides only about thirty to forty units; *logements-foyers* in France are rarely larger than eighty units.[98]

In Vienna, which is subdivided into over twenty districts, large congregate housing projects are being built in each of the districts so that residents will still be able to remain within reasonable proximity to their former neighborhoods.

The larger housing projects, such as some of Sweden's blocks of service flats, do inevitably lead to some age segregation, especially when, because of their size, they must be located on the outskirts of town, where land costs are cheaper. Where possible, Swedish authorities try to locate pensioners' housing in town centers, and in some cases, they have imaginatively located community facilities such as libraries and meeting rooms on the premises of the residential complex so that all age groups interact routinely.

Pensioners' flats, that is, ordinary apartments intended for use by the elderly, are usually located in typical multi-family homes dispersed throughout a residential area. And mention has already been made of the policy of some municipalities in Sweden not to build blocks of service flats larger than ten to fifteen units in order to avoid age segregation.

Homes for the aged face even greater difficulty in attempting to remain integrated within the larger community. They share the problems of sheltered housing complexes, and their residents are usually older and frailer and less likely to get out. What some homes have done to combat this isolation is to create day centers for use by older people in the community. In Sweden, pensioners and others can use the food and podiatry services available in homes for the aged.

It remains unclear, though, to what extent older people from the community actually mix with their institutionalized peers. There is a fear of being identified with the residents. This fear was imaginatively overcome in one British home through the opening of a bar, which was open at certain hours to the community at large. It proved to be quite a popular experiment.

IMPLICATIONS FOR THE UNITED STATES

At the national level, the United States is doing relatively little to better the housing situation of the elderly. No emphasis is being placed on either rehabilitating existing stock or encouraging new construction. Yet there is little doubt about the extent of the housing need among the elderly—one estimate is that as many as 3.5 to 4 million elderly households are maintained in sub-standard conditions.[99]

Federal housing policies that affect the elderly are now limited to rent subsidies, which are estimated to benefit only one-third of all those entitled to them (among all age groups), and Section 202 housing.[100] This program provides low-interest loans to non-profit sponsors of housing for the elderly. In all there have been only about 120,000 units built, and new construction is now limited to about 17,000 units a year.[101] The U.S. government no longer provides loans to the elderly for rehabilitation purposes, and it never has had a national policy with regard to sheltered or congregate housing.

Some developments that are more interesting are taking place at the local level, including property tax deferral programs, circuit breaker legislation, the development of granny annexes or Elderly Cottage Housing Opportunity (ECHO housing), accessory apartments and reverse equity. The experience of other countries in some of these areas would clearly have relevance to the United States, and the federal government could play a useful role in studying how these programs have operated abroad, funding and evaluating some demonstration projects in the United States, and disseminating information regarding success and failures. Such a minimal role for the national government might appeal in this time of budgetary retrenchments.

However, there is little doubt that other countries have been able to make a broader dent in meeting the shelter needs of their older populations through the acceptance of a greater public responsibility for the adequacy of their nations' housing. A combination of consumer and production subsidies and some direct construction by the public sector have all proven necessary to achieve a range of housing options that can meet the heterogeneous needs of the elderly.

Low-interest loans and loan guarantees have been particularly important in helping to retool existing housing stock and stimulate the construction of a variety of new housing—from ordinary homes and apartments scattered throughout the community to concentrations of sheltered housing. By and large, governments in western industrialized countries have set policy guidelines and assisted in the financing of new construction; they have left it up to the private sector—both non-profit and for-profit organizations—to actually construct and manage new housing. This dependence on the private sector would seem to be compatible with America's free market ideology, but it still requires a degree of governmental commitment that the United States has been reluctant to make.

While there is little question that the housing policies followed by many European countries are expensive, in the long run is the United States pursuing a cost-effective policy by neglecting its existing housing stock, discouraging the construction of intermediate housing alternatives which might decrease the need for more expensive nursing home care, and providing no incentives to families to encourage co-residency? Unfortunately, the costs of not acting are rarely calculated.

NOTES

1. United Nations, *Human Settlements and the Aging,* report of the U.N. Centre for Human Settlements (Habitat) for the World Assembly on Aging (A/Conf. 113/25, May 26, 1982), pp. 5–6.

2. United Nations, *Housing, Environment and Aging,* report of the Secretary-General for the World Assembly on Aging (A/Conf. 113/13, April 28, 1982), p. 6.

3. U.N., *Human Settlements and the Aging,* p. 6.

4. Ibid., p. 12; and *Aging in the United Kingdom,* report prepared for the World Assembly on Aging (London: Department of Health and Social Security, 1982), p. 8.

5. U.N., *Housing, Environment and Aging,* p. 24; and M. Powell Lawton, ''Environments and Living Arrangements,'' in *International Perspectives on Aging: Popu-*

lation and Policy Challenges (New York: U.N. Fund for Population Activities, 1982), p. 172.

6. Conversation with Leo Baldwin, Senior Housing Program Coordinator, American Association of Retired Persons, October 1982.

7. James M. Rubenstein, "Housing the Elderly in France and the Netherlands" (paper presented at the annual meeting of the Gerontological Society of America, Dallas, Tex., November 1978), p. 16.

8. *Report from Ireland,* prepared for the World Assembly on Aging (Dublin: National Council for the Aged, 1982), p. 12.

9. *Ageing in the United Kingdom,* p. 9.

10. Rubenstein, "Housing the Elderly in France and the Netherlands," p. 14.

11. Ibid., p. 15.

12. Ibid., p. 13.

13. Ibid.

14. Ibid., p. 16.

15. Ibid., p. 14.

16. Ibid., p. 16.

17. Ibid., p. 17.

18. Ibid., p. 12.

19. Ibid., p. 18.

20. E. Jay Howenstine, *Foreign Experience in the Financing of Housing for the Elderly* (Washington, D.C.: U.S. Department of Housing and Urban Development, (1973), p. 8.

21. M. Powell Lawton and Sally Hoover (eds.), *Housing Choices for Older Americans* (New York: Springer Publishing Co., 1981), p. 12.

22. Henning Friis, "Social Programmes for the Aged in Denmark," *EURAG Newsletter* (June 1980):4.

23. Conversation with Leo Baldwin.

24. Don Ove Pedersen, "Housing Problems of the Elderly," *Danish Medical Bulletin* 29, No. 3 (March 1982):118.

25. Howenstine, *Foreign Experience in the Financing of Housing for the Elderly,* p. 8.

26. Pedersen, *"Housing Problems of the Elderly,"* p. 118.

27. Howensteine, *Foreign Experience in the Financing of Housing for the Elderly,* p. 16.

28. Rubenstein, "Housing the Elderly in France and the Netherlands," pp. 9–10.

29. Ibid., p. 9.

30. *Aging in France,* report prepared for the World Assembly on Aging (Paris: Ministère des Affaires Sociales et de la Solidarité Nationale, 1982), p. 29.

31. *Ageing in the United Kingdom,* p. 8.

32. Ibid.

33. "Housing—Public Expenditure Cuts," Briefing No. 15 (March 1981), Courtesy of Age Concern England, pp. 8–9.

34. *Ageing in Norway,* report prepared for the World Assembly on Aging (Oslo: Ministry of Health and Social Affairs, 1982), p. 25.

35. *Ageing New Zealanders,* report prepared for the World Assembly on Aging, 1982, p. 40.

36. *Netherlands National Report on Aging Policy,* report prepared for the World

Assembly on Aging (Rijswijk: Ministry of Cultural Affairs, Recreation and Social Welfare, 1982), p. 11.

37. *La Voix du Retraité* (December 1980 and January 1981).

38. *Presse-und Informationsdienst des KDA* (September 1981).

39. *Ageing New Zealanders*, p. 69.

40. *Report on the Situation of the Elderly in the Federal Republic of Germany*, report prepared for the World Assembly on Aging (Berlin: German Center of Gerontology, May 1982), p. 11.

41. *Christ im Alter* (August 1974).

42. *Années-Documents CLEIRPPA* (December 1976).

43. Lawton, "Environments and Living Arrangements," p. 164.

44. *Ageing International* 9, No. 3 (Autumn 1982):14.

45. *Sweden Now*, No. 3, 1981.

46. Anthea Tinker, *Housing the Elderly: How Successful Are Granny Annexes?* Housing Development Directorate occasional paper (London: Department of the Environment, January 1976), pp. 30–31.

47. Australia's 'Granny Flats' Capture U.S. Interest," *Ageing International* 8, No. 4 (Winter 1981):11.

48. Ibid.

49. Ibid.

50. Ibid.

51. Ibid., p. 12.

52. Sheila Peace, " 'Small Group' Housing in the Community, Part II: Variations on Sheltered Housing," *Ageing International*, 8, No. 2 (Summer 1981):16.

53. Ibid.

54. Ibid., p. 18.

55. Ibid., p. 19.

56. Ibid.

57. Ibid.

58. Leonard F. Heumann, "Sheltered Housing for the Elderly: The Role of the British Warden," *Gerontologist* 20, No. 3 (June 1980): 319.

59. Ibid.

60. Ibid.

61. Ibid.

62. Rubenstein, "Housing the Elderly in France and the Netherlands," p. 19.

63. Ibid.

64. Heumann, "Sheltered Housing for the Elderly," p. 319.

65. Age Concern England, *Information Circular* (July 1975).

66. Margret Dieck, "Residential and Community Provisions for the Frail Elderly in Germany—Current Issues and Their History," *Gerontologist* 20 No. 3 (June 1980):262.

67. *Foreign Programs for the Elderly*, HUD International Special Supplement No. 10 (Washington, D.C.: U.S. Department of Housing and Urban Development, December 1973), p. 7.

68. Rubenstein, "Housing the Elderly in France and the Netherlands," p. 25; and Heumann, "Sheltered Housing for the Elderly," p. 322.

69. *Just Another Age*, report prepared for the World Assembly on Aging (Stockholm: Ministry of Health and Social Affairs, 1982), p. 28.

70. Heumann, "Sheltered Housing for the Elderly," p. 328.

71. Ibid., p. 325.

72. Ibid., p. 328.

73. John McRae, "Elderly Housing in Northern Europe," (paper presented at the annual meeting of the Western Gerontological Society, Tucson, Ariz., April 1978), p. 6.

74. Rubenstein, "Housing the Elderly in France and the Netherlands," p. 19.

75. Ibid., p. 26.

76. Ibid.

77. Heumann, "Sheltered Housing for the Elderly," p. 320.

78. Ibid.

79. Dieck, "Residential and Community Provisions," p. 269.

80. Ibid., p. 264.

81. Heumann, "Sheltered Housing for the Elderly," p. 319.

82. *CIGS Newsletter* (November 1979).

83. *Aging in Norway,* p. 27.

84. Robert L. Kane and Rosalie A. Kane, *Long-Term Care in Six Countries: Implications for the U.S.* (Bethesda, Md.: U.S. Department of Health, Education, and Welfare, Public Health Service, National Institutes of Health, 1976), p. 180.

85. Ibid., pp. 179–180.

86. Dieck, "Residential and Community Provisions," p. 269.

87. Ibid., p. 270.

88. *Just Another Age,* pp. 28–29.

89. James M. Rubenstein, "Housing Policy Issues in Three European Countries" (paper presented at the annual meeting of the Gerontological Society of America, Washington, D.C., November 1979), p. 10.

90. Ibid., pp. 15–16.

91. Ibid., p. 11.

92. U.N., *Human Settlements and the Aging,* p. 6; and Lawton, "Environments and Living Arrangements," p. 174.

93. M. Powell Lawton, "The Relationship of Age Mixing to Security in Housing for the Elderly" (paper distributed at the International Symposium for Housing and Environmental Design for Older Adults, Washington, D.C., December 1973), p. 4.

94. *Leeftijd* (May 1981).

95. U.N. *Human Settlements and the Aging,* p. 12.

96. Einer Engberg, "Special Housing Requirements for the Elderly and the Handicapped" (paper distributed at the International Symposium for Housing and Environmental Design for Older Adults, Washington, D.C., December 1973), p. 9.

97. *Ageing International* 9, No. 3 (Autumn 1982):13.

98. Heumann, "Sheltered Housing for the Elderly," p. 322; and Rubenstein, "Housing the Elderly in France and the Netherlands," p. 25.

99. Conversation with Leo Baldwin, October 1982.

100. Ibid.

101. U.S., Senate, Special Commission on Aging, *Congressional Action on the Fiscal Year 1983 Budget: What It Means for Older Americans* (Washington, D.C.: Government Printing Office, November 1982), p. 37.

8

Family Support Patterns, Policies and Programs

Mary Jo Gibson

The growing interest in recent years in the role of the family in providing support to its older members is by no means confined to the United States. Partly as a result of humanitarian concerns and partly as a result of escalating long-term care costs, virtually every developed nation seeks to prevent unnecessary or premature institutionalization of the elderly. And the family has been recognized as a critical factor in helping older persons remain in the community.

As in the United States, evidence from other industrialized nations shows the same general pattern—family members continue to be the major social support of the elderly. Although co-residence of the elderly with their adult children is not the norm in most developed nations, family members maintain a high degree of contact with older relatives, with whom they exchange many forms of assistance. In fact, family members—especially spouses, daughters, and daughters-in-law—provide the bulk of the care received by the elderly who are chronically ill, and the care provided through family sources far outweighs that which is provided through public and voluntary sectors combined.

The caregivers, who are primarily women, experience considerable stress. Recent research from nations such as the United Kingdom, Japan, and West Germany buttresses evidence being accumulated in the United States that the caregivers themselves need "back-up" support.

Examining the programs and policies supportive of family caregivers available in other developed nations provides ideas for a number of options which might be adapted for use in the United States. These include innovative approaches to providing respite care, group programs for family members, and various forms of financial assistance.

This chapter is based on a paper presented at the joint meeting of the Gerontological Society of America and the Canadian Association of Gerontology, Toronto, November 11, 1981.

The question of what is the proper "mix" of public and family responsibility for the care of the elderly is a matter of policy debate in many developed nations, and some of the salient issues in this debate are discussed below.

LIVING ARRANGEMENTS AND PATTERNS OF CONTACT

Although co-residence between elderly persons and their adult children is still common in a few industrialized nations, such as Japan, the pattern in most developed nations is for older persons to maintain their own residences, either out of preference or necessity. Even in countries not yet fully modernized, such as Poland and Yugoslavia, where co-residence between young and old is still widespread, the preference in both generations seems to be toward separate quarters, in order to maintain privacy and independence, a state that Leopold Rosenmayr has called "intimacy at a distance."[1] In Poland, although 67 percent of older people live with their children,[2] 62 percent of older persons surveyed in 1970 also believe that the generations should live separately if possible.[3]

In Czechoslovakia the proportion of persons aged 70 and over living with their children decreased by 8 percent between 1968 and 1978, while the trend toward generations living separately but in the same neighborhood intensified.[4] In Japan the proportion of the elderly living alone has been slowly but steadily increasing, particularly in urban areas such as Tokyo.[5]

The fact that the majority of the elderly do live in separate households in most developed nations does not mean that family ties have been undercut. Data from a number of industrialized nations indicate that older persons typically live in close geographic proximity and have a high degree of contact with their children. In the United States, for example, the majority of the elderly either live with or near an adult child, and this proportion has remained fairly stable over a twenty-year period (59 percent in 1957, 61 percent in 1962, and 52 percent in 1975).[6] While the proportion of those living with an adult child decreased over the same period (from 36 percent in 1957 to 18 percent in 1975), the number of those living within a ten-minute drive from at least one of their children increased. Additionally, 77 percent of those with surviving children had seen one of them within the week prior to the interview, and this proportion remained fairly constant over a twenty-year-period.[7]

Very similar data were reported recently from Canada. In a 1980 survey of elderly persons in Regina, Saskatchewan, 18 percent of those with children shared a household with them; 75 percent had a child living in the city; of these, 80 percent saw at least one child weekly.[8]

Likewise, 75 percent of a sample of persons over age 75 in the United Kingdom who had children saw one of them once a week or more, as did 67 percent of those between the ages of 64 and 75. Interestingly, a clear majority of the British respondents said they did not want to see their children more frequently.[9] In France, three quarters of the urban population age 65 and over in the provinces live close to their families.[10] And in an urban industrial area in

Sweden, 80 percent of 70-year-old Swedes surveyed in the city of Gothenburg had seen their children within the last week.[11]

Austria serves as an example of a developed nation where the percentage of older people living with children is relatively high by most western standards. According to 1979 "microcensus" data, 43 percent of Austrians age 60 and over with surviving children live with a child either in the same household or same house. Another 27 percent live within a half-hour's distance, and 76 percent of these see the nearest child at least weekly.[12]

A number of demographic variables have been reported as predicting the sharing of a residence with an adult child, including socio-economic status, sex, marital status, cultural background, and rural-urban residence. More older women than older men share a home with a child, and this proportion increases with age. For example, in the United Kingdom, it is reported that 41 percent of women aged 85 or over live with a child or another relative.[13] These sex differences in living arrangements may be due to women's greater longevity and the fact that fewer older men are likely to be widowed at a time when increasing health problems and diminished mobility make living alone untenable.

Ethel Shanas found that the living arrangements differ by social class and that sharing a home with adult children is more commonly a working class than white collar phenomenon in both the United Kingdom and the United States.[14] Co-residence is more common among the lower socio-economic classes in Austria.[15] And a twelve-year longitudinal study in Israel showed that co-residence is more common among those who grew up in traditional societies, such as immigrants from near Eastern nations, than among European immigrants.[16] However, frequency of contact with at least one child not living with older parents was found to be the same for both Israeli groups.

Although "intimacy at a distance" may be the preference, "living under one roof" is frequently the reality, especially in rural areas, where co-residence is more common than in urban areas. Three-generational families are still common in rural areas of eastern Europe, notably Bulgaria, Poland, Romania, and the U.S.S.R.[17] For example, 1977 data from Romania indicate that 50 percent of the elderly in rural areas live with offspring, compared to 10–30 percent in urban areas.[18] Data from Austria also support the view that joint living between older children and parents is more frequent in rural than urban areas. Although a majority of older Austrians in rural areas share a household with a child, this proportion drops to 14 percent in Vienna, in part due to the high (32 percent) proportion of childless elderly there.[19]

While sharing a household with a child appears to be more common in rural than in urban areas, this does not mean that ties between generations in urban areas are dissolving. Bent Frijs-Madsen reports that older people in Copenhagen who have only one child, and do not live with the child, were more than twice as likely (72 percent) to have seen the child recently as their counterparts in rural areas (41 percent).[20] (This fact is probably explained by the fact that families living separately live at greater distances in rural areas.)

Hence, although co-residence between the generations is not the typical pattern in most industrialized nations, there has not been a massive breakdown in family support. Numerous studies indicate that most older persons live near at least one child, with whom they are in frequent contact even in highly urban areas. And several studies suggest that the children initiate face-to-face contact more frequently than the older parents do.[21]

In fact, when it becomes difficult or impossible for older relatives to maintain their own residences, some evidence suggests that families in developed nations remain willing to take the old into their homes. Although a 1978 survey in the United States showed an overwhelming preference for having an elderly relative live *nearby* but not *in* the respondent's home, over 80 percent of the 652 persons surveyed were willing to take care of an older relative, including the ill and isolated, in their own home under some circumstances.[22] While the proportion of elderly living with children in Japan is high (approximately 75 percent) compared to other developed nations, a recent cross-cultural study between the United States and Japan revealed *no* significant differences between respondents in the two countries in the sense of responsibility toward parents, nor in their willingness to accept a dependent parent in their home.[23] In fact, Americans were more willing to take in an older relative other than a parent than were Japanese families.[24]

Thus, co-residence between the elderly and their offspring is only one measure of the degree of family support available. Nonetheless, the myth that families in developed countries abandon their aging parents persists. A recent survey of three generations of American women found that, although they themselves believed strongly in filial support, they did not think others did, and they subscribed to the notion that children do not take as much care of their elderly parents today as in the past.[25]

As a historical footnote, research done in Europe and the United States suggests that what really constitutes the myth is the idea that in the past the extended family assumed greater responsibility for its older members than is the case today. Although family sizes in the United States were indeed larger in the pre-industrial era (the average size of households in 1790 was 5.8, compared to 2.81 in 1978), this was due to high fertility rates rather than the number of live-in older relatives.[26] In Europe, evidence also shows that the nuclear family comprising only two generations has been the dominant type of household since pre-industrial times.[27] When joint living did occur, it was typically as much a function of economic necessity as of strong emotional ties. It has even been suggested that today's "modified extended families" care for older relatives more extensively and for longer periods than ever before because chronic disabilities have replaced acute illnesses as the most prevalent health problem of older adults.[28]

FAMILY HELPING PATTERNS

Research on family helping patterns in western nations, as well as in more traditional societies, has documented the existence of a complicated matrix of mutual aid and service flows between generations. Additionally, research from Eastern Europe indicates that patterns of interaction and help between the elderly and their children in socialist countries are similar to those in the west.[29]

Assistance Provided by Older Persons

Family support, of course, is two-directional; older persons are not passive recipients in the family network, but themselves provide financial and other forms of help to younger family members. Several studies indicate that providing financial assistance to children seems to be a particularly common practice. In a sample in Regina, Canada, three times as many elderly persons reported giving financial assistance to children as reported receiving it.[30] Similarly, in Austria older persons surveyed in 1979 reported giving more financial support to their children than they received; one-quarter said they gave such assistance to their children.[31] The types of assistance provided to children appear to differ somewhat by social and economic class. While baby-sitting is a common role of elderly parents among the inner city poor in the United States and among the lower urban working classes in Europe, the affluent more frequently provide financial assistance, with goods and money being passed down from the older to the younger generations through gifts and inheritances.[32] The elderly also provide less tangible forms of assistance, such as advice and counsel. In a 1976 French study, 40–50 percent of adult children interviewed said they asked their parents for advice in important matters.[33]

Assistance Received by Older Persons

Although in many cases help and services are more frequently provided by older persons to children and grandchildren than the other way around, this situation often reverses during extreme old age, with its accompanying health problems.[34] For example, it is reported from the Federal Republic of Germany that the very old are usually the ones to receive family support, and most of this support is connected with housekeeping tasks.[35] Similarly, a nationwide Austrian study concluded that although elderly people report roughly the same amount of help received from and given to children, this depends upon their health status.[36] Old people in poor health receive three times the amount of assistance as those in good health.

Studies from a number of nations have documented that services important to older people, such as physical care, shelter, escorting, and help with household tasks, are commonly provided by children and other kin. For example, the survey in Austria found that adult children accounted for three-fifths of all help received by the elderly with household tasks, shopping, and so on.[37] In Canada, 76 percent of a sample of 224 older persons said they had a child or other relative who would provide them with help if needed with health care, shopping, and the like. Fifty percent were currently receiving such help.[38]

Although in most developed nations financial support appears to be more typically given by parents to adult children than the other way around, financial support by children to older relatives in rural regions and working class families is common in the Federal Republic of Germany.[39] However, even though financial assistance is offered, frequently reasons of self-esteem lead older persons to cut their consumption rather than accept support from family members or claim social welfare benefits to which they are entitled.

The amount of care provided by families to ill elderly relatives in most developed countries far outweighs that provided by the public or voluntary sectors. Help from families comprises approximately 80 percent of all home health care received by ill older persons in the United States, with the major types of assistance being personal care, homemaker services and transportation.[40] A 1977 U.S. General Accounting Office report on home health care, based on data collected in Cleveland, Ohio, found that at the "greatly impaired level," into which around 17 percent of those over 65 fall, the costs of maintaining the older person at home equalled or exceeded the costs of institutionalization.[41] Yet the study also found that families and friends provide over 70 percent of the value of services received by these older persons.[42] It is concluded that the financial costs of maintaining the ill elderly at home have been largely hidden.

The 5 percent of persons age 65 and over who are in institutions at any one time in the United States are outnumbered two to one by equally disabled older persons who live in the community, primarily in the homes of their families, a proportion that did not change markedly between 1962 and 1975.[43] In fact, a large number of those who are institutionalized are single persons who either have never married or have no close relatives.

In the Federal Republic of Germany, there are three times as many ill persons of all ages being cared for at home by the average nuclear family as are receiving care in institutions, and four times as many are being cared for at home in larger family settings.[44] It is also reported that assistance to older Germans needing the highest degree of help far exceeds the volume of such services provided in institutions or through the formal service sector.[45] In Japan, it is estimated that approximately nine times as many impaired older people are being cared for at home as in institutions.[46] Similarly, in Poland, considerably more bedridden people are being cared for in private households than in hospitals and nursing homes.[47]

This general pattern of family care for the elderly in developed countries does not exclude even the severely mentally disabled. Estimates in the United States and United Kingdom indicate that most older persons with senile dementia live in the community, and that family members are their principal caregivers. In the United States, approximately six times the number of persons with senile dementia in nursing homes are maintained at home by kin.[48]

Not only is family care the predominant pattern: it also seems to be the pattern desired by the elderly. In times of crisis caused by ill health or the death of a spouse, it is to family members that the elderly most frequently turn for assistance. In fact, studies from a number of nations indicate that older persons in need of help turn first to spouses, then to children, then to other relatives, and only last to formal agencies for assistance.[49] For example, 64 percent of older Austrians living with a child and 46 percent of those with a child living within 30 minutes distance expected a child to provide nursing care in the event of a long-term illness.[50] (The percentages were considerably higher in the case of short-term illnesses.) And in a study conducted in a midwestern city in the United States, kin help, especially for personal and home health care, was found to be the kind of help most preferred by older persons if they were not able to perform these tasks themselves. Most of the elderly did not want help from government sources, except for assistance with income needs, such as social security.[51] Similarly, 75 percent of 272 retired workers surveyed in a large industrial town in Poland said they would turn first to the family in situations of real necessity.[52]

IMPACT OF THE CAREGIVING ROLE

While caring for an ill older parent can be a positive experience with many rewards, research studies conducted in a number of countries, including the United Kingdom, the United States, Japan, Australia and West Germany, indicate there are many stresses related to the caregiving role. These appear to be primarily associated with the isolated and confining nature of the role, the effects of caregiving on the mental and physical health of the responsible family members, and financial difficulties.

The day-to-day responsibilities for the care of an elderly relative usually fall on one person—generally a spouse, a daughter or a daughter-in-law. Even if there are other family members in the household or geographically accessible, a pooling of responsibilities generally does not occur.[53] In many cases, there are no other family members in the household to share the burden of care. In Japan, for example, it is reported that a higher proportion of impaired older persons are living with an unmarried than a married child.[54] In one Japanese study of families reporting difficulties related to caring for an elderly relative, those who experienced the most difficulty were unmarried children, who typically held jobs outside the home, and spouses, who themselves might be old and infirm.[55] Similarly, in a study of elderly persons discharged from hospitals in the United States, 63 percent were found to be receiving care from persons who were elderly themselves.[56]

Daisaku Maeda has estimated that about 25 percent of the caregivers to the bedfast elderly in Japan are themselves aged 60 or over. He cites a 1976 survey which found that two-thirds of impaired old people in Japan are being cared for in families experiencing serious difficulties; that is, the primary caregiver is over age 60 and/or chronically ill, and/or employed full time, and/or caring for another impaired person, and/or caring for a young baby or child.[57] At the same time, these caregivers had little or no assistance with their caretaking tasks. Because of these circumstances, in some cases the impaired older person was not receiving care or the quality of care was poor. A complicating factor is that home help services in Japan are subject to a strict income test, and it is usually only the impaired elderly who live alone or with an aged spouse who are eligible for such assistance.

Recent research in Australia and New Zealand also illustrates the problems encountered by primary caregivers to ill or disabled older persons. Interviews with 140 primary carers to severely and moderately disabled older persons living in Melbourne and Adelaide, Australia, revealed that care of the severely disabled frequently appeared to take over the carers' own personal and family life.[58] Of the carers; 41 percent were concerned with their own loss of privacy and freedom; 18 percent experienced anxiety and sleeplessness; and 17 percent were worried about the impact on their own families. Forty-four percent of these primary carers were themselves aged 60 or older.[59] In Christchurch, New Zealand, it was found that two-thirds of a sample of primary carers experienced some ill effect on their health, including fatigue, anxiety and general health deterioration.[60]

Another important factor in looking at the degree of burden on families is the duration of the support provided, which is often remarkable. For example, in the Federal Republic of Germany, most of those aged 80 and over who need nursing care by family members at home have been in that situation for up to five years, more than one-third for six to twelve years, and almost one-eighth over thirteen years.[61] Similarly, 66 percent of the carers of severely disabled older persons in Australia had been caring for that person for five or more years, as had 47 percent of the carers of the moderately disabled.[62] In the United Kingdom, research conducted by the Equal Opportunities Commission found almost half of the carers to older relatives had cared continually for over five years.[63] In the United States in a survey of 614 families who were living with and caring for a disabled older relative, slightly more than half of the disabled elders also had multiple symptoms of mental impairment such as forgetfulness, confusion and poor judgment. Despite their severe impairments, these older persons had been receiving care from family members for an average of six years.[64]

In the United Kingdom, an estimated 300,000 single women were living at home in 1978 in order to look after elderly infirm parents or other relatives. A survey of 350 of these single women showed that about half could not work outside the home because of their obligations to their relatives, resulting in both isolation and financial hardship; for instance, 25 percent had not taken a vacation for one to five years, and 11 percent had not taken one for eleven to fifteen years.[65] Similarly, a survey of persons caring for old people in New South Wales, Australia, revealed that 73 percent of the caregivers had not had a night away from their responsibilities for over six months and that 87 percent of the daughters caring for mothers were not in paid employment.[66]

Many women employed outside the home also care for ill older parents and have difficulties balancing these duties with their other work, family and community responsibilities. In the United States, Patricia Archbold investigated a sample of 30 women who were caring for severely functionally impaired parents, including some who were employed full-time outside the home and some who were not.[67] She identified two primary groups: (1) the "care providers," who themselves provide the services their parents require, and (2) the "care managers," who locate the needed services and then manage their provision by others. Although care provision was found to be in many ways more physically and emotionally difficult than care management, the care managers also experienced many stresses, such as time limitations, career interruptions and financial problems. Because of the high cost of purchasing services, even the professional women in the sample found they had little money at the end of the month. Many were drawing on their own savings and investments, which increased their anxiety about their own old age.[68] Both the care managers and the care providers also reported difficulties in their marital relationships which they attributed to caregiving.[69]

There is some evidence that the psychological burden of caregiving is frequently at least as difficult to bear as the physical burden. One American study showed that there was a clinically depressed family member in one of four households where a dependent older person resided and that one in eight older persons who required time-consuming help from another person was clinically depressed.[70] In the Federal Republic of Germany, a study investigating 140 children living with an older relative suffering from chronic physical or mental illness indicates that personality changes in the parent were a primary influence on the degree of burden experienced by caregivers. Persons who were living with a physically vigorous older person with some form of senile dementia seemed to be the most vulnerable. These caregivers manifested a large number of psychosomatic complaints and low life satisfaction. Compared to this group, relatives of chronically physically ill older persons, even those who were incontinent or bedridden, experienced lower degrees of burden.[71] In Japan, it was found that 81 percent of families caring for relatives with senile dementia complained about the mental and physical stress they experienced in caring for their older relative, and 36 percent cited lack of sleep as a major problem.[72]

Researchers in the United States and United Kingdom also have explored the factors contributing to feelings of burden on the part of family members caring for older relatives with senile dementia. In one study of twenty-nine caregivers in the United States, feelings of burden were *not* found to be related to the extent of behavior impairment manifested by the relative, but were instead related to the frequency of visits from other family members.[73] In contrast, preliminary data from a recent United Kingdom study of twenty-one supporters of persons with senile dementia found that the frequency of contact supporters had with relatives and friends, and the amount of help they received, were *not* associated with caregiver morale.[74] This study also came up with the surprising finding that the greater the impairment of the relative, the higher the caregiver's morale.[75] (The researcher speculates that when dementia is newly started, the supporter is uncertain as to whether the deviant behaviors are self-motivated; this uncertainty is distressing and lowers morale.) Many of the caregivers in this sample found some of the behaviors manifested by their relative so distressing that they could cope with them only by selectively ignoring them.

In a survey of 112 family caregivers to elderly mentally infirm persons who were attending five psychogeriatric day hospitals in Scotland, C. K. Gilleard and others found that the most frequent problems relate to the inability of the dependent older person to be left alone and to disruptions in the caregiver's personal life.[76] Data from a subsample of forty-six supporters indicates that there is a strong correlation between the emotional and personal demands placed on the caregiver (for example, demands for attention, disruptions in social life and family conflicts) and a negative emotional state. In fact, only the presence of these "demand problems" was significantly predictive of whether the relative was still in the community or in institutional care at six-, twelve-, and eighteen-month follow up. (The older relatives' physical dependency, physical disabilities and even aggressive behavior failed to relate significantly to outcome.) Further studies are now in progress to investigate the effectiveness of psychogeriatric day care in providing "time out" from these demands. Similarly, a recent survey of 614 caregivers to disabled elders in the United States revealed that the caregivers who experienced the most problems were those caring for mentally impaired relatives whose behavior disrupted the household. Although this study found that families generally cope fairly well, certain types of families seemed to experience more difficulties in caring for an older relative. These were typically three-generation households in which the primary caregiver was called upon to meet her husband's and children's needs as well as those of the impaired older person. Another especially problematic situation was when the primary caregiver was a daughter-in-law.[77]

Some families caring for impaired older persons reach a crisis point and decide to institutionalize their relative. Usually, this decision is made as a last resort, after families have exhausted their coping abilities and resources. The decision to institutionalize a relative has been called "a nadir of life" because of the great emotional conflict it generates in both young and old. An analysis of factors leading to the decision among a group of fifty caregivers in the United Kingdom revealed that the majority had undergone a prolonged period of stress—in 62 percent of the cases, the caregivers had had their sleep disturbed by their relative on a regular basis; 52 percent reported depression or anxiety; 42 percent had experienced restrictions in their social life; and 33 percent felt unable to leave their relative alone for more than an hour.[78]

SUPPORT FOR FAMILIES OF THE ELDERLY

Outlined below are examples of some of the policies and programs which are designed to serve as incentives to family care in industrialized nations and some of the services to help alleviate part of the stress of caring for older relatives. These include various forms of financial assistance to families, respite care, and group programs for families. Housing assistance, such as low interest loans to families to adapt a dwelling to accommodate an older relative and "granny annexes," is also an important supportive service for families; it is discussed in Chapter 7.

Financial Assistance

Most of the industrialized nations in the west (the United States, Canada, and the Federal Republic of Germany are exceptions) provide a "constant" attendance allowance, a cash benefit paid on behalf of permanently disabled persons who require either full- or part-time care by another person at home, under their old age and invalidity insurance programs.[79] This benefit is normally used to hire a nurse or to reimburse family members for the costs incurred in caring for a relative.

There is, however, wide variation among nations in the qualifying conditions for constant attendance allowances. Some programs require total (100 percent) disability; in others, including many Scandinavian countries, allowances are paid for lesser degrees of disability.[80] Some nations, such as Switzerland, apply an income test, and in France, the income of the family as well as the beneficiary is calculated in the means test.[81]

Benefit levels also vary widely. Many nations calculate the constant attendance supplement as a percentage of the base amount of the invalidity (disability) pension, and hence its adequacy is linked to that of the base pension. In Denmark, for example, disability pensions are high relative to those of many other nations, and the constant attendance supplement in 1979 equalled the full disability pension.[82] In contrast, Japan's disability pensions are relatively low, and the constant attendance supplement came to only one-fourth of the disability pension.[83] Several European nations use a flat-rate formula, based on the degree of incapacity, to calculate the benefit. In Belgium, the benefit in 1979 ranged from $414 a year (minimum) to $828 (maximum);[84] in East Germany, it ranged from $132 a year (minimum) to $1,500 (maximum).[85]

In the United Kingdom, both the elderly disabled person and his or her caregiving relative can receive an allowance. In 1980, the constant attendance allowance to the elderly beneficiary ranged from $28 per week (minimum) to $42 per week (maximum).[86] Additionally, a son, daughter, or other relative (although generally not a married woman) can receive an invalid care allowance if the person spends at least thirty-five hours a week looking after an older relative who receives a constant attendance allowance; the caring relative's allowance is considered taxable income. In 1980, the invalid care allowance was $32 per week.[87] Legislation enacted in 1981 enables persons who are not related to the disabled persons to claim the allowance.[88] And legislation was also recently enacted in the United Kingdom permitting women and men who drop out of the labor force to care for an elderly or disabled relative to be credited with social security contributions for the period, up to twenty years, that they remain at home.[89]

Recently, a group of charities in the United Kingdom has begun campaigning for an extension of the invalid care allowance to married and cohabiting women, who form 75 percent of the carers.[90] The National Council for the Single Woman has also submitted a recommendation to the government that would remove certain limitations on the invalid care allowance.[91] Currently, it takes dependents six months to qualify for an attendance allowance, which is a necessary precondition for the invalid care allowance. Hence the council is recommending that entitlement to the invalid care allowance should not depend on payment of the attendance allowance to the person needing care, and that the invalid care allowance should not be taxed.

While the constant attendance allowance is provided as part of many social security programs, in some nations similar payments to family members caring for older relatives are provided through other sources. In the Federal Republic of Germany, for example, the Federal Public Assistance Law permits the reimbursement of relatives or neighbors providing nursing care to the low-income infirm elderly.[92] In Finland, the Ministry of Social Affairs and Health has recently launched home care allowances in 11 of the country's 450 municipalities, providing local authorities with grants covering half of the costs of the allowance.[93] The allowance is paid either directly to the older person, who can use it to obtain the services he or she needs, or to the primary caregiver.

While the United States does not provide a constant attendance allowance benefit under its Social Security program, the U.S. Veterans Administration does provide "housebound" or "aid and attendance" allowances to eligible veterans and their widows. These are payable respectively to veterans who are permanently housebound due to disability or to those who are in need of regular aid and attendance by another person. Veterans who are 100 percent disabled due to a service-connected disability received a basic benefit in 1982 of $1,130 per month.[94] If they were eligible for the "aid and attendance" allowance, they received an additional amount, ranging from $270 per month to $2,093 per month in 1982, depending upon the severity of the disability.

Veterans who do not have a service-connected disability may also be eligible for veteran's benefits based on non-service connected disability and need. For example, single veterans whose income fell below $5,328 per year in 1982 were eligible to have their income supplemented up to this limit. In addition, if the veteran was entitled to a housebound allowance, the income limit (and potential supplement) was raised from $5,328 to $6,513; if the veteran was eligible for an aid and attendance allowance, the income limit was raised to $8,424. These programs can provide substantial financial assistance to eligible veterans and their families.

Tax reductions for family members who support elderly dependents are available in the United States and Japan. In the United States, persons who contribute more than half of the total support to an elderly relative whose income is less than $1,000 a year (exclusive of tax-exempt income such as Social Security) can count them as a dependent. In 1980, this exemption was $1,000, the same as for other dependents, such as children. In Japan, the income tax credit for families whose older parent(s) live with them is considerably higher than the credit for other dependents, although the amount is small in comparison to the amount actually needed to support an old person at home.[95]

Sweden is an example of a nation which provides several layers of financial support for invalid care. First, disabled persons of any age who are covered under the invalidity (disability) program can receive a constant attendance allowance equal to 60 percent of the base amount of their invalidity pension.[96] Second, family members performing the equivalent of home help services are reimbursed at the same rate as other home help aides, approximately $10 per hour, including benefits, by the municipal government.[97] The reasoning behind this is not only to stimulate family assistance and relieve the formal home help service, but perhaps to encourage the family caretaker to enroll as a paraprofessional in the home help service at some point in the future. The caregiver's allowance is thus also viewed as a form of training assistance. In 1982, relatives employed as home helpers numbered 10,500 out of a total of about 70,000 home helpers.[98]

Community Programs for the Infirm Elderly

A number of services, such as home help/home health assistance and day care or day hospitals, can be critical in helping ill older persons remain in their own home or that of their family. (See Chapters 4 and 6 for a discussion of these services in other developed countries.) Although these services do not have the family as their target group, their availability is a major factor in reducing the burden on the family caregiver and, especially in health-related areas, providing necessary skilled "back-up" support.

An important issue here is whether the services are universally available to all, regardless of income, or whether they are means-tested. If they are means-tested, and if the income of the family as well as that of the older person is considered in the means test, elderly persons with family support will be excluded. Even where the services are universally available, in times of budget cuts they may be limited to those not living with family members or without other family support.

For example, in Japan, elderly persons who pay income tax or whose children pay income tax are not eligible for the public home help service,[99] yet this is not a service which is widely available through the private sector. And in times of scarce resources and budget cuts, nations such as the United Kingdom, which generally believe in universally available services, give priority to low-income individuals and those without family or other informal support.[100]

As in the United States, treatment of patients in the home by physicians is not common in most developed countries, and this can pose a formidable problem for the bedfast elderly and their caring relatives. (The United Kingdom and the U.S.S.R. are two countries where home visits for older patients are still fairly common.)

Services for Family Caregivers

Respite Care

One of the most necessary services for families providing direct care to their ill older relatives is some form of respite care to enable the caregiver to have a night away from home or take a vacation. Respite stays at nursing homes or other residential settings for older persons who are being cared for by family members are becoming increasingly widespread in many nations, and especially in northern Europe. According to Sheila Peace the reasons are two-fold.[101] First, the principle of keeping the frail elderly in the community as long as possible often succeeds or fails depending on the degree of interaction between professionals and family members. Family members will frequently go on caring for elderly relatives suffering even from severe mental impairments, as long as they can be assured of respite care and support in times of crisis. Second, in-patient beds and residential beds are becoming scarce commodities, and innovations in short-stay care are needed in order to prevent the blocking of much-needed long-term-care beds.

In New Zealand, persons caring for disabled elderly persons are now entitled to four weeks holiday through the Disabled Persons Relief Scheme.[102] The ill persons are placed in suitable accommodations or given alternative care in their homes to relieve the caregivers. France began experimenting with providing temporary placements in institutions in 1978 by making an initial 400 beds available; the costs were covered through social security.[103] Denmark also provides short-term stays in nursing homes; these are called "temporary relief accommodations." Japan recently substantially expanded its program of providing short-term stays at nursing homes for bedfast older persons who are being cared for by relatives.[104] Short stays for persons with senile dementia whose families face emergency situations, such as childbirth or illnesses, also are now available at two nursing homes in Tokyo through a program developed by the municipal government.[105]

In the United Kingdom, many geriatric hospital departments, if approached by the invalid's doctor, will arrange for a few weeks of holiday care in a hospital bed. Some hospitals will book periods of in-patient care, alternating with periods of nursing care at home.[106] For example, the family may care for the elderly patient for a four-week period, followed by his or her admission to a "respite bed" for two weeks. In fact, several geriatricians in the United Kingdom now base their service on the use of short-term beds and negotiate the time of discharge with the family at the point of admission; for example, the family agrees to take care of the patient for a four-week period, followed by his or her admission to a "respite" bed for two weeks.[107] The utilization of in-patient beds to provide these care alternatives still appears to be rare in the United States.[108]

Some problems have emerged in providing respite stays. Family members have difficulty locating those temporary accommodations which are available, and most nursing homes and other residential settings have insufficient space to meet the many requests they receive. In the United Kingdom, the National Council for the Single Woman and her Dependents now provides national listings of homes offering suitable placements. And in the Federal Republic of Germany, a Caritas home in Dortmund-Dern came up with an innovative approach to the problem of insufficient space. Nine residents of the home whose condition had stabilized volunteered to spend several weeks at another home outside of the city so their beds could temporarily be used by older persons needing more intensive levels of care. The latter's families were then able to take a vacation, and the residents who changed sites were pleased with their own "vacation."[109]

Another approach to the problem of insufficient space at nursing homes is to develop homes designed solely for short-term stays. In Switzerland, the city government of Zurich runs a "pensioners hotel" for short stays by older persons whose relatives are away, who are convalescing following hospitalization, or who need temporary accommodations for other reasons.

In the United Kingdom, short-term homes are being developed under voluntary auspices. David Hobman found that such "purpose built" short-stay residential establishments can offer some important advantages over respite stays in long-term establishments, where "short stay persons" frequently may remain outsiders.[110] One such short-term home is run by a voluntary association, Age Concern Norfolk, and is jointly funded by the county council social services department and the health authority. This home provides twenty-one residential and ten day care places. Some residents are accepted on very short notice, literally "overnight," to allow a relative to meet a domestic or professional obligation. Annually, the center serves 900 people, whose average length of stay is two weeks.[111]

Yet another alternative to institutional short-term care is to provide temporary placements for elderly persons in the private homes of qualified individuals. Such schemes, sometimes called "assisted lodgings," are a rapidly growing innovation in the United Kingdom. For example, the Liverpool Personal Service Society, a voluntary agency, runs what is essentially a short-term foster care program. The foster caregivers, most of whom are women in their early 60's, enjoy the opportunity to use their skills in their own homes while making some extra money, and they also enjoy the fact that they can have an elderly person with them as frequently or infrequently as they like.[112] Foster caregivers meet regularly to exchange experiences and provide each other with support. The family caregivers have been able to have a break from their caring responsibilities while knowing their relative is being well looked after in a one-on-one situation.

A family support scheme in Avon, run by Age Concern, is another example of a short-term foster care program.[113] Volunteer "hostesses" are carefully assessed by the organizers to make certain their personalities and homes are suitable. Initially, only older persons who were alert and relatively mobile were accepted into the program in order to prevent strain on the hostesses, but now some persons who are incontinent or mentally confused are accepted. The weekly cost to clients is £35, which covers the costs to the hostesses but does not provide them with any profit.[114] Initiated on a pilot basis in 1980, the scheme has expanded to include the entire county of Avon.

In a recent national survey of both voluntary and statutory provision of permanent and respite foster care for the elderly in the United Kingdom, Patricia Thornton and Jeanette Moore concluded that these schemes work well and should be expanded.[115] (Fourteen such programs were identified in 1979). The schemes help free institutional beds, offer personalized service to older persons with high levels of dependency,[116] and are cost-effective. A high level of physical care and emotional support was provided by the foster caregivers, who were predominantly older women, and most elderly clients were satisfied with the service they received.[117] Those who had also experienced local authority residential care preferred the individual attention they received from the foster caregivers. In the opinion of Thornton and Moore, the advantages of the respite foster care approach include its flexibility and the opportunity it provides to combine the resources of statutory and voluntary agencies with those of caring individuals in the community.

There are also thirty-one "crossroads care attendant" schemes in Britain, which provide part-time care attendants to support families of the disabled.[118] Although the service is available to families of disabled persons of any age group, the great majority of those served are elderly. The care attendants, who are generally women, are paid on an hourly basis and given basic and continuing training. The service itself, which may be funded and organized under voluntary and/or statutory auspices, is free to families regardless of their economic circumstances. Families see the schemes as filling an important service gap, and they point to the flexibility in the types of tasks the attendants perform and the "unsocial" hours they work.[119]

Finally, several other forms of respite care are provided under voluntary auspices in Britain. A 1981 survey of schemes that "support the carers" identified a wide range, including day care, night sitting, sleeping in, mutual aid, counseling, and education programs.[120] For example, in a number of areas, volunteers are used extensively in providing day care to the elderly mentally ill. And a particularly innovative approach to home care relief in Sheffield uses volunteers to provide respite to relatives of patients discharged from a psychogeriatric ward.[121] The volunteers are introduced to the families while the patient is still in the ward so that they can provide on-going practical and emotional support.

Night-sitting services provide relief for one of the most common complaints associated with caring for a very ill older relative—that is, having to get up several times during the night to respond to the latter's needs. Although the services are not widespread, in several nations they are still more common than in the United States. The city of Stockholm, for example, provided over three hundred thousand hours of night care assistance a year to elderly persons in 1978.[122] A "go to bed patrol" helps persons get ready for and into bed, and a "night patrol" returns to give them any medications they need, turn them in their beds and so on. There are trained "night care" assistants in several communities in the United Kingdom as well.

Group Programs for Families

A relatively new approach to strengthening family networks is group support and training programs for families of the elderly. In the United Kingdom, the United States, Canada, Australia and the Federal Republic of Germany, several programs have been initiated to lessen the isolation of family members by putting them in touch with others in similar situations in order to share coping strategies and impart useful information and skills training related to the needs of their older relative. The target groups of these programs may include families who are anticipating a caregiving role, those who are the primary caregivers to mentally and/or physically impaired elderly, and those whose relatives are in institutions.

In the United States, the Natural Support Program of New York City's Community Services Society offers several forms of group support to families. These include

1) Educational groups, which provide education and skills training for more effective caregiving;

2) Peer support facilitated by community professionals and para-professionals, in which members give each other emotional support and advice about problems associated with caring for their older relatives; and

3) Self-help groups, which may evolve out of mutual aid groups and provide their own leadership from among the caregiver members.[123]

In Australia, the New South Wales Council on Ageing sponsors monthly "carer" groups, which help family members learn about services which are currently available and serve as advocates for instituting new ones.[124]

In the United Kingdom, the United States and the Federal Republic of Germany, programs also have been developed specifically for relatives of the mentally impaired elderly. In the United States, the Alzheimer's Disease and Related Disorders Association (ADRDA) is sponsoring family support groups around the nation. The rapid growth of this national organization is testimony to the need it fills. Formed in 1979 and initially composed of seven family support groups which had sprung up autonomously around the country, ADRDA has grown to more than 58 chapters, representing over 250 local family support groups.[125] In addition to assistance in organizing family support groups, ADRDA sponsors educational forums for both lay and professional people regarding Alzheimer's Disease, advises government agencies about the needs of afflicted families, and promotes national research.

In the Federal Republic of Germany, Jens Bruder reports on over two years of group work with 140 women caring for older persons with senile dementia.[126] In addition to giving emotional support to the caregivers, the group provided information on the behavioral changes of the relative and opportunities for the caregivers to discuss their reactions to them. Some of the most important discussion topics included changes in filial role and the caregivers' guilt feelings. The groups also provided counsel and support for those who eventually had to institutionalize their relative.

Group programs for relatives of residents at nursing homes and long-term care facilities are also becoming increasingly widespread. For example, groups for family members of psychogeriatric nursing home patients in the Netherlands have helped relatives accept their loved one's placement in an institution.[127] Spouses and children met in separate groups because of the differing nature of their concerns. Discussion topics addressed the relatives' guilt feelings (guilt was so strong among spouses that only one of fifty partners had been able to tell their spouses that they were planning to admit them to the nursing home), how frequently to visit, modes of interacting with their relative, and concerns about the nursing home.[128]

Self-evaluations of small group programs for families of the institutionalized elderly at the Health Sciences Centre Hospital in British Columbia, Canada, reveal that such groups reduce the stigma and guilt surrounding institutionalization, help family members cope with changes in their relative's behavior, and lessen their isolation.[129] While such discussion groups for families of nursing home residents are being developed in a number of nations, others are being targeted on families whose relatives are on waiting lists for institutional placement, which are frequently long. For example, as long ago as 1978 the Maimonides Hospital and Home for the Aged in Montreal, Canada, began helping such families to evaluate the pros and cons of institutionalization and cope with the difficult emotions associated with making the decision to institutionalize a relative. The program became an integral part of services offered to families of persons awaiting admission to the home.[130]

In the United Kingdom, St. James Hospital in Portsmouth has been the base for offering a number of services which help "care for the carers." These include intermittent relief admissions, long-term day hospital care, and a relatives' psychotherapy group.[131] The great majority (80 percent) of those who attend the relatives' group have a loved one afflicted with senile dementia, and they attend the group right up until their relatives' death as a means of coping with their feelings of anger, resentment and guilt. St. James is planning to extend its supportive services to family members to include day hospitals that are open seven days a week, weekend relief admissions, a "tucking in" and "waking up" service, and a traveling day hospital to reach those in rural areas.

In Denmark, the Jutland Technological Institute has developed an interesting model for improving relationships among the aged, their families and the staff of nursing homes. In its Family Participation Project, eleven nursing homes initiated a number of experiments to increase interaction among these groups and their staff met frequently to exchange ideas and experiences.[132]

The experiments undertaken by the homes included

1) "Family contracts," in which relatives identify the ways they wish to contribute to and participate in the life of the nursing home. Many relatives feel a real need to be active in the nursing home, but may be reluctant to take the initiative for fear of being a bother.

2) Various forms of family education, including counseling groups, peer support and discussion meetings, and intake procedures more sensitive to the needs of families.

3) Relatives' Nursing Home Councils to advise management about matters affecting the quality of life in the home. In some of the larger nursing homes, councils were formed at the ward level.

4) "Network meetings" for the elderly residents, staff and family members, to address sensitive issues which frequently lead to a breakdown in communication, such as loss of residents' belongings, inadequate care, families' fears about criticizing staff, and so on.

5) "Family care" projects, in which the homes provided more opportunities for intergenerational interaction, such as making the home more attractive for visiting children by creating playrooms.

An evaluation revealed that these experiments were highly successful—all but two of the homes developed workable approaches to increasing family involvement in the life of the home.[133] Although the staff initially increased its workload in order to get relatives involved, the benefits far outweighed the extra staff time. For example, one of the positive side effects of increased family participation was increased resident interaction. "When relatives get to like each other and meet under friendly conditions, it becomes easier for residents to like each other too." Finally, the cost of the entire project—$20,000—was considered minimal in light of the benefits. The results of these various experiments were disseminated widely among both professionals and in Denmark's popular press.

POLICY ISSUES

The question of what is the proper "mix" of public and family responsibility for the care of the elderly is a matter of policy debate in many developed nations. Some issues which seem central to the debate include the extent to which families should be considered financially responsible for the care of aged members, whether the development of social services and institutional facilities serve as substitutes for—and perhaps disincentives to—family support, and exactly what policies and programs serve as incentives to family care.

Mandating Filial Responsibility

Because of escalating Medicaid expenses for institutional care, it has been proposed in the United States that children whose parents are in nursing homes be required to pay a portion of their expenses. Most other industrialized nations have abolished legal requirements obligating filial financial responsibility for elderly parents, or are in the process of doing so. Vienna, for example, recently repealed the provision that children be responsible for the costs incurred by their parents, and the Austrian Senior Council has urged all other Austrian states to do the same.[134]

In those nations which still have legal requirements regarding filial support, there have been many difficulties in enforcing family obligations. In Japan, for example, families are required to subsidize the costs of nursing home care received by older relatives. However, a special legal provision—the "division of household" clause—allows exceptions to this requirement if this is considered in the best interest of the older person. According to one report, this clause is frequently invoked by welfare workers.[135] In Yugoslavia, children are legally required to take care of their older parents if the parents are ill and without income. In practice, however, few older persons are willing to report their children for non-support.[136] These examples underscore some of the problems of attempting to enforce filial responsibility, and also some of the reasons why such obligations have been abolished in many other nations.

Research conducted in the United States leads to the same conclusions. As Sandra J. Newman found in her review of the history of filial support legislation at the state level in the United States neither existing evidence nor intuition suggests that family solidarity is developed or nurtured by mandated financial contributions.[137] Similarly, Alvin Schorr reports that the filial contributions required in many states under the former old age assistance program (the predecessor of today's Supplementary Security Income Program) did not lead to significant public cost savings.[138] Such provisions were difficult and expensive to administer. At most, they appear to have deterred some old people from applying for assistance because they did not want to burden their children with this requirement. Further, the provisions appear to have impacted most heavily on the already poor. James J. Callahan also concluded recently from a review of national data that "expanded asset tests with introduction of legal responsibility for selected children of institutionalized adults are not promising sources of large additional sums of money."[139]

Despite such evidence, the last several years in the United States have seen renewed interest in requiring, by law or regulation, some filial responsibility for the costs relatives incur in nursing homes. Although several such measures have failed in Congress, Medicaid statutes have recently been reinterpreted by the Reagan Administration to allow states to force adult children and other relatives to pay for the cost of nursing home care.[140]

Disincentives to Family Care

More common in developed countries than legal requirements for filial responsibility are provisions which take into account the family's resources when needy older persons apply for aid. Where such provisions exist, families actually can be penalized for the decision to live with or care for older relatives. In the United States, for example, Supplemental Security Income benefits are reduced by one-third if the aged person lives in another person's household. According to Schorr, it is unlikely that such a reduction (which equalled $63 per month in 1978) actually leads many poor older persons to choose to live alone.[141] Instead, those who are most affected are parents and children who must share dwellings out of economic necessity, and the reduction simply results in increased financial and other strains on the family.[142] Interestingly, within the meaning of the law, any aged person who "owns the shared dwelling in whole or in part," or who pays "any portion of the rent," is not considered to be living in another person's household. Hence those who are penalized are older persons and their families who are unable to manipulate the definition, that is, the most impoverished and least educated. Yet another disincentive to multigenerational living in the United States is the consideration of the income of family members who live with the low-income elderly when determining the latter's eligibility for food stamps.

It is also possible for family support to be undercut if services are not carefully structured. While chronically ill older persons in the United States receive little financial reimbursement under Medicare and Medicaid for in-home services, Medicaid provides full reimbursement to the financially destitute for long-term institutional care. And several studies have illustrated how these policies indeed may function as disincentives to home and family care of the elderly.[143]

In Israel, Hannah Weihl reports that older persons who are living with their children must forfeit claims to welfare services for which they would have otherwise been eligible. One example of this involves access to nursing home care. Because of the scarcity of nursing home facilities in Israel, the final criterion for deciding who among the chronically ill will be admitted is primarily whether the client lives with relatives or alone.[144] Similarly, Robert M. Moroney found that services in the United Kingdom which could be used to support families caring for impaired elderly relatives were not provided to such families but rather to individuals where there was no viable family support.[145] While these examples may legitimately be seen as cases of scarce resources being targeted on those in greatest need, they also raise issues about penalizing families who choose to care for their elderly members.

Services as Complementary to and Supportive of Family Care

While disincentives to family care exist in some nations, evidence is building that services and other incentives can be created which increase both family willingness and capacity to care for older relatives. For example, in the United States, research conducted by Marvin Sussman indicated that over 90 percent of the respondents in two Midwestern cities, ranging in age from 18 to 64, responded positively to the possibility of both financial and other incentives provided by the government to encourage family care of the elderly. Over half of the respondents in one city said they would participate in such a program.[146] Families also said they would prefer a monthly check to cover the expenses and extra time spent to care for an older relative rather than other forms of economic support, such as tax deductions and low-interest loans.[147] Reasonably priced and accessible medical care was the most desired service support.

As debate continues in the United States about the cost implications and appropriateness of providing direct subsidies to families caring for disabled elderly members, many other nations are currently providing such payments. In some instances, the payments are so low they would not be expected to serve as incentives, but in other cases, they are quite substantial. The impact of these payments, however, does not seem to have been evaluated systematically, and it is not clear whether or to what extent they actually serve as incentives to family care. Similarly, and somewhat surprisingly, the ''aid and attendance'' allowance program of the U.S. Veterans Administration has not been evaluated.

The few pieces of evidence available from other countries suggest that families who might be eligible for these programs may not be utilizing them widely. One report from the United Kingdom estimated that, in 1973, a relatively small proportion of the disabled elderly who were living with their children received a constant attendance allowance.[148] And although economic support from the local government is available in Denmark to families caring for the elderly with extensive nursing needs, it is reported that the program is used by only a limited number of families. In both cases, it was unclear from the available information whether families were not aware of the programs, whether they were not applying for other reasons, whether their applications had been rejected or whether there were other reasons. (On the other hand, families in California, who could be reimbursed for in-home services given to disabled or impaired older relatives under Title XX of the U.S. Social Security Act made extensive use of the option.)[149]

The availability of other benefits, such as social security credits for the years caregivers remain at home, may prove to be as significant factors as the allowances themselves in stimulating family care of the elderly. (The United Kingdom and Sweden now provide such credits.) Family members who drop out of the labor force to care for elderly relatives not only sacrifice wages, but can be jeopardizing their own economic security in old age if they receive no social security credits. If health insurance coverage is not available to the caregiver, this can also be an important financial cost.

There are many unanswered questions about the extent to which direct payments to families are in themselves sufficient incentives to family care. For some families, the availability of other supportive services, such as home health care and respite relief, may be at least as important as receiving financial support. Marvin B. Sussman's finding that families who were already taking care of an elderly person were more concerned about obtaining quality medical care and other social services than receiving a monthly check supports this reasoning.[150] More recently, Amy Horowitz and Lois Shindelman found that over 80 percent of a sample of 203 primary caregivers in the United States preferred a service program, most notably home help and home medical care, to financial support.[151] (Interestingly, financial supports elicited a negative reaction from a sizable group of respondents, primarily those most likely to need them, such as the least educated, the oldest and those with the lowest incomes.) According to Horowitz and Shindelman, these findings are consonant with a number of other studies which suggest that financial stress seems to be of less consequence to families than the social and emotional impact of caregiving.[152] Similarly, Archbold found strong congruence between "care providers" and "care managers" in their ranking of the services they needed most.[153] Both groups ranked assistance by a homemaker with nursing and personal care for their older relative as the most critical form of assistance, followed by respite care.

On the other hand, Joseph Hörl and Leopold Rosenmayr found that only one-fifth of a sample of households giving aid to an older person in Austria anticipated that home help services would alleviate the burden. Surprisingly, households receiving home help assistance expressed feelings of burden more frequently (48 percent) than did those who were not receiving such help (34 percent).[154] The researchers speculate that older persons in households receiving home help, which represented only 2 percent of responding households, may have had more severe impairments than those which did not. They conclude that, whatever the explanation, it seems clear that providing supportive social services to families cannot take away *all* of the burden experienced by kin.

Such examples underscore the complexity of determining what factors influence perceptions of burden by families caring for older relatives, and their perceptions of the types of supportive services which would be most helpful to them. Clearly, families and their older relatives have very heterogeneous abilities and needs, and what is sufficient to encourage one family to adopt or continue a caregiving role may not be so for another. And, of course, the optimum "mix" of services varies within subgroups in the same nation as well as among nations.

Services as a Substitute for Family Care

The issue of whether increased social services and institutional care options for the elderly serve to undercut traditional family caring responsibilities is emotionally charged in developed as well as developing countries. In the United States, this has been called "the myth of service substitution." Despite some evidence to the contrary, many policy-makers, the general public, and some social service practitioners continue to believe that public services substitute for rather than complement family care of the elderly. The issue is an important one because such attitudes discourage the provision of supportive services which could encourage families to adopt a caregiving role, assist them in continuing it, and improve the quality of care they are able to provide to their older relatives.

There has not been much systematic research in this area, probably because of its complexity and the difficulty of developing appropriate measures for this phenomenon. The evidence which is available from other nations, however, generally suggests that the availability of public services for the elderly need not undercut family responsibility. In Denmark, for example, the introduction of a wide range of home help and other community services has not led to decreasing contact with or assistance to elderly parents on the part of adult children. National surveys conducted in 1962 and 1977, following the expansion of home help services, showed the same general picture. In both years, around 70 percent of persons aged 62 and over had seen a child during the week prior to the interview, and well over half of the elderly received various forms of assistance from their children.[155] Henning Friis concludes that there is no reason to expect that the further expansion of in-home services will undermine family support. Instead, he sees such expansion as strengthening the capabilities of families to care for their older members.[156]

Similarly, the widespread availability of home helpers and other public services for the aging in Sweden does not appear to have undercut family support of the aging. The recent Swedish national report to the U.N. World Assembly on Aging explicitly refutes the charge that the extension of public services has undermined the willingness of Swedes to help older relatives when they become ill. The report cites a recent study showing that 50 percent of adult children surveyed said they would prefer to look after an ill parent themselves and that 75 percent have the practical means to give support in the event of a lengthy illness.[157] These results are corroborated by prior studies showing that there are considerably more aged people in Sweden receiving help from relatives and friends than from the public home helpers and that nearly one-third of Swedish pensioners receive daily help from family or friends.[158]

By the same token, in a recent Canadian survey, the researchers found "no indication that the introduction of services where a viable family support system already exists undermines the amount of help provided through the informal network of family and friends." Of older persons in Regina who reported receiving formal help within the four weeks prior to the interview, 92 percent also reported receiving help from children and relatives, almost all within the same time period.[159] It is concluded that formal agency support appears to be an extension of, rather than a substitute for, services already provided. Frequently, the formal help appeared to be filling service gaps, especially in cases where older persons required intensive and frequent assistance.

In the United States, research conducted by the Community Service Society of New York, which provides an extensive array of services to families caring for the disabled elderly, found that the majority of families did not reduce their level of support because of the introduction of formal services. Of the 23 percent of families who did do less, many had been providing very high levels of support and had been encouraged by agency staff to use homemakers for respite. In only three of the forty-eight families followed for two years did the level of support decrease in both years.[160] In fact, aggregate support provided by families was as likely to increase as decrease over the study period. The researchers conclude that ''the substitution effect appears to be of a very low order,'' and is ''in many instances a socially desirable consequence of the introduction of the service.''[161]

In the United Kingdom, Moroney has also concluded that there is no factual basis to support the charge that increases in services for the elderly through the welfare state have encouraged a discernible shift in patterns of family care.[162] Although the rates of institutionalization of the elderly in the United Kingdom increased between 1951 and 1971, most of this increase can be attributed to changes in the age structure of the population and not to decreasing willingness of families to care for their ill older relatives. The percentage of persons aged 74 and over increased by 117 percent in the same period, and the majority of persons admitted to institutional care come from this group. And in the United Kingdom, as well as in the United States and many other nations, the institutionalized elderly are more likely to lack potential family support—for example, because they are childless or unmarried—than the general elderly population.

Similarly, Maeda (1981) concludes that although the United States has a higher rate of institutionalization (around 5 percent) of older persons than does Japan (1.4 percent), this is explained by differences in the demographic structures of the older populations of the two countries and *not* by differences in filial responsibility toward older parents.[163] (No significant differences between the two nations in levels of responsibility for the care of an older parent were found in Maeda and Sussman's 1980 cross-national study.) There are many more childless elderly in the United States than in Japan, leading to higher rates of institutionalization. It should be noted that rates of institutionalization may also differ because access to such care is more limited in Japan.

There is also no evidence that Medicare and Medicaid have led the elderly to enter institutions in disproportionate numbers in the United States. In fact, the percentage of those aged 65 and over in institutions has remained roughly the same since the period prior to the introduction of these programs (that is, 4 percent in 1966 and about 5 percent in 1980).[164] This small percentage increase can be accounted for entirely by the increase in persons aged 75 and over during the same period. Despite public concern about the escalating cost of institutional care, rising costs are due primarily to increased prices for the care and not to increased utilization.[165] In fact, one can question why the proportion of the institutionalized aged has not increased more rapidly, given the institutional bias in Medicare and Medicaid coverage and the shortage of community and home care services in the United States. The answer, according to Schorr, is that older persons and their families "conduct a private, unheralded guerrilla war" in order to remain outside of institutions despite the many obstacles.[166]

In summary, data on the issue of service substitution are still fairly sparse. The bulk of the evidence which is available, however, suggests that providing publicly funded services does not necessarily undermine family support and is probably a response to needs that have manifested themselves for some time.

The Issue of Cost

One issue which evokes considerable concern in the United States and other nations is the potential cost of providing any large-scale program of services or direct payments for families of the aging. In fact, several researchers in the United States have concluded that any universal policy that would help all families presently providing care would be foolhardy because of the immense cost arising from additional demand.[167] All of the proposals for various incentives to families (cash, tax deductions and packages of home care and social services) also face the problem of creating an adequate assessment or "gatekeeping" procedure to determine client eligibility.[168] Even if a way could be found to limit services or payments to older persons who are seriously impaired, it has been argued that cost savings might not be achieved. The Health Care Financing Administration in the United States has estimated that between 60 percent and 80 percent of the care received by the impaired elderly is provided by family members who are not compensated, and the value of services rises with the level of impairment.[169] Even assuming that the cost of home care is less than that of institutional care, subsidized home care is likely to lead to higher overall demand and higher public costs.[170] Further, public officials who want to control institutional care costs can do so more directly—if not very humanely—by limiting access to such care and by setting tight limits on the number of long-term-care beds they authorize. (This is currently happening to some extent at the state level in the United States.)

CONCLUSIONS

While there are legitimate concerns about how to develop economically feasible policies and programs for families, public cost savings should not be the sole or even the primary consideration in providing increased supportive services for families. The issue also involves many considerations of social equity. There is ample evidence which indicates that families, and particularly women, are currently providing by far the largest part of the care received by the dependent elderly in many nations. These families are subject to emotional, physical and financial stresses. Although a number of important questions about the cost-effectiveness of particular services or policies are unanswered, this should not obscure the fact that many beleaguered families are in need of some measure of formal support. What is rarely pointed out is that we also do not know the long-range implications for the public purse of *not* attempting to buttress families in their caregiving efforts.

As Anton Amann has argued, research in all the nations where it is available indicates that the family is playing an important role within the system of care and is a crucial element in every well-balanced system of care.[171] While bureaucracies are generally more effective in establishing standardized, formal programs and services, the family is the prototype for personal, informal and non-standardized services.

Thus, the issue becomes how to develop policies which strike a balance between the highly valued resources of both families and formal agencies. In some nations, such as the United States, public policies may actually serve to undercut rather than strengthen the families of older persons. Not only is there no explicit public policy designed to support families in these nations, but the presence of family members may be the declared reason for withholding a service.[172] (As Kamerman has pointed out, even in those nations which have an explicit family policy, such as Sweden, France and the Federal Republic of Germany, the policy is focused on families with young children and policies for the aging are generally not a component.)

Why has no family policy for the aged been developed in nations such as the United Kingdom and the United States? Kamerman suggests that there are persistent fears that whatever the government does to help the family, which is viewed as a "fragile institution," will undermine it and increase its dependency on government.[173] This assumption leads to the conclusion that social services should be provided only to individuals who are deviant and not to members of "normal" families. Additionally, political advocacy efforts for the aging in these nations have deliberately separated the elderly from their families in their successful fight to increase pensions, provide health care, and so on. According to Kamerman, one consequence has been to remove the aged still further from society and from their families and to penalize those who wish to care for their older relatives. Regardless of the pros and cons of developing an explicit policy for families, it does seem reasonable to expect that nations should carefully consider the potential impact upon family relations with older relatives when they develop policies and structure programs and services.

A Comparative Perspective

It is clear from the above review of policies and programs supportive of family caregivers abroad that several other nations have moved beyond the rhetoric of family support. For example, home health and home help services are far more widely available in a number of nations, especially those in Scandinavia, than in the United States. Further, the United States is one of the only industrialized nations that does not provide a constant attendance allowance program as part of its Social Security program. The provision of respite care, both in institutional and in community settings, also appears to be more widespread in some nations, such as the United Kingdom, than in the United States.

Despite the relative backwardness of the United States in these areas, there are some encouraging recent developments. For example, 1981 legislation now allows states to expand the provision of community-based and in-home services, including home health aides, homemaker services and respite care for families caring for the dependent elderly, under Medicaid. While this so-called Medicaid waiver program is too new to have yet been implemented on a nationwide basis, preliminary analysis indicates that both homemaker/chore services and respite care are falling within the top four additional services being requested by states.[174] (The other two most frequently requested services are case management and adult day care, both of which could also be beneficial to families.)

There is additional impetus for the provision of respite care at the state level. Of twenty-four states responding to a survey conducted by the New York State Senate Committee on Aging in 1981, five (Texas, Wisconsin, Connecticut, Florida and South Carolina) were found to have made substantial programmatic efforts or to have enacted enabling legislation.[175] New York State also passed legislation in 1981 authorizing a demonstration respite care program.

One area in which the United States can perhaps serve as a model to other nations is in the formation of self-help support groups of families of persons with senile dementia. The Alzheimer's Disease and Related Disorders Association provides impetus at the national level for the rapid proliferation of local support groups for families. This expansion is an indicator of families' need for assistance in coping with the stresses involved in caring for a severely mentally impaired relative. It is also an example of how informal action can complement and expand the limited formal services available to a very needy group.

The Future

The search for ways to encourage family support of the ill elderly is likely to remain a critical one in the years to come. Although families in developed nations are currently absorbing significant proportions of the cost of caring for the dependent elderly, it is not clear that they will continue to do so in the future. A number of demographic trends, including changes in the age structure of the population and in family composition as well as increases in the number of women working outside the home, may produce changes in future family care patterns.

In most developed nations, the proportion of the "very old," those 75 years of age and over, within the elderly population is increasing rapidly. Persons in this age group are the heaviest consumers of health and social services and may have offspring who are themselves the "young old," with declining energy, health and finances. In the United States, recent national data indicate that 40 percent of persons between the ages of 55 and 59, and 20 percent of those aged 60–64, have at least one parent living.[176]

Major changes in fertility rates would also impact on future family care patterns of the aging. Although many experts have foreseen a long-run continuation of low fertility in the United States, which would mean fewer children to support their aged parents in the future, there is recent evidence that this trend is reversing itself dramatically, at least in the short run. About all that one can conclude is that fertility rates are largely unpredictable. According to demographer Judith Treas, there is likely to be a future of "well spaced booms and busts creating cycles of boon and bane for intergenerational support systems for the elderly."[177]

Changes in family composition may also limit the ability of families to care for their older members. In the United States, for example, it is projected that the number of households containing unattached individuals (those who have not married or are divorced or widowed) will nearly equal the number of households of married couples by 1990.[178] If these trends continue, many persons who have borne the sole responsibility of caring for a child in their young adult years may find themselves bearing the sole responsibility of caring for an ill older parent in their middle years.

The recent increase in the proportion of working married women is a cross-national phenomenon. In some countries, these increases have been dramatic. Between 1951 and 1971 in Britain, labor force participation rates of married and widowed older women doubled.[179] There have been rapid increases in the United States and Japan as well. In the United States, 42 percent of women aged 55–64 are in the labor force.[180] However, as of yet, there is no evidence that women are moving away from their traditional responsibility of family care for the elderly. A recent survey of three generations of American women showed that the younger women felt even more strongly about filial responsibility than did their mothers and grandmothers and that working as well as non-working middle generation women were providing necessary services to their mothers.[181]

While these trends may make it more difficult for families to care for elderly relatives in the future, family support is now and no doubt will remain the preferred option for many. In fact, when placed in historical perspective, family care patterns seem to be remarkably resilient. As Rosenmayr has pointed out, the family as a system of mutual support between generations has already survived the changes in life style throughout and after the industrial revoluton.[182]

Because of rapidly escalating public health care budgets in many nations, it is likely that finding new ways of buttressing natural and perhaps surrogate families in their caregiving efforts will also remain in the best interests of society as a whole, as well as of families and their older relatives.

Hopefully, economic concerns will not obscure the basic issue, which is that policies should be designed to reflect the forms of care that families and their older relatives *prefer*. Not all families are capable or desirous of caring for dependent older relatives. Yet in the current political and economic climate of fiscal austerity, there are indications that a number of governments are making extravagant claims about the capacity of the family to meet the needs of the elderly. And in some nations, such as the United States, programs and policies which might support families in their caregiving role and encourage them to continue it are conspicuous primarily by their absence. In the United States, some persons fear that proposals for a "new federalism," under which the responsibility for institutional long-term-care costs under Medicaid would be transferred to the states, would lead them to restrict access to institutional care without increasing community and in-home services. This raises the specter of increasing numbers of chronically ill older persons who are in need of institutional care being left to their own resources or those of their families. Many families simply may not be in a position to absorb the burden of care without major sacrifices and some unintended negative consequences.

Such consequences were explicitly recognized in the national report of the Federal Republic of Germany for the World Assembly on Aging. It cautions that we must not underestimate the potential long-term costs of not giving support to caregivers and other family members who provide help to older relatives over a prolonged period.[183] Rather, positive family relations are best promoted by mutual financial independence between generations and the provision of aid which helps avoid excessive strain on families.

Significantly, the need to buttress families in their caregiving efforts was underscored at the recent U.N. World Assembly on Aging. A report of the secretary general, a key background document for the assembly, emphasized that relief should be provided so that families are not indirectly penalized by society for caring for their aged members, and that the cost of these policies should not be the major concern.[184] Delegates from the 121 nations meeting in Vienna went on to recommend in the International Action Plan adopted at the assembly that the family as a whole, including its male members, should take over and share in the burden of care of older relatives and that countries should implement measures to assist families who wish to keep elderly relatives at home.[185] These recommendations signal the growing international recognition that ways must be found for families and the public sector to balance and complement their resources and responsibilities for the care of the elderly.

NOTES

1. Leopold Rosenmayr, "The Family—A Source of Hope for the Elderly," in Ethel Shanas and Marvin B. Sussman (eds.), *Family, Bureaucracy, and the Elderly* (Durham, N.C.: Duke University Press, 1977), p. 139.

2. Jerzy Piotrowski, "Old People, Bureaucracy, and the Family in Poland," in Shanas and Sussman, *Family, Bureaucracy, and the Elderly*, p. 166.

3. Ibid., p. 164.

4. International Union of Local Authorities, "Care of the Aging: A Question of Increasing Dimensions," June 1981, p. 20. Mimeographed.

5. Erdman Palmore, *The Honorable Elders: A Cross-Cultural Analysis of Aging in Japan* (Durham, N.C.: Duke University Press, 1975), pp. 39–40.

6. Ethel Shanas, "Social Myth as Hypothesis: The Case of the Family Relations of Old People," *Gerontologist* 19, No. 1 (1979):6–7.

7. Ibid.

8. Senior Citizens' Provincial Council, *Regina Social Support Study* (Saskatchewan, Canada; 1981), pp. 2–18.

9. Mark Abrams, *Beyond Three Score and Ten* (London: Age Concern England, March 1978), pp. 22–23.

10. P. Paillat and C. Wibaux, "Les citadins âgés"(Paris: I.N.E.D., Travaux et Documents no. 52), quoted in I. Simeone et al., "The Evolution of the Family and the Health of Elderly People," (paper presented at the WHO preparatory conference for the U.N. World Assembly on Aging, Mexico City, December 8–11, 1980), p. 36.

11. A. Svanborg, "Seventy-Year Old People in Gotenburg: Population Study in an Industrialized Swedish City," *Acta Medica Scand., Supplement* 611 (1977):5–37.

12. Josef Hörl and Leopold Rosenmayr, "Assistance to the Elderly as a Common Task of the Family and Social Service Organizations," *Archives of Gerontology & Geriatris* 1 (1982):77.

13. Sally Greengross, "Caring for the Carers," in Frank Glendenning (ed.), *Care in the Community: Recent Research and Current Projects* (Stoke-on-Trent, England: Beth Johnson Foundation Publications, 1982), p. 20.

14. Ethel Shanas, "The Family and Social Class," in Shanas et al., *Old People in Three Industrial Societies* (New York: Atherton Press, 1969), pp. 237–238.

15. Simeone, "The Evolution of the Family."

16. Hannah Weihl, "Cultural Differences and Situational Constraints on the Interaction Between Aged Parents and Their Adult Children" (paper presented at the 12th International Congress of Gerontology, Hamburg, July 12–17, 1981, abstract).

17. United Nations, *Aging in the Context of the Family*, report of the Secretary General for the World Assembly on Aging (A/Conf. 113/11O, April 29, 1982), p. 8.

18. A. Ciuca, "The Elderly and the Family," in G. Dooghe and J. Helander (eds.), *Family Life in Old Age* (The Hague: Martinus Nijhoff, 1979), p. 49.

19. Hörl and Rosenmayr, "Assistance to the Elderly," p. 79.

20. Bent Frijs-Madsen, "Denmark," in Erdman Palmore (ed.), *International Handbook on Aging* (Westport, Conn.: Greenwood Press, 1980), p. 79.

21. L. Roussel, "La Famille après le mariage des enfants," (Paris: P.U.F., 1976), p. 40, quoted in Simeone, "Evolution of the Family."

22. Marvin B. Sussman, "Social and Economic Supports and Family Environments for the Elderly," final report to the U.S. Administration on Aging, January 1979, mimeographed.

23. Daisaku Maeda and Marvin B. Sussman, "Japan-U.S. Cross-Cultural Study on the Knowledge of Aging, the Attitude Toward Old People, and the Sense of Responsibility for Aged Parents," research abstract, Department of Sociology, Tokyo Metropolitan Institute of Gerontology, February 1980, pp. ll–12.

24. Daisaku Maeda and Marvin B. Sussman, "Japan-U.S. Cross-Cultural Study on the Knowledge of Aging, the Attitude Toward Old People, and the Sense of Responsibility for Aged Parents," *Japanese Journal of Gerontology* (March 1980):93.

25. Elaine M. Brody et al. "Three Generations of Women: Comparisons of Attitudes and Preferences for Service Providers" (paper presented at the annual meeting of the Gerontological Society of America, San Francisco, Calif., November 1979).

26. *Population Issues* (March/April 1979).

27. Leopold Rosenmayr, "Socio-cultural Change in the Relation of the Family to Their Older Members" (paper presented at the 10th International Conference of Gerontology, Deauville, France, May 26–28, 1982), p. 1.

28. Greengross, "Caring for the Carers," p. 21.

29. Rosenmayr, "The Family—A Source of Hope," p. 143.

30. Senior Citizens' Provincial Council, *Regina Social Support Study*, p. 22.

31. Hörl and Rosenmayr, "Assistance to the Elderly," p. 86.

32. Marjorie Cantor, "The Configuration and Intensity of the Informal Support System in a New York City Elderly Population" (paper presented at the annual meeting of the U.S. Gerontological Society, New York, October 1978).

33. Roussel, "La Famille après le mariage des enfants," p. 40.

34. H. Worach-Kardas, "Family and Neighbourly Relations—Their Role for the Elderly," in Dooghe and Helander (eds.), *Family Life in Old Age*, p.46.

35. *Report on the Situation of the Elderly in the Federal Republic of Germany*, report prepared for the World Assembly on Aging (Berlin: German Center of Gerontology, May 1982), pp. 49–50.

36. Hörl and Rosenmayr, "Assistance to the Elderly," p. 82.

37. Ibid., p. 82, Table 4.

38. Senior Citizens' Provincial Council, *Regina Social Support Study*, p. 23.

39. *Report on the Situation of the Elderly in the Federal Republic of Germany*, pp. 49–50.

40. National Center for Health Statistics, "Home Care for Persons 55 and Over, July 1966-June 1968," *Vital and Health Statistics*, Series No. 10, No. 73 (1972), quoted in Stanley Brody et al., "The Family Caring Unit: A Major Consideration in the Long-Term Support System," *Gerontologist* 18, No. 6 (1978):556–561.

41. U.S. General Accounting Office, *Home Health—The Need for a National Policy to Better Provide for the Elderly*, HRD–78–79 (December 30, 1977), p. 9.

42. Ibid., p. 10.

43. Shanas, "Social Myth as Hypothesis," pp. 7–8.

44. *Altenhilfe* (1979), p. 10.

45. *Report on the Situation of the Elderly in the Federal Republic of Germany*, p. 50.

46. Daisaku Maeda, "The Cultural Forces Encouraging and Supporting Caregivers in Japan" (paper presented at the 12th International Congress of Gerontology, Hamburg, West Germany, July 12–17, 1981), p. 4.

47. Piotrowski, "Old People, Bureaucracy, and the Family," p. 169.

48. Miriam Aronson and Robert Katzman, "Afterword: Making the System More Responsive," *Generations* (Fall 1982):47.

49. Senior Citizens' Provincial Council, *Regina Social Support*, p. 27; and Hörl and Rosenmayr, "Assistance to the Elderly," p. 91.

50. Hörl and Rosenmayr, "Assistance to the Elderly," p. 88.

51. Victor G. Cicirelli, *Social Services for the Elderly in Relation to the Kin Network* (final report to the NRTA-AARP Andrus Foundation, May 1979), pp. 156–157.

52. Worach-Kardas, "Family and Neighbourly Relations," p. 42.

53. Colleen L. Johnson, "Impediments to Family Supports to the Dependent Elderly: An Analysis of the Primary Caregivers" (paper presented at the annual meeting of the U.S. Gerontological Society, Washington, D.C., November 1979).

54. Yutaka Shimizu et al., "Difficulties of Families Living with and Caring for Impaired Old People" (paper presented at the International Congress of Gerontology, Tokyo, Japan, August 1978).

55. Yutaka Shimizu and Misako Honma, "Problems in the Familial Domestic Care

of the Impaired Elderly and Their Relationship to Family Type,'' *Japanese Journal of Gerontology* (March 1978).

56. Johnson, ''Impediments to Family Supports,'' p. 5.

57. Maeda, ''Cultural Forces,'' pp. 3–4.

58. Australian Council on Ageing and Australian Department of Social Security, ''Older People at Home: Summary of Work in Progress'' (July 1982), p. 49.

59. Ibid., p. 51.

60. *Ageing New Zealanders*, report prepared for the World Assembly on Aging (1982), p. 56.

61. *Situation of the Elderly in the Federal Republic of Germany*, p. 50.

62. Australian Council on Ageing, ''Older People at Home,'' p. 51.

63. Equal Opportunities Commission, ''The Experience of Caring for Elderly and Handicapped Dependents: Survey Report, 1980,'' quoted in Greengross, ''Caring for the Carers,'' p. 19.

64. S. Walter Poulshock, Gary T. Deimling and Linda Noelker, ''The Effects on Families of Caring for the Impaired Elderly in Residence,'' *Bulletin of the Benjamin Rose Institute* (Summer 1982).

65. Age Concern England, Information Circular (August 1978), p. 6.

66. New South Wales Council on Ageing report, quoted in *Growing Older* (September 1976), pp. 21–22.

67. Patricia Archbold, ''Impact of Parent-Caring on Women'' (paper presented at the 12th International Congress of Gerontology, Hamburg, West Germany, July 1981), pp. 3–4.

68. Ibid., p. 10.

69. Ibid., p. 8.

70. Barry Gurland et al., ''Personal Time Dependency in the Elderly of New York City: Findings from the U.S.-U.K. Cross-National Geriatric Community Study,'' *Dependency in the Elderly of New York City* (Community Council of Greater New York, 1978), p. 29.

71. Inge Luders, ''Social Work for the Elderly and Family Support'' (paper presented at the 12th International Congress of Gerontology, Hamburg, West Germany, July, 1981).

72. *Rojin no fukushi to hoken* (June 1981), pp. 3–5.

73. Steven Zarit et al., ''Relatives of the Impaired Elderly: Correlates of Feelings of Burden,'' *Gerontologist* 20, No. 6, (1980):652–653.

74. Mary Gilhooly, ''Social Aspects of Senile Dementia,'' in Rex Taylor and Anne Gilmore (eds.), *Recent Trends in British Gerontology* (Hampshire, England: Gower Publishing Co., 1982), pp. 68–70.

75. Ibid., p. 67.

76. C. J. Gilleard et al., ''Problems of Caring for the Elderly Mentally Infirm at Home'' (paper presented at the 12th International Congress of Gerontology, Hamburg, West Germany, July 1981).

77. Poulshock et al., ''Effects on Families,'' p. 2.

78. J.R.A. Sanford, ''Tolerance of Senility in Elderly Dependents by Supporters at Home: Its Significance for Hospital Practice,'' *British Medical Journal* 3 (1975):472–473.

79. Martin A. Tracy, ''Constant-Attendance Allowances for Non-Work Related Disability,'' *Social Security Bulletin* (November 1974):32–37.

80. Ibid., p. 34.

81. Ibid., p. 35.

82. U.S., Department of Health and Human Services, Social Security Administration, *Social Security Programs Throughout the World 1979*, Research Report No. 54, p. 63.

83. Ibid., p. 127.

84. Ibid., p. 21.

85. Ibid., p. 87.

86. Age Concern England publication (1980), pp. 58–59.

87. Ibid., p. 61.

88. Age Concern England, Information Circular (1981), p. 4.

89. Elizabeth Kirkpatrick, "Social Security Benefits for Women in the Federal Republic of Germany, Switzerland, and the United Kingdom," in *Social Security in a Changing World* (Washington, D.C.: U.S. Social Security Administration, September 1979), p. 114.

90. Age Concern England, Information Circular (August 1982), p. 7.

91. Heather McKenzie, "The Single Woman as a Carer," in Glendenning (ed.), *Care in the Community*, pp. 137–139.

92. *Aktiver Lebensabend* (September 1976).

93. *Aging in Finland*, report prepared for the World Assembly on Aging (Helsinki: Ministry of Social Affairs and Health, 1982), p. 58.

94. Information provided by the U.S. Department of Veterans Benefits, Compensation and Pension Service, Policy Division, Washington, D.C., in a conversation with author, September 1982.

95. Maeda, "Cultural Forces," p. 7.

96. U.S., Department of Health and Human Services, *Social Security Programs*, p. 227.

97. Tullia van Sydow, First Secretary, National Swedish Board of Health and Welfare, personal communication with author, October 1980.

98. *Just Another Age*, report prepared for the World Assembly on Aging (Stockholm: Ministry of Health and Social Affairs, 1982), p. 31.

99. Mikio Mori, "Services in Japan," in Morton Teicher et al. (eds.), *Reaching the Aged: Social Services in Forty-Four Countries* (Beverly Hills, Calif.: Sage Publications, 1979), p. 195.

100. Robert M. Moroney, *The Family and the State: Considerations for Social Policy* (London and New York: Longman Group, 1976).

101. Sheila Peace, "Mental Health and the Elderly in Other Industrialized Nations," background paper prepared for the White House Conference on Aging, p. 13.

102. *Age Concern New Zealand*, (1981), p. 3.

103. *Ageing International* 5, No. 2 (Summer 1978):3.

104. Maeda, "Cultural Forces," p. 8.

105. *Rojin no fukushi to hoken* (November 1981), p. 22.

106. John Agate, *Taking Care of Old People at Home* (London: George Allen and Unwin, 1979), p. 83.

107. Peace, "Mental Health and the Elderly," p. 14.

108. Valeria L. Remnet, "Alternatives in Health Care Services," in Pauline Ragan (ed.), *Aging Parents* (University of Southern California, Ethel Percy Andrus Gerontology Center, 1979) p. 217.

109. *Altenhilfe*, No. 1, 1981, p. 20.

110. David Hobman, "Caring for the Caregivers of the Elderly" (paper presented at the 12th International Congress of Gerontology, Hamburg, West Germany, July 1981), p. 4.

111. Ibid., p. 5.

112. Sue Newton, "What Shall We Do With Granny?" *New Age* (Summer 1980): 29.

113. Barbara Rees, "The Family Support Scheme in Avon," in Glendenning (ed.), *Care in the Community* p. 107.

114. Ibid., pp. 109–110.

115. Patricia Thornton and Jeanette Moore, *"The Placement of Elderly People in Private Households"* (research monograph, Leeds, England: Department of Social Policy and Administration, 1980), p. 66.

116. Ibid., p. 73.

117. Ibid., pp. 97–98.

118. D. Phillips, "The Crossroads Care Attendant Scheme," in Glendenning (ed.), *Care in the Community*, pp. 113–116.

119. Ibid., p. 115.

120. Age Concern England, "Caring for the Carers: A Preliminary Directory of Initiatives" (April 1982), p. 1.

121. Ibid., p. 20.

122. International Council of Homehelp Services, *Information Bulletin* (June 1980), p. 21.

123. Iris Hudis and Miriam Buchsbaum, "Components of Community-based Group Programs for Family Caregivers of the Aging," *Strengthening Informal Supports for the Aging* (Community Service Society of New York, 1981):38–39.

124. New South Wales Council on Ageing, 1979.

125. Jerome H. Stone, "The Self Help Movement: Forming a National Organization," *Generations* (Fall 1982):39–40.

126. Jens Bruder, "Group Work with Women Who Care for a Demented Relative within a Multi-generational Household" (paper presented at the 12th International Congress of Gerontology, Hamburg, West Germany, July, 1981).

127. L. Cahn et al., "Conversation Groups Composed of Family Members of Psychogeriatric Nursing Home Patients" (paper presented at the 12th International Congress of Gerontology, Hamburg, West Germany, July 1981), p. 1.

128. Ibid., pp. 2–4.

129. Pamella Ottem and Kathleen Moorby, "Potential in Relatives of the Institutionalized Elderly" (paper presented at the annual meeting of the Gerontological Society of America and the Canadian Association of Gerontology, Toronto, November 1981).

130. Carole Brandwein and Rena Postoff, "A Didactic and Therapeutic Model of Intervention in Working with the Adult Children of Aged Parents" (paper presented at the annual meeting of the Gerontological Society of America, San Francisco, Calif., 1977).

131. Pearl D.J. Hettiaratchy, "Hospital-based Initiatives in Caring for the Carers, Including a Relatives' Psychotherapy Group in Portsmouth," in Glendenning (ed.), *Care in the Community*, pp. 130–133.

132. Knud Ramian, "Development of Family Participation in Nursing Homes" (paper presented at the annual meeting of the Gerontological Society of America, San Diego, Calif., November 1980), pp. 1–10.

133. Ibid., pp. 6–7.

134. *Rentner und Pensionist* (June 1979).

135. K. Makizono, "Division of Household" (paper presented at the International Congress of Gerontology, Tokyo, Japan, August 1978).

136. D. Nada Smólic-Krkóvic, "Aging, Bureaucracy, and the Family," in Shanas and Sussman (eds.), *Family, Bureaucracy, and the Elderly*, pp. 81–82.

137. Sandra J. Newman, "Government Policy and the Relationship Between Adult Children and Their Aging Parents: Filial Support, Medicare, and Medicaid" (paper presented at the annual meeting of the Gerontological Society of America, San Diego, Calif., November 1980), pp. 5–6.

138. Alvin Schorr, *Thy Father and Thy Mother: A Second Look at Filial Responsibility and Family Policy* (Washington, D.C.: U.S. social Security Administration, July 1980), pp. 3, 28.

139. James J. Callahan et al., "Responsibility of Families for Their Severely Disabled Elders," *Health Care Financing Review* (Winter 1980):35.

140. Conversation with Jack Christy, legislative representative for the American Association of Retired Persons, December 1983.

141. Schorr, *Thy Father and Thy Mother*, pp. 29–30.

142. Ibid.

143. U.S., General Accounting Office, *Entering a Nursing Home—Costly Implications for Medicaid and the Elderly*, PAD–80–12 (November 1979).

144. Hannah Weihl, "The Household, Intergenerational Relations, and Social Policy," in Shanas and Sussman (eds.), *Family, Bureaucracy, and the Elderly*, p. 130.

145. Moroney, *The Family and the State*.

146. Sussman, "Social and Economic Supports," p. 48.

147. Ibid., p. 24.

148. Moroney, *The Family and the State*.

149. Callahan et al., "Responsibility of Families," p. 46.

150. Sussman, "Social and Economic Supports," p. 23.

151. Amy Horowitz and Losi Shindelman, "Social and Economic Incentives for Primary Caregivers" (paper presented at the annual meeting of the Gerontological Society of America, San Diego, Calif., November 1980), p. 7.

152. Ibid., p. 12.

153. Patricia Archbold, "Caring for the Caregivers" (paper presented at the 12th International Congress of Gerontology, Hamburg, West Germany, July 1981), pp. 6–8.

154. Hörl and Rosenmayr, "Assistance to the Elderly," p. 92.

155. Henning Friis, "The Aged in Denmark: Social Programmes," in Teicher et al. (eds.), *Reaching the Aged*, p. 206.

156. Ibid, p. 207.

157. *Just Another Age*, pp. 54–55.

158. Ibid.

159. Senior Citizens' Provincial Council, *Regina Social Support Study*, p. 24.

160. Dwight L. Frankfather, Michael J. Smith, and Francis G. Caro, *Family Care of the Elderly* (Lexington, Mass.: Lexington Books, 1981), p. 72.

161. Ibid.

162. Moroney, *The Family and the State*, p. 127.

163. Maeda, "Cultural Forces," p. 6.

164. Schorr, *Thy Father and Thy Mother*, p. 32.

165. Callahan, "Responsibility of Families," p. 35.

166. Schorr, *Thy Father and Thy Mother*, p. 33.

167. Sheldon S. Tobin and Regina Kulys, "The Family and Services," in Carl Eisdorfer (ed.), *Annual Review of Gerontology and Geriatrics* (New York: Springer Publishing Co., 1980), p. 394.

168. Schorr, *Thy Father and Thy Mother*, p. 37.

169. U.S., Health Care Financing Administration, Committee on Labor and Human Resources report to accompany S. 234, March 1982, Community Home Health Services Act, p. 24.

170. Frankfather et al., *Family Care of the Elderly*, p. 101.

171. Anton Amann, *The Status and Prospects of the Aging in Western Europe*, Eurosocial Occasional Paper No. 8 (Vienna, 1981).

172. Sheila B. Kamerman, "Public Policy for the Elderly: The Dilemmas in a Family Policy Perspective," *Strengthening Informal Supports* (1981):14.

173. Ibid., p. 17.

174. Conversation with Joel Cohen, Research Associate, the Urban Institute, Washington, D.C. October 1982.

175. New York State Senate Committee on Aging and New York State Senate Select Committee on Interstate Cooperation, *Perspectives on Respite Care for the Elderly* (July 1981), p. 3.

176. NRTA-AARP national survey, Data Resources Unit, Washington, D.C., (July 1981).

177. Judith Treas, "The Great American Fertility Debate: Generational Balance and Support of the Aged," *Gerontologist* 21, No. 1 (1981):98–102.

178. George Masnick and Mary Jo Bane, *The Nation's Families: 1960–1990* (Cambridge, Mass.: Joint Center for Urban Studies of MIT and Harvard University, 1980), p. 57.

179. Age Concern England, *Profiles of the Elderly* (Mitcham, Surrey: Age Concern, 1977).

180. U.S., Department of State, *U.S. National Report on Aging for the World Assembly on Aging* (Washington, D.C.: June 1982), pp. 68–71.

181. Elaine M. Brody et al., "Three Generations of Women," p. 23.

182. Rosenmayr, "Socio-Cultural Change in the Relation of the Family," p. 11.

183. *Report on the Situation of the Elderly in the Federal Republic of Germany*, pp. 50–51.

184. United Nations, *Aging in the Context of the Family*, p. 11.

185. United Nations, *International Plan of Action for the World Assembly on Aging* (A/Conf., 113/mc/L.27, August 4, 1982), pp. 26–27.

9

Educational Opportunities

Mary Jo Gibson

The need for providing a range of educational opportunities for the elderly—from courses to promote intellectual and personal growth, to training for employment needs, to education for retirement years—has been recognized in all industrialized nations. Currently, such opportunities exist, at least for a limited number of older persons, in all developed countries. At the same time, there have been some common problems in extending these opportunities, for example, how to encourage the low-income elderly who have limited educational backgrounds to participate in the programs which are offered. Outlined below are examples of some of the educational programs for older persons which are being offered in other industrialized nations and some of the policy issues these countries are facing as they attempt to widen these opportunities.

GENERAL EDUCATIONAL OPPORTUNITIES

Universities of the Third Age

There are now over 150 *universités du troisième âge* ("universities of the third age," U3A) in Europe, Latin America and Japan.[1] These locally run universities, located in a variety of settings, offer an array of courses for the elderly. The first U3A was organized in France in 1973 as an extension of the regular programming of the University of Toulouse. There are now roughly fifty-two such universities in France, the majority of which are offshoots of established universities.[2] Many, however, do not have a formal university connection, and frequently they are sponsored by clubs and associations of retired persons. The Club des Retraités M.G.E.N. (Association of Retired Teachers) in Paris, for example, organized over 200 hours of course work per week in 1978 for over 2,500 students.[3] And other U3A's are also being managed by the elders themselves.[4]

The courses cover a wide variety of subjects, including the humanities and current events, studio arts and crafts, pre-retirement education, preventive health and gymnastics. Some programs, such as that of the University of Toulouse, offer free medical checkups for students as well. The fees for the courses, which are largely subsidized by local and national governments, are usually nominal. In general, the courses do not have eligibility requirements and are not taught with the same rigor and demands as formal university classes. Grades and examinations have largely been eliminated. However, in those "universities of the third age" which are based in university settings, older students may also enroll in the standard university courses.

Although the U3A were originally designed solely for the elderly, there have been attempts at age integration too. For example, the Interage University in Grenoble and Everyman's University in Dijon, the names of which refute the segregation inherent in the words "third age," are open to all age groups, with a special focus on those groups not likely to be found in traditional university settings.[5]

Who is most likely to attend a U3A? Data from several studies suggest that participation is linked to one's class and educational background. A profile of the student body at the U3A in Amiens showed that the great majority of students were women, primarily those who were formerly employed, many as civil servants.[6] Relatively few blue collar workers and farmers were found among the U3A student populace. At the same time, the U3A did not seem to attract the educational elite; it drew fewer persons who had completed advanced studies than had completed primary studies (40 percent) or secondary studies (54 percent). Similarly, in a study conducted at the U3A in Aquitaine, the majority of students were women who had some high school or more advanced education, which is certainly not the norm for the average older French man or woman.[7] Hence a picture emerges of the "typical" U3A student as an older woman who has been active outside the home and who is relatively well educated.

What attracts these students? According to one study, the initial motivation is primarily intellectual and cultural, with students typically expressing particular interest in lectures, trips, art, and cultural activities.[8] As Gautrat and Tugendhaft have noted, for those who did not have an opportunity to attend university when they were young, going to the university in later life can be a sort of "revenge" for missed learning opportunities, especially for women who were forced to submerge intellectual interests.[9] While the initial attraction appears to be primarily "learning for learning's sake," several studies also indicate that many students are also drawn by an opportunity to widen their social contacts.[10] Involvement in the U3A frequently develops into greater involvement in community affairs and volunteer work.[11]

Although relatively few studies have been conducted on the impact of the U3A, the research that has been done suggests that students indeed benefit from the experience. For example, one study indicated that the students showed a high level of satisfaction and did not miss classes.[12] The lack of tests and competition afforded them an opportunity to engage in intellectual pursuits for their own sake, without academic or peer pressure. Students also appreciated the more egalitarian relationships between students and teachers than those they remembered from their youthful schooling. Yet another source of satisfaction was the opportunity to improve one's body through exercise and sports. Many U3A's offer various forms of physical exercise, through which they help "modify the cognitive one-sidedness of traditional university curriculum."[13]

At the University of Amiens, students praised the opportunity to study subjects they had not studied before. Four-fifths said that their involvement at the U3A had produced a positive effect on their lives in general and had led to greater social contact and increased activities outside the university.[14] Similarly, loneliness and depression were found to decrease among regular participants at a U3A in Warsaw, and practically two-thirds of the student body became more active in outside organizations as a result of their university involvement.[15]

Hence the evidence that is available suggests that the impact of the U3A on students is positive. At the same time, many of the U3A's are seen to have a beneficial effect on the broader university community. Reaching out to the elderly can help to "democratize" the student body and help stimulate interest in aging among other faculties and among the students. For example, the initiation of exercise courses for the elderly at one U3A prompted medical students to use older subjects to study the physiology of aging.[16]

Nonetheless, U3A's have been criticized by some as being "elitist" because they primarily attract the relatively well educated. To meet this charge, some U3A's are trying to broaden their base through less traditional outreach methods. For example, in Lyons, the U3A reaches out to the elderly in the community to determine what subjects would most interest them.[17] Students at the U3A themselves canvas community residents and senior club organizers to determine how the U3A can better meet their needs. The university makes an effort to "bring the classroom to the students" and organizes classes in any section of the city for 30–50 seniors who wish to study a particular subject. There are also growing examples of U3A's which utilize radio broadcasts and correspondence courses for the homebound and provide transportation to campus, all measures that could increase participation by groups typically not reached.

Educational Opportunities in Scandinavian Nations

"Folk high schools" and "study circles" have for many years provided the greatest number of adult education opportunities in Scandinavia.[18] The folk high school, a type of boarding school, is a specifically Scandinavian form of adult education, and the oldest form of adult education in these nations. Groups of adult students meet in a residential setting, generally for short periods such as one to three weeks, and study special topics. The schools are run by local governments or non-profit associations, and there is a high degree of student participation in determining the curriculum and planning and implementing the educational process.

In Denmark, there are approximately 85 folk high schools, all of which are run as independent private bodies. Although the state pays 85 percent of their operating expenses, it has no influence over course content and methods.[19] In Sweden, there are around 110 folk high schools, which served about 150,000 students in 1978–1979.[20]

Although there are no statistics available on the percentage of older persons who attend folk high schools, it is reported that in Denmark there has been an explosive growth in courses for the aging at these schools. In 1977 a total of 141 courses was offered, ranging from humanities and science to various creative activities. In 1980, the elderly comprised about 10 percent of all students at these schools.[21] Four high schools have been founded specifically for pensioners. It is also reported that Danish folk high schools offer special courses for older persons combining study and leisure during the summer months. Recently some of these colleges have recognized that many older persons wish to interact and learn with younger persons as well as their own peers, and have organized courses of one to three weeks' duration which mix older and younger students.[22] Course offerings have included literature, history and science, and there have been seminars on economics, music and graphic design.

Ensomme Gamles Vaern, one of the oldest and largest voluntary associations serving the elderly in Denmark, has been successful in running a day high school for the elderly. The school serves both the "well" elderly and those who are physically and mentally impaired, and it offers most of the classes and activities found in high schools for younger people. For example, there is an extensive curriculum as well as activities such as orchestra, newspaper, debate, gymnastics and frequent outings. The school has helped older persons sustain their interests, gain self-esteem (many of the students did not have the opportunity to complete high school during their youth), and improve their morale.[23]

In Sweden, where it is estimated that around one-third of the adult population is engaged in some form of study, the most popular and extensive form of adult education is the study circle.[24] These informal groups are organized by voluntary educational organizations and pensioners' associations, and most are subsidized by the local and national government. Study circles for older persons are primarily sponsored by the Pensioners' National Organization of Sweden (PRO), which in 1976 sponsored almost 9,000 study circles, reaching some 90,000 participants.[25]

The national subsidy for study circles covers a bit more than 45 percent of their cost, with the remainder coming from fees and municipal grants. (The tuition fees paid by students are very low.) Study circles for groups designated as high priority educational targets, such as older persons with less than a seventh grade education and handicapped persons, receive higher national subsidies.[26]

Much of the appeal of study circles is that the students determine the subject or issue to be studied, and the circle leaders, who have some administrative and coordinating tasks, serve as facilitators rather than as teachers. To be eligible for public subsidies, the circles must have between five and twenty members and meet for at least twenty class hours spread over at least four weeks. Popular subjects are the humanities, the arts, civics and foreign languages. Some courses are taught in conjunction with planned group travel abroad.

The concept of the study circle appears to be spreading to other nations. A Scottish Retirement Education working group, established at the initiative of Age Concern Scotland, is proposing the establishment of study circles for older persons, based on common interests or hobbies as a decentralized model for extending educational opportunities.[27] In the proposed model, the circles would be run by the elderly themselves, with the role of professional educators confined to that of coordinating the training of older volunteer teachers and helping older persons get in touch with a circle appropriate to their interests.

Educational Opportunities in Other Nations

In Austria, all universities have now opened their doors to older persons who are not seeking academic degrees.[28] The demand for such opportunities has been unexpectedly high, even though many of the elderly have only limited educational backgrounds. No specific educational requirements or formalities are required on the part of Austrian elders wishing to attend university lectures as auditors. (Older persons who have completed secondary school and wish to obtain a university degree are encouraged to matriculate.) Additionally, the universities of Vienna, Graz and Salzburg have opened counseling offices for older persons who wish to attend lecture courses.[29]

Older Austrians, along with other adults in Austria, also have access to further educational opportunities through adult colleges, which are scattered throughout the country. Many of these colleges organize special courses and programs. In Vienna, 12 percent of the elderly were enrolled in adult colleges in 1977.[30] The most popular courses are in the humanities, folklore and geography.

Recently, some educational institutions have begun offering specific training programs for grandparents (for example, in modern math and foreign languages) to enable them to better help their grandchildren with their studies.[31]

In addition, the Conference of Austrian Adult Education intends to introduce an "educational passport," which will register all forms of adult education which have been taken over the life span, including those for no formal credit. The passport is expected to provide easily accessible evidence of acquired skills and aid in educational counseling efforts.[32]

In Japan, the demand for classes for the aging continues to outstrip the supply, although classes for the aging offered under governmental and voluntary auspices have expanded greatly in recent years. Public funds have been used since the early 1970's to make a variety of short classes (approximately thirty-six to fifty hours of study) available to the elderly. They cover material designed to help them understand social change and the younger generation, maintain health, and enrich their use of leisure time. Participants are encouraged to plan and manage their own classes in cooperation with senior clubs and schools. In 1974–1975, over 1,500 classes were organized in about 40 percent of Japan's cities, towns and villages; approximately 2 percent of the population over age 65 participated.[33] Additionally, the Japanese Institute for Gerontological Research and Development has been sponsoring "universities for the elderly" since 1976. These universities also provide short courses to raise the educational level of the elderly; popular courses deal with longevity, current events and religion.[34]

As in the "universities of the third age," the students who tend to participate are relatively educationally advantaged. A survey conducted in four schools serving the Japanese aging indicates that two-thirds of the students (aged 65–74) had finished eleventh grade or gone beyond it, which is higher than the average educational level of persons in this age group.[35] Further, half of the participants lived alone or just with their spouses, which is also not the norm in Japan, where around 70 percent of the elderly live with an adult child.

In the United Kingdom, emphasis is being placed on an adult education model which has potential for reaching the elderly, that is, the Open University, although participation by the aging to date remains relatively low.[36] The essence of the Open University is distance learning, or the opportunity to learn in one's own home by making use of the media and the mails, as well as special tutorial sessions. It has provided thousands who never had the opportunity to attend courses in a normal campus setting with the opportunity to obtain advanced degrees. Again, however, it is the relatively educationally advantaged who are most likely to enroll.

In part due to the example of Britain's Open University, fifteen American universities and colleges are collaborating with public broadcasting stations and cable systems to allow adult learners to earn undergraduate bachelor's degrees on a part-time basis. The National University Consortium, which opened in 1980, is the first such national system.[37] Adults enrolled in the program receive instruction through printed materials, television broadcasts and optional tutoring.

Reflective of their interest in preventive health and biomedical research, the socialist countries of Eastern Europe have placed particular emphasis on health education as a means of involving older persons in continuing education. In the U.S.S.R., for example, a number of cities have organized "universities of health and longevity" within the framework of health education. Weekly courses for older persons are held during fall and winter months and incorporate the latest ideas in gerontology and preventive medicine.[38] In the German Democratic Republic, health education is an important component of a course in nature and society for 1,400 seniors at the Veterans College of Karl Marx University in Leipzig. Older citizens are also a key target of URANIA, the East German society for spreading popular scientific knowledge. In 1980, 15 percent of

URANIA's activities in Leipzig were aimed at citizens of advanced age.[39] Encouraging older persons to provide accounts of personal experience was used as a method of stimulating participation. Popular topics are history and culture, gerontology and foreign travel.

New Horizons, in Canada, although not an educational program as such, is an interesting decentralized model for promoting educational projects. The program, which is funded by the federal government, provides groups of ten or more older persons with small grants of several thousand dollars for projects of use to their peers or to the wider community.[40] Many educational projects have been funded under the program, such as health promotion activities, oral history and film making on topics of interest to the elderly.

Increasing Participation by the Elderly in Educational Opportunities

In the area of continuing education for the aging, one major problem common to most industrialized nations is that the rates of participation by older persons in adult education opportunities are much lower than those for other age groups. In the United States, for example, where a wide variety of courses are offered in many settings, less than 4 percent of persons aged 65 and over participated in any type of education activity in 1981.[41] And national surveys conducted in 1976 and 1977 in Great Britain show that only 2 percent of those between the ages of 45 and 69 and 1 percent of those aged 70 and over had participated in any educational or leisure-time class.[42] Further, most of those who do participate tend to be the more affluent and better educated. Similar results are reported in many other developed nations. In fact, there are still many unanswered questions about why relatively few older people, and especially those with limited educational backgrounds, enroll in the available programs and what are the best ways to encourage them to do so.

According to British researcher Mark Abrams, the low participation is in part due to class differences and the prior educational experiences of various cohorts of the elderly. Seventy percent of the British citizens now aged 50 to 64 finished their full-time education before reaching age 15. There are many working-class adults in this age group who have an unfavorable image of education and think of everything connected with it as dull and painful.[43] Because of class and sex differences in mortality rates, the 65 to 79 age group has proportionately more women and middle-class individuals than the 50 to 64 age group. Taken by themselves, these factors would seem to predict greater participation on the part of the 65 to 79 group. Instead, its participation decreases slightly. Abrams interprets this decline as being due to the very negative image of education held by this age group, which is worse than that of the 50 to 64 age group.

Abrams suggests that measures that might increase participation by older members of the working class include courses that build upon their skills and interests and enable them to exercise skills and hobbies acquired during working life. Local history courses, for example, could draw directly on their pasts.[44] Age-homogeneous classes might be less threatening than heterogeneous classes, where the fear exists of "looking silly." Finally, it may be important that teachers be the age peers of the older working-class students and stress strong student participation.

Yet another deterrent to participation is the mismatch between educational supply and demand. What is offered frequently fails to interest many older persons. Other possible reasons for low rates of participation include lack of awareness of available programs, problems in access to the programs (such as transportation difficulties or restrictive fees) and anxiety about formal education. Additionally, motivating older persons without much formal education to participate may require personal contact and individualized counseling to help overcome fears of failure and to identify the courses or programs which are personally rewarding. Simply publicizing educational offerings through brochures and the media may not be sufficient.

The Federal Republic of Germany is one nation that has an atypically high rate of participation by older persons in adult education. Approximately one-third of the population aged 60 and over participates in educational opportunities offered by decentralized "popular high schools" (*Volkshochschulen*) or by the church, traditionally the most important providers of education in Germany outside the compulsory school system.[45] The offerings at the popular high schools that appeal most to older students are language courses and those involving some form of physical exercise. Courses in politics, history and religion dominate the offerings by church institutions, although many offer physical exercise classes as well.

According to researcher Karl Schmitz-Moorman, there has been relatively little demand for age-segregated classes for older persons in the Federal Republic of Germany.[46] Recently, however, demand for something comparable to the "universities of the third age" is beginning to be apparent. Within the last two years, the universities of Dortmund, Marburg and Frankfurt have begun sponsoring U3A's. These universities are trying to structure their offerings so that they do not duplicate those available elsewhere. For example, the University of Frankfurt offers a full academic program leading to formal degrees to older persons. In contrast, the University of Dortmund is concentrating on training older people to be service providers to their peers. Forty retirees have enrolled at Dortmund in a four-semester course to be trained as "experts in problems of age" in order to eventually help their age peers.[47] The university sees these students as being prepared for two possible "careers"—that of animator, involving group work with older persons to stimulate hidden skills and talents, and that of advisor or counselor to a variety of institutions serving the aging.

Sweden is another example of a nation that has had some success in increasing the participation of older persons in adult educational opportunities. In 1974, only 8 percent of persons between the ages of 65 and 74 were involved in any form of adult education (primarily study circles), but by 1977, the number had increased to nearly 17 percent.[48] (The participation rate by women pensioners was consistently double that for men.) This doubling of participation in a three-year period considerably exceeds the growth rate of enrollment in general adult education. The dramatic increase is due in part to a concerted effort by national pensioners' organizations, which serve as a channel for most of the educational activities directed to older adults, to publicize the various opportunities available. The members of these organizations have also helped older persons find programs and study circles which are individually satisfying.

It has also been Sweden's experience that the chief beneficiaries of adult education are the already well educated and that, unless the government undertakes active outreach, these forms of education can actually widen the learning gap in the community.[49] Sweden has perhaps made the most concerted effort on behalf of its "under-educated" adult population of any industrialized nation. National educational policy focused on this group during the 1970's, and the Swedish Board of Education's outreach efforts have concentrated on recruiting educationally disadvantaged adults in work places and residential areas through personal contacts. (Although using personal contacts to interest persons in adult education is not new and has a long history in Swedish popular education, the government has now begun to earmark state funds for this purpose.) More recently, the Swedish government has identified older persons with no more than a seventh grade education as a special target group for outreach efforts by study circles.[50]

Sweden is not alone in targeting some of its efforts in continuing education for older persons on those with little formal education. In the Federal Republic of Germany, the Ministry of Education and Science has now completed a three-year demonstration project designed to reach older persons who typically do not participate in any kind of formal educational program. The results are encouraging. Special outreach teams and group work, organized by the Deutsches Zentrum für Altersfragen (German Center for Aging Issues), have been successful in involving the poor and persons with little formal education in special programs that focus on their day-to-day concerns and interests.[51]

It has not been easy to reach the sometimes skeptical target audience. Special animators were first trained in how to make contact with these groups of older persons and dispel their distrust about educational participation. Success was in large measure dependent upon personal contacts and patience. In some cases it took several months to obtain enough participants to set up a discussion group.

In the discussion groups, animators replaced traditional adult educational methods with a looser structure in which participants sought to improve their understanding about their own problems by interacting with persons experiencing similar difficulties. Over the fifteen-month period that the groups met, project leaders found that a surprising degree of initiative, dedication and interest can be stimulated among older people who are not educationally advantaged.[52]

Finally, the Danish television administration recently experimented successfully with a new way to reach the elderly and other poorly educated groups.

Recognizing that the aging are predominant consumers of television programs in general and information programs in particular, they designed a television-based course in elementary Danish to engage the interest of adults with poor educational backgrounds. (The course led up to a level comparable to the highest classes in the general school.) The results were positive; 59 percent of those who participated were aged 50 and over and 11 percent were aged 67 and over. Further, more of those who were 60 and over completed the course than did those in younger groups.[53]

Implications for the United States

It is primarily in formal higher education that we find the greatest expansion of educational opportunities for older persons in recent years in most developed nations. The United States which has led the way in opening university classes to the elderly at no or minimal charge, has certainly been a leader in this area. Of all U.S. colleges and universities (1,449 institutions), 45 percent had established free or reduced tuition programs for older persons by 1979, and 22 percent of the fifty states had enacted legislation that permitted tuition waivers or reductions for older persons in state-run universities.[54]

The United States has also pioneered the successful model of Elderhostel, a low-cost summer residential program in which the aging devote a week to combined study and leisure activities. By the summer of 1981, approximately 400 colleges and universities around the country were sponsoring Elderhostel programs, attended by nearly 40,000 older persons.[55] Recently, Elderhostel has expanded to include Canadian and European institutions, and it is now experimenting with winter sessions.

In Europe and in the United States, debate continues about the merits of age segregation versus age integration in education for older persons. While many of the first efforts seem to have focused on developing special programs and classes for older persons (for example, the "universities of the third age"), there are now increasing attempts to integrate age groups in various educational settings. The opening up of several "universities of the third age" to all age groups, as well as regular university classes to older persons, are examples of these efforts in Europe.

The United States, which is probably as advanced as any nation in providing age-integrated learning opportunities, was cited in the U.N. Educational, Scientific, and Cultural Organization (UNESCO) report prepared for the 1982 World Assembly on Aging as one nation where it is common to find elderly persons and younger persons attending classes together.[56] This is no doubt due in large part to the widespread opening of university and college classes to the older population, as well as to the growing number of intergenerational "bridge" programs in other educational settings.

While expanding opportunities for formal education to the aging is clearly meeting a real need, to which the rapid expansion of institutions such as U3A and Elderhostel attests, these reach only a relatively educationally privileged minority of older persons. The number of elderly reached in the United States by any type of educational activity remains quite small (2.4 percent in 1978 and 3.1 percent in 1981), although the rate of increase during this time span (39 percent) is encouraging.[57] These figures compare favorably with those from the United Kingdom (1–2 percent being reached in 1976–1977) and Japan (2 percent in 1974–1975), but not so favorably with the Federal Republic of Germany (33 percent in 1981) and Sweden (17 percent in 1977). It should be noted that reliable cross-national statistics for comparative purposes are not available. Comparisons made on the basis of the figures cited above must be made with caution because of possible differences in defining what constitutes an "educational activity," whether age 55, 60 or 65 is used in defining an older person, and the years for which statistics are available. Nonetheless, the figures serve as a very rough yardstick for comparative purposes.

What these figures suggest is that a few other nations have succeeded in extending learning opportunities to a relatively broader spectrum of their older population than has the United States. Their success has apparently been due to increasing learning opportunities in non-traditional settings. (Even in the United States about 65 percent of all courses taken by the elderly are in non-traditional settings, such as private community organizations, and only 35 percent are in all of the traditional settings combined, including two- and four-year colleges, secondary schools and vocational schools.)[58]

Sweden succeeded in doubling the participation of older persons in adult education within a relatively short period. This dramatic increase appears to be due to an outreach strategy which involves personal contacts with other older persons by members of national pensioners' organizations. Perhaps more fully utilizing the skills of the elderly themselves in an outreach capacity might be a promising approach for the United States to adopt, and national voluntary organizations might play an expanded role in channeling some of these efforts. The most popular form of adult education in Sweden is the study circle in which students determine the subject to be studied and the way in which the course is structured. The informal and flexible nature of this approach would seem especially appealing to persons who are not accustomed to formal academic methods, and particularly to older persons with limited educational backgrounds.

The reasons for the high rate of participation by the elderly reported in the Federal Republic of Germany are not clear on the basis of the information available, but appear to be linked to the diverse offerings provided through "popular high schools" and churches. The idea of expanding educational offerings and outreach through churches may hold potential in the United States where a majority of older persons regularly attend church or synagogue services. (A 1981 nationwide survey indicated that 53 percent of Americans 65 and over had attended church or synagogue services within the previous two weeks.)[59]

Making better use of the mass media in promoting education for the aging is another under-utilized means of increasing educational participation by older persons outside of conventional institutional frameworks. In fact, technological advances make it probable that in the near future homes can become educational resource centers, with the possibility of two-way communication between learner and teacher. Such advances would have especially important implications for the homebound elderly and could buttress efforts being explored in such programs as Britain's Open University and the Danish Television Administration. The potential of the mass media for promoting education of the aging was recognized at two recent international conferences on education, an Anglo-French seminar held at Wye College in the United Kingdom,[60] and an international seminar on education and aging organized by the Austrian National Commission for UNESCO in 1979.[61]

Several other conclusions drawn at the UNESCO seminar have important implications for expanding learning opportunities to older learners.

1) In teaching the elderly, emphasis should be placed on group work and participation by the learners in the teaching process in order to take advantage of their life experience.

2) The learner should be able to choose homogeneous or mixed-age groups according to his or her personal preferences.

3) Educational opportunities should be provided through a broad range of formal and informal institutions, including colleges and universities, third age universities, clubs, study circles, institutions for the aged, and the work place.

The problem of low rates of participation by older persons with limited educational backgrounds appears to be a thorny one practically everywhere. Interestingly, it is in the two nations which already have the highest reported rates of educational participation by seniors, the Federal Republic of Germany and Sweden, that we find efforts at the national level to reach older persons with limited educational backgrounds. The experience of these two countries in targeting outreach efforts on the "under-educated" should prove instructive for the United States. In Sweden, an important component of this effort is the use of higher public subsidies to stimulate the recruitment of the underprivileged. This grows out of the recognition that if educational institutions are not compensated for the extra cost they must bear to recruit those who are truly hard to reach, they will be forced to focus on more easily accessible groups.

Despite its importance, adult education and particularly education for the aging are rarely priority items relative to other state expenditures. In fact, education for the aging tends to be viewed by policy-makers as a "frill" rather than as a right, and rarely as a necessity. There are, however, indications in several nations, including the United States, that older persons are increasingly turning to education for vocational reasons and as a means of improving job skills they need in order to ensure their livelihood.[62]

Even if education for the aging is generally still not a high priority at the national level, it is receiving growing attention at the international level. The

1982 U.N. World Assembly on Aging recognized the right of the aging to education, and its recommendations may serve as impetus for national action in this area. According to the International Plan of Action adopted at the assembly,

educational policies should reflect the principle of the right to education of the aging, through the appropriate allocation of resources and in suitable educational programmes. Care should be taken to adapt educational methods to the capacities of the elderly, so that they may participate equitably in and profit from any education.[63]

Among the other areas emphasized in the plan's recommendations are utilization of the mass media as a means of promoting participation by the aging in educational activities and increasing participation by the aging in formulating and designing these activities. Finally, the plan underscores the importance of recognizing and encouraging the contributions that the aging themselves make as educators and as the transmitters of knowledge and values to younger generations.

In the years to come, the rate of participation by older persons in adult education will probably increase as future cohorts of better-educated elderly are motivated to engage in continuing education. At the same time, advocacy efforts by the elderly themselves may place pressure on governments and educational institutions to expand the range of options available to meet the diverse needs of older persons. Associations of the elderly in France, for example, are lobbying to broaden the interpretation of the 1971 Continuing Vocational Education Act to include learning opportunities which promote intellectual and personal growth across the lifespan and are not limited to those under age 65. And in the United Kingdom, the recently formed Forum on the Rights of Elderly People to Education promises to be an active and persistent advocate for the educational needs and rights of older persons in order to ensure that these are met in public policy.[64]

EMPLOYMENT-RELATED EDUCATIONAL OPPORTUNITIES

Training for Older Workers

In comparison with the United States, most other industrialized nations have more systematic manpower training opportunities for workers and potential workers.[65] (In the United States and Australia, such programs are generally limited to specific target populations, such as young adults or the impoverished.) And a few nations make special provisions for older workers. The Federal Republic of Germany, for example, provides training subsidies for up to a year to firms willing to hire unemployed older workers. Under the 1973 Promotion of Employment Act, unemployed older workers in Germany taking part in advanced training or retraining courses may be paid an allowance equivalent to 140 percent of the unemployment benefit.[66] Along with other benefits, the allowance may equal 87.5 to 95 percent of their former net wage. The Ministry of Labor pays all or part of the direct and indirect training expenses, as well as the social insurance contributions. Unemployed older workers who have not obtained any vocational training certificate are a special target.

In Japan, the Ministry of Labor has established some training incentives to help deal with the serious problem of unemployment among middle-aged and older workers. (Japan has had an unrealistically low retirement age of 55, but the government has been bringing steady and successful pressure to bear on industry to extend the retirement age to 60 by the year 1985.) Individuals scheduled to retire within three years are eligible for special vocational training to enable them to switch occupations. Entrance fees and tuition are paid by the government. In 1979, 10,000 older persons took advantage of this training.[67]

In addition, employers in Japan who have fixed the retirement age of their employees below age 60 are required to set up a "Replacement Support Plan," whose staff work closely with the public employment bureau to help older workers find other jobs following retirement from their firms.[68] A Pre-Retirement Vocational Lecture and Training System established in 1973 provides incentive grants to employers who allow their workers to attend daytime training courses.[69] This act provides vocational lectures and training to give workers the knowledge and skills they need for reemployment. Japan also provides training grants to firms willing to hire unemployed older workers age 45 or over.[70] On-the-job training for older workers is encouraged through governmental grants to employers, which in 1979 averaged about $60 a month for six months per employee hired. Some 20,000 older workers or handicapped persons profited from this opportunity each month.[71] On an individual basis, some Japanese firms offer their older employees a variety of courses to facilitate their prospects for alternative employment, in accounting, for example, or provide financial assistance so that they can obtain certification in other fields, such as small business consultation, commodities distribution, and so on.

In Sweden, there are special training provisions for workers age 50 and over who face unemployment or difficulty holding a job. Companies who hire these workers are paid special temporary training grants by the Labor Market Board, and there are special "adjustment" courses available to older persons seeking employment.[72]

Paid Educational Leave

The importance of paid educational leave has been recognized by the ILO, which urges that it be adopted as a principle of national labor policy everywhere.[73] The possibility for paid educational leave is, in fact, provided either through law or through collective bargaining agreements in a number of European nations, including France, Sweden, the United Kingdom and the Federal Republic of Germany.

In most nations, paid educational leave generally supports training for vocational purposes rather than for the pursuit of general academic educational goals.

In France, for example, the types of training which are state approved include training for persons who wish to obtain higher qualifications for their current jobs, for those who wish to change jobs and for those who need "refresher" training to update skills during times of technological and structural change in the economy.[74] Access to these forms of training, of course, can help older persons, as well as younger workers, remain in their current jobs or change careers.

In Sweden, although national legislation has established the right of workers to educational leave, there are no provisions for the payment of salary during the leave period. However, special subsidies through study grants are available to workers. These grants are financed through a payroll contribution by employers which has been in effect since 1976.[75]

Although the United Kingdom and the Federal Republic of Germany do not have national legislation establishing this right, paid educational leave is nonetheless fairly widely available to workers. In the United Kingdom, such leave is commonly financed by employers or, in some cases, is arranged through collective bargaining agreements between unions and employers. A 1979 survey of paid educational leave in England and Wales, however, indicated that although approximately 17 percent of the work force received such leave in 1976–1977, older workers were under-represented.[76] Additionally, professional and scientific workers and supervisors were more likely to receive such leave than clerical and manual workers.

In the Federal Republic of Germany, there are laws in five of the Laender (states) which establish the general right of workers to take educational leave.[77] (However, in two of these states the opportunity is restricted to workers under the age of 25.) Although other German states do not have such laws, some individual firms in these states also make provisions for paid educational leave. Overall, it has been estimated that 10 percent of employees in Germany are eligible for educational leave, although not all who have the right are fully aware of it.[78] As in the United Kingdom, older workers are under-represented among those actually receiving educational leave.

Implications for the United States

A recent comparison of adult vocational educational opportunities in nine industrialized countries concluded that most European nations have progressed further than the United States in developing education and training programs for workers, and especially for blue collar workers.[79] In addition, paid educational leave, which allows workers to periodically upgrade their skills, is a far more common practice in Europe than in the United States. In the United States, employers are generally reluctant to give their employees time off for education and training, and paid educational leave is primarily limited to sabbaticals for university professors. There is also no effective incentive system in the United States to encourage employers to expand their own education and training programs.

What accounts for the United States' relative backwardness in manpower training? First, all of the national training systems reviewed in the cross-national study cited above were found to rely on contributions from employers to help finance the training efforts, a model which American business and industry have been reluctant to accept.[80] Further, the trade union movement in the United States has been a less forceful advocate for expanding training options than have been its European counterparts. In Scandinavia in particular, strong trade unions and employee associations have been powerful forces in creating training opportunities for workers.

Despite these wider opportunities for the general population of adult workers in European nations, it is not clear that older workers have had equal access to the programs which are available. France, for example, has had legislation since 1971 providing for "continuing vocational education" at no "out-of-pocket" expense to the worker, but in practice the provisions exclude older persons and are applied primarily to the young, migrants and women. Ministry of Labor statistics indicate that more than half of the trainees (57 percent) in 1978 were under 25 years of age.[81]

Even in a nation such as the Federal Republic of Germany, which has special provisions to promote the training of older workers as part of the federal Promotion of Employment Act, less than 1 percent of the workers who benefited under the act in 1973 were over 55 years of age.[82] Similarly, in Denmark, any adult who is employed or seeking employment is eligible to apply for semi-skilled worker training, which generally consists of short courses (about 144 hours) in a particular skill area. Yet in 1976, of 350,000 total participants, only 7 percent were over age 50.[83] In order to meet the problems of technological unemployment, "reconversion training" is being sponsored by private companies, labor exchanges, and labor market organizations. Again, older workers were sharply under-represented in these programs, with only 9 percent of participants in 1972–1973 being over age 50.[84]

In several countries where paid educational leave for workers is commonly provided through collective bargaining, it appears that only a relatively small proportion of older workers benefit from these policies. In the United Kingdom, for example, persons under 30 years of age were found to be eight times more likely to obtain out-of-house paid educational leave than those over 50.[85]

Exactly why older workers are under-represented in some of these programs is not clear from the information available. In the case of France, the broadly written 1971 legislation makes no special provision for older workers. Since that time, economic recessions and rising unemployment among youth appear to have limited the act's implementation to youth and certain other "high priority" groups.

In the case of the Federal Republic of Germany, which did enact special legislative provisions for the training of older workers, why so few older persons have benefited is even less clear. It is possible that older persons themselves may be reluctant to take part in the training programs which are open to them for a variety of reasons, such as anxiety about formal education. Low participation may also be the result of training programs which are directed to individual companies' short-term needs rather than to longer range skills development, and the fact that older workers' needs have not been taken into account.[86] If training for the older worker is to be successful, some of the following factors should be considered:

- the impatience of older workers with long training periods;
- the preference of older workers for personalized instruction and on-the-site job training that has clear practical applications;
- the potential contribution that older workers can make to the design of their courses;
- the importance of linking the training to its impact on other employment conditions, such as wage scales, production standards, and so on.[87]

Provisions in the pension legislation in both France and Germany which facilitate converting unemployment benefits to an old age pension several years before the normal retirement age may also serve as a disincentive to pursuing a training program. And if older persons and trainers believe that jobs will not be available once the training is completed, this is no doubt a significant disincentive to older persons participating or being chosen to participate in training. Finally, it is possible that, since access to training programs depends upon the discretion of individual program administrators, non-participation by the elderly may be the result of age discrimination.

Thus, extending education and training opportunities to older workers appears to be a complex problem in most industrialized nations. Even where there is legislation to promote the training of older persons, there is no guarantee it will be implemented. Increasing training and retraining opportunities may also require removing various disincentives to work in pension legislation and, ultimately, on changing societal attitudes about the occupational competence and contributions of older persons.

Finland, which has a long history of continuing education opportunities, found that older workers (persons over age 40) who are given training and retraining opportunities have a high success rate in later placements.[88] Over 75 percent of older workers who participated in training programs were subsequently placed in jobs corresponding to their education. This certainly suggests that vocational training programs can be very successful in promoting the employment of the ''older'' worker.

PRE-RETIREMENT EDUCATION

The importance of pre-retirement education and planning is recognized in almost all developed countries. It remains, however, in the early stages of development practically everywhere, and the percentage of persons being reached by these programs in most nations still remains low. According to estimates by the International Labour Office, less than 5 percent of future retirees actually attend such courses in the countries where they are most widespread.[89] Further, the great majority of these courses are for persons who are just on the eve of retirement. Even in the United States, which has the longest tradition of pre-retirement education, relatively few individuals are being reached and there are many unresolved issues about the structuring and content of the programs.

Only two nations, Norway and the United Kingdom, have national organizations concerned solely with promoting pre-retirement education and coordinating measures related to it. Only in Norway is pre-retirement education becoming as common as orientation sessions for new employees. Norway is also the only country where the national organization promoting pre-retirement education is a semi-official public agency. The Norwegian National Preparation for Retirement Council obtains 90 percent of its budget from the Ministry for Social Affairs. It represents a range of private associations, four government ministries, the Employers' Federation and the trade unions.[90] It arranges and publicizes pre-retirement programs throughout the nation, trains leaders to teach the courses, and promotes research. The other industrialized nation with a national association concerned solely with pre-retirement issues is the United Kingdom. The Pre-Retirement Association of Great Britain and Northern Ireland did much of the pioneer work in the field and has the support of both trade unions and employers' federations.[91] It has been instrumental in encouraging local authorities and employers to organize pre-retirement courses, conducts its own specialized seminars, and supplies training seminars to organizers and trainers. Most local education authorities in Britain now provide pre-retirement courses, as do many private firms.[92]

Although the Netherlands does not have a national association promoting pre-retirement education, a national working group was set up in 1973 to coordinate and encourage pre-retirement activities. A "retirement in sight" project was established at the national level in 1975, and by 1978, approximately ninety pre-retirement courses were being offered at adult education institutes and centers in local neighborhoods. Participants obtain five to eight days' paid leave during the last few years preceding retirement to take these courses.[93]

France is stimulating pre-retirement planning through incentives to employers, who can deduct the cost of approved pre-retirement programs from their obligatory payroll tax (around 2 percent) to fund the country's system of continuing vocational education.[94] The French parliament ruled that pre-retirement education falls within the 1971 law on "continuing vocational education"; this means that individuals may take such courses on a paid educational leave basis underwritten by the state or by their employers.[95] Although France does not have a national organization promoting pre-retirement, these financial incentives certainly serve as a stimulus. The National Institute for Active Retirement (Institut National pour la Retraite Active, INRAC) is only one of a number of organizations assisting those wishing to develop pre-retirement planning programs. Courses have been held successfully through old people's clubs and universities of the third age, and in mobile units in isolated rural areas.

In Canada, the initiative in promoting pre-retirement education has been taken at the provincial level. In 1978, the government of Alberta developed a province-wide plan to assist its residents in preparing for retirement.[96] It insured that retirement training courses were offered in all parts of the province and also educated the public and employers about the advantages of early planning for retirement years. More recently in Canada, a series of eight half-hour television programs entitled "Tomorrow is Now" has been shown over thirty community stations. The shows were accompanied by free public information about pre-retirement planning.[97]

In the nations of Eastern Europe, the organizational bases for pre-retirement education programs are workplaces, trade unions, and health facilities. The mass media play an important role in disseminating information useful in preparing for retirement, as do popular science lectures.[98]

Program Content, Structure and Duration

There is general agreement that spouses should be included in pre-retirement courses and that courses can be offered through a variety of settings, such as at work, as part of continuing education programs, or in community centers. (Several areas in Finland and France have even experimented with using mobile units to bring courses to persons living far from population centers.) However, there is less agreement about the content, structuring and duration of the courses.

There is wide variation in the content of the courses available, within as well as between nations. Some programs primarily emphasize factual information about the financial aspects of retirement, such as pension benefits, while others have broadened their scope to include not only health-related issues and the use of leisure time, but the psychological adjustments in retirement as well. According to the ILO, the trend increasingly appears to be toward broad course objectives and content, and away from mere information on finances.[99]

The length of pre-retirement courses also varies widely—from one-day sessions to ongoing programs continued over a number of years. A recent comparison of pre-retirement programs offered by a sample of British and U.S. firms showed that although there was a preponderance of programs of short duration (six months or less) in both nations, a larger percentage of U.S. firms had programs which extended for periods of two years or more.[100] British programs, however, were found to be less restrictive—for example, 93 percent of the British programs were open to hourly as well as salaried employees, compared to 75 percent in the United States.

Nor is there universal agreement about the best way to structure participation in the programs. A review of pre-retirement programs offered by a number of firms in Europe, conducted by the Council of Europe in 1977, indicated that most firms mix participants from different occupations in their courses.[101]

However, some firms, especially in the United Kingdom and France, prefer to group participants in their programs by occupation because of the assumed greater homogeneity of their concerns, similarity in their pension benefits, and so on.

One question which has emerged in the area of pre-retirement planning is the best time for workers to begin participating in the programs. It has been the experience of some nations that the closer one is to retirement age, the more reluctant one becomes to undertake pre-retirement planning—a reflection of psychological "denial" of the impending change in one's life. Considerations such as these have led some planners to recommend that pre-retirement education be started a number of years before the normal retirement age, perhaps five or ten. Many have even advocated that knowledge about aging and retirement be built into the school curriculum at an early age. Pro Senectute, for example, the largest voluntary association serving Switzerland's elderly, has distributed material about aging to school teachers throughout the country for use in their classrooms.[102]

In Israel, the pre-retirement program offered by the Israeli Military Industries has evolved from an initial one-day seminar to an extensive "phased" program involving employee participation for at least five years prior to retirement.[103] Sessions for persons in younger groups (for example, ages 55–63) focus on more general and long-range concerns about the aging process, such as social and health adjustments, while those for the 64–65 age group concentrate on the more immediate concerns older persons face as they near retirement. Since some research has indicated that retired persons tend to pursue only those leisure activities which were initiated prior to retirement, courses in leisure activities (such as landscaping and ceramics) are offered in the earlier phase of the program so that they can become practiced roles. The course content is thus structured in such a way as to facilitate the adoption of new roles and activities. A particularly innovative feature of the Israeli Military Industries' program is that it purposely selects and trains young employees to serve as pre-retirement counselors so they can begin to prepare for their own retirement at a relatively early age.

Program Effectiveness

To date, there has been very little research in any nation on the long-range effectiveness of pre-retirement education. A recent review of the handful of evaluations that have been conducted of retirement preparation programs in the United States concluded that there is little proof in either direction as to their effectiveness.[104] One of the few longitudinal studies ever done on the efficacy of such programs also suggests that their real value appears to be limited to the pre-retirement stage itself; the long-range impact was found to be minimal.[105] As programs of longer duration and broader content are implemented and evaluated in other nations, as well as in the United States, it should become easier to judge the effectiveness of alternative approaches in helping to bring about good adjustments in retirement.

Recommendations of International Organizations

Although relatively small proportions of persons are currently being reached by pre-retirement education programs in most industrialized nations, the field has grown rapidly over the last several decades. This expansion has been not only quantitative, as more and more programs have been offered in different settings, but qualitative, as the content of many courses has been broadened to include topics related to psychological and personal adjustments to the aging process as well as "bread and butter" concerns.

There is little doubt that pre-retirement education will greatly expand in the future under the impetus of what is already happening in the field and of promotion by organizations such as the United Nations and the Council of Europe, which have already recommended some policy guidelines in this area to their member nations. Recognition of the importance of pre-retirement education at the international level was first given by the Council of Europe in 1972, when it required its committee of ministers to draft proposals for more effective methods of preparation for retirement.[106]

The Council of Europe working group on pre-retirement education recommended in 1977 that until the idea of pre-retirement preparation is widely accepted, particular attention be focused on certain groups at high risk of experiencing difficulties in adjusting to retirement.[107] These include persons who, because of their working conditions—often hard manual labor—have had the least opportunity to develop leisure activities; self-employed persons; and persons for whom work is the main justification in life.

In order to reach these groups, the Council encouraged local action, such as that initiated by some municipalities in the United Kingdom and the Federal Republic of Germany, and neighborhood initiatives. The advantages of these local efforts are that they usually reach women first, which makes them a more effective means of involving couples than courses aimed at workers in their place of employment. Additionally, self-employed persons and those who have already begun retirement with no preparation can attend the sessions.[108]

The United Nations, in turn, has recommended that the idea of preparation for retirement be considered within its wider societal context, making it possible to realize the hopes for both leisure and continued activity that are aroused by a well-conceived program of retirement preparation. Thus, expanding options for additional social roles for the elderly, as well as developing more flexible working conditions in later life, should be considered a part of retirement preparation.[109]

The United Nations has also recommended that pre-retirement training start around age 50 and be accompanied by flexible retirement policies and efforts to adapt the job to the worker. In the International Plan of Action adopted at the 1982 U.N. World Assembly on Aging, governments are encouraged to take measures that will ensure a smooth and gradual transition from active working life to retirement, including pre-retirement courses and lightening the work load by promoting a gradual reduction in work time.[110]

By easing the transition to retirement, such measures can help workers avoid "retirement shock" and allow them to develop new interests in part-time or voluntary work and leisure activities to be explored during retirement years.

Implications for the United States

Pre-retirement education was pioneered in the United States after World War II, and it has remained one of the leaders in the field ever since. Serious experimentation with retirement preparation courses next began in the United Kingdom in the late 1950's, followed by most other industrialized nations in the 1960's.

Since the early 1970's there has been a rapid increase in retirement preparation courses offered by industry in the United States, out of response to a recognized need for more careful retirement planning and to the effects of inflation on retirees' income. A review of the current status of such programs in industry in the United States indicates that more than 33 percent of the responding companies have formal programs, and many more are working to establish them.[111] Further, more than half of these programs were rated as "comprehensive" in content and format rather than as "narrow."[112] Similarly, according to a 1979 survey of the nation's largest corporations, programs increasingly cover a wide range of social and psychological issues and are being offered five or more years prior to retirement.[113]

Despite these optimistic signs, several important problems remain, including the degree of employee participation in the programs. In one survey, only a third of the 134 companies reported a participation rate of 75 percent or better.[114] Another third reported rates below 50 percent, which were attributed by their chief executive officers and personnel directors primarily to employees' "fears of facing retirement." There are also continuing concerns about the quality of many of the programs offered, a problem which is exacerbated by the lack of qualified personnel to develop and implement the programs. Employers may be eager to "get a program on the books," turn to the first consultant available, and end up with a poorly conceived program that is damaging to the sponsoring institution. Finally, although program sponsorship has grown fairly rapidly over the last decade in the United States, several observers have sounded a note of caution about the probability that this will continue in the future.[115] In the current economic situation, pre-retirement education programs may assume a lower priority in corporate boardrooms unless a direct link can be shown between such programs and employee productivity.

The United States is itself serving as a model for groups in other nations which wish to develop pre-retirement programs. For example, Action for Independent Maturity (AIM), a division of the AARP and the largest developer of pre-retirement programs and publications in the United States, has received requests from and supplied materials to many organizations in Japan, Mexico,

Canada, and several European nations. AIM's group program, which is being used by over 3,000 corporations and other organizations in the United States, has also been filmed in operation and broadcast on Japanese national television.[116]

The experience of other nations with retirement preparation programs, however, does hold relevance for the United States. Because of the uneven quality of pre-retirement programs offered in the United States and the lack of a central point where information may be obtained on what constitutes a sound program, it has been suggested that a federal agency concerned with pre-retirement planning be created to stimulate broad-based intervention.[117] The experience of Norway is instructive here. Norway is the only nation where pre-retirement education is widespread, and it is also the only country with a national association which is backed by government funding. The association represents a number of different interests, including employers, trade unions, government ministries and private organizations. It remains to be seen, however whether even such a semi-official public agency would be an acceptable model to America's largest corporations, a majority of whose leaders indicated in a nation-wide survey that they felt the government should basically stay out of the pre-retirement field.[118]

Another national stimulus to retirement preparation is provided by France, which allows employers to deduct the costs of approved pre-retirement courses from their mandatory payroll tax to fund the nation's system of continuing vocational education. It is possible that some system of tax incentives to employers who institute pre-retirement courses would serve as a viable option in the United States.

Both in the United States and in other developed nations, a number of observers have noted that adequate preparation for old age must be a lifelong process and should not be delayed until a few years prior to retirement.[119] This suggests that emphasis should be placed on developing an educational system (from elementary school on) that stresses the mastery of the tasks of all life phases. In order to do this, classroom teachers must be sensitized to issues concerning the aging and encouraged to find ways of weaving a lifespan perspective into their curriculum. In Switzerland, Pro Senectute, the nation's largest voluntary organization serving the elderly, has distributed material on aging to classroom teachers on a nation-wide basis. While there are localized examples of such efforts in the United States as well, these should be greatly expanded. The ultimate goal is to subsume "pre-retirement courses" as such within continuing education across the lifespan, although it is clear that in the short run such courses fulfill a real need.

Yet another approach to retirement preparation emphasizes the need for reorganizing the worlds of work, education and leisure so that these three components are better balanced across the lifespan. The current segmentation of life into periods of intense work, followed by enforced leisure, has been widely criticized in practically all developed nations. Even the idea of "pre-retirement programs" has been criticized by some as a means of encouraging the elderly to passively "adjust" to retired life by accepting more limited status, roles and income. Further, an international seminar on the problems of preparation for old age, held in Zurich in 1980, cautioned against using retirement preparation as an excuse for not lobbying for changes in the relationship between work and education that will lead to true "lifespan education." [120] Norway is dealing with the charge of passivity by encouraging participants to become social activists during their retirement years, working to promote changes beneficial to all age groups.

As we have seen, both the United Nations and the Council of Europe have recommended that flexible or progressive retirement be considered a part of pre-retirement planning. Although a number of companies in Europe, as well as in the United States, have experimented with progressively reducing working time as employees near retirement age, it is not clear that these reductions in work time have been closely coordinated with the pre-retirement training programs themselves. This may prove a fruitful approach to explore, since such a marriage could allow workers to actually experience what they are learning about in their planning sessions, for instance by discovering satisfying ways to use increased leisure time and finding alternative roles to replace their full-time occupational roles.

NOTES

1. "Education permanente et Troisième âge," *3 Age* (May/June 1981):13.
2. M. C. Vanbremeersch and A. Margarido, "Les Etudiants de l'université du 3° âge de l'université de Picardie," *Gérontologie et Société* 13 (June, 1980):123–148.
3. "Education permanente," p. 13.
4. "Learning, Education, and Later Life," statement from an Anglo-French seminar held at Wye College, University of London, July/August 1980.
5. *Années-Documents CLEIRPPA* (October 1977).
6. Vanbremeersch and Margarido, "Etudiants de l'université du 3° âge," pp. 123–148.
7. B. Delage, "Essai de vérification de l'hypothèse de démocratisation au travers de deux initiatives prises an faveur des personnes âgées," unpublished manuscript, Talence, France, Maison des Sciences de l'Homme, domaine universitaire, 1978, quoted in Charlotte Nusberg, "Educational Opportunities for the Elderly in Industrialized Countries outside the United States," *Educational Gerontology* 8 (July/August 1982):404.
8. Vanbremeersch and Margarido, "Etudiants de l'université du 3° âge," pp. 123–148.
9. M. Gautrat and M. Tugendhaft, "Recherche sur l'Acquisition des Connaissance du Troisième Age," *Gerontologie* (July 1980):14.
10. Vanbremeersch and Margarido, "Etudiants de l'université du 3° âge," pp. 123–148, and Gautrat and Tugendhaft, "Recherche sur Connaissance," p. 15.
11. Vanbremeersch and Margarido, "Etudiants de l'université du 3° âge," pp. 123–148.
12. Gautrat and Tugendhaft, "Recherche sur Connaissance," p. 15.
13. "Learning, Education and Later Life."

14. Vanbremeersch and Margarido, "Etudiants de l'université du 3° âge," pp. 123–148.

15. *Presse und Informationdienst des KDA* (January/February 1978).

16. "Exemple d'Antenne d'Université: Montargis," *Gérontologie et Société* (June-July 1980):150.

17. "Les universités du 3° âge," unpublished manuscript, Service Documentation ANEP/IRNIS (June 1980); quoted in Nusberg, "Educational Opportunities," p. 405.

18. "Adult Education in Sweden," fact sheet prepared by the Swedish Institute (October 1980), pp. 1–4.

19. Richard Peterson et al., "Adult Education in Nine Industrialized Countries," report prepared for the National Center for Education Statistics, mimeographed. (Princeton, N.J.: Educational Testing Service, 1980), Vol. 2, p. 58.

20. Ibid., p. 117.

21. J. Bruun Pederson, "Information, Education and Related Activities," *Danish Medical Bulletin* 29, No. 3 (March 1982):110.

22. *Gérontologie et Société* (June/July 1980).

23. Raymond Glasscote, Jon E. Gudeman and Donald Miles, *Creative Mental Health Services for the Elderly* (Washington, D.C.: Joint Information Service of the American Psychiatric Association and the Mental Health Association, 1977), pp. 47–48.

24. "Adult Education in Sweden," p. 2.

25. Peterson, "Adult Education in Nine Countries," Vol. 1, p. 165.

26. "Adult Education in Sweden," p. 2.

27. *Education Guardian* (May 5, 1981).

28. United Nations Educational, Scientific, and Cultural Organization (UNESCO), *Education and Aging*, report for the World Assembly on Aging (A/Conf. 113/20, March 10, 1982), p. 21.

29. *Rentner und Pensionist* (June 1978).

30. Ernst Gehmacher, "Educational Questions Concerning the Elderly," report commissioned by UNESCO (Vienna, Austria, December 1978), p. 76.

31. UNESCO, "Education and Aging," p. 21.

32. Gehmacher, "Educational Questions," p. 78.

33. Kazufusa Moro-Oka, *Recurrent Education: Japan* (Paris: OECD, 1976), p. 27.

34. *Welfare and Health of the Aged* (July 1977).

35. Keiko Ishida, "A Case Study of Education for the Elderly," *Japanese Journal of Gerontology* 2 (1980).

36. Nusberg, "Educational Opportunities," p. 405.

37. National University Consortium news release (College Park, Md.: University of Maryland, 1980).

38. Dmitri F. Chebotarev and Nina N. Sachuk, "A Social Policy Directed Toward the Health and Welfare of the Aged in the Soviet Union," *Journal of the American Geriatrics Society* 27, No. 2 (February 1979):56–57.

39. Horst Mohle, "Gerontological, Psychological, and Pedagogical Fundamentals of Adult Education—Their Application in Work with Older Adults" (paper presented at the International Congress of Gerontology, Hamburg, West Germany, 1981), pp. 8–9.

40. Nusberg, "Educational Opportunities," p. 406.

41. U.S., Department of State, *U.S. National Report on Aging for the U.N. World Assembly on Aging* (June 1982), p. 80.

42. Mark Abrams, "Education in Later Life" (paper presented at 5th Bolton College of Adult Education meeting, Bolton, England, February 1980), p. 3.

43. Ibid., p. 9.

44. Ibid., pp. 21–22.

45. Karl Schmitz-Moorman, "Education and Study in Old Age in Germany" (paper presented at the 12th International Congress of Gerontology, Hamburg, Germany, July 12–17, 1981).

46. Ibid.

47. *Altenhilfe* (November 1981).

48. Peterson, "Adult Education in Nine Countries," Vol. 1, p. 165.

49. "Adult Education in Sweden," pp. 3–4.

50. Ibid.

51. *Verstehen, Anknüpfen, Entwickeln: Animatorische Bildungs Arbeit mit Sozial und Bildungsbenachteiligten Älteren Menschen* (Bonn, West Germany, Ministry for Education and Science, 1981).

52. Ibid.

53. Pederson, "Information, Education," pp. 110–111.

54. U.S., Department of State, *U.S. National Report for the World Assembly* (Washington, D.C.), p. 80.

55. Ibid., p. 87.

56. UNESCO, "Education and Aging," p. 29.

57. U.S., Department of State, *National Report for the World Assembly*, pp. 80–81.

58. Ibid.

59. *Aging in the Eighties: America in Transition* (Washington, D.C.: National Council on the Aging, 1981), p. 24.

60. "Learning, Education, and Later Life," p. 9.

61. Austrian Commission for UNESCO, report on an international seminar, "Educational Questions Concerning the Elderly" (Vienna, September 25–27, 1979), p. 7.

62. U.S., Department of State, *National Report for the World Assembly*, pp. 87–88.

63. United Nations, "Draft Report of the Main Committee," International Plan of Action for the World Assembly on Aging (A/Conf. 113/mc/L.27, August 4, 1982), p. 32.

64. *Age Concern England Information Circular* (March 1981), p. 3.

65. Peterson, "Adult Education in Nine Countries," Vol. 1, p. 273.

66. OECD, *Socio-Economic Policies for the Elderly* (Paris, 1979), p. 52.

67. *Nihon Keizai Shimbun.*

68. "Socio-Economic Policies for the Elderly: Questionnaire," p. 35.

69. OECD, "Questionnaire and Analytical Synthesis Report for Socio-Economic Policies for the Elderly" (SME/SAIR, E/80.02, May 19, 1980).

70. OECD, *Socio-Economic Policies*, p. 59.

71. *Nihon Keizai Shibun* (November 26, 1979).

72. Peterson, "Adult Education in Nine Countries," vol. 1, p. 109.

73. Ibid., pp. 285–286.

74. Ibid., p. 117.

75. Ibid., p. 133.

76. Ibid., Vol. 2, pp. 153–154.

77. Ibid., p. 76.

78. Ibid., Vol. 1, pp. 114–115.

79. Ibid., pp. 283–284.

80. Ibid.

81. Ibid., p. 123.

82. OECD, *Socio-Economic Policies*, p. 53.

83. Peterson, "Adult Education in Nine Coutries," Vol. 1, p. 109.

84. Ibid.

85. Ibid., Vol. 2, p. 153.

86. Ursula Engelen-Kefer, "Managing the Older Worker Out of the Labor Market: The West German Experience," *Industrial Gerontology* (Winter 1973):47.

87. *Older Workers: Work and Retirement* (Geneva: International Labour Organization, 1979), p. 31.

88. OECD, "Questionnaire and Analytical Synthesis," p. 82.

89. United Nations, *Transitions Between Professional Life and Retirement*, report of the ILO for the World Assembly on Aging (A/Conf. 113/16, February 1982), p. 22.

90. Fred Kemp, "The Need for Preparation for Retirement," in *Preparation for Retirement: Its Significance and Present Status in Europe* (symposium sponsored by the Norwegian Institute of Gerontology, November 1977), p. 39.

91. Peterson, "Adult Education in Nine Countries," Vol. 1, p. 167.

92. Ibid., Vol. 2, p. 156.

93. G. H. Kroes, "Preparation for Retirement in the Netherlands" (unpublished manuscript, November 1976), pp. 7–8.

94. Kemp, "Need for Preparation," p. 41.

95. Peterson, "Adult Education in Nine Countries," Vol. 1, p. 157

96. *Alberta Council on Aging News* (November 1977).

97. Canadian Association of Gerontology, *Information Bulletin* (Winter 1980).

98. Dmitri F. Chebotarev, Nina N. Sachuk and N. V. Verzhikovskaya, "Status and Condition of the Elderly in Socialist Countries of Eastern Europe," report prepared for the World Assembly on Aging (Kiev: Institute of Gerontology, 1982), pp. 42–43.

99. ILO, *Transitions*, p. 23.

100. Janet M. Rives and Sidney R. Siegel, "Out to Grass: A Transatlantic Look at Pre-Retirement Programmes," *Personnel Management* 2 (February, 1980), pp. 42–43.

101. Council of Europe, *Preparation for Retirement* (Soc. 76, 4– E, Strasbourg, France, 1977), pp. 32–33.

102. *Dynamic Years*, (July/August 1979), p. 26.

103. Israel Military Industries, Manpower Development Department, "Pre-Retirement Counseling," undated booklet.

104. Sandra K. Olson, "Current Status of Retirement Preparation Programs," *Aging and Work* 4, No. 3 (1981):182.

105. Francis D. Glamser, "The Impact of Preretirement Programs on the Retirement Experience: A Longitudinal Experiment" (paper presented at the annual meeting of the U.S. Gerontological Society, Washington, D.C., November 1979).

106. ILO, *Transitions,* p. 22.

107. Council of Europe, *Preparation for Retirement*, p. 30.

108. Ibid., p. 31.

109. *U.N. Bulletin on Aging* 2, No. 1, (July 12, 1977).

110. United Nations, "International Plan of Action of the U.N. World Assembly on Aging" (A/Conf. 113/MC/L. 27, August 4, 1982), p. 31.

111. Olson, "Current Status of Retirement Programs," p. 181.

112. Ibid.

113. Research and Forecasts, Inc., "Retirement Preparation: Growing Corporate Involvement," *Aging and Work* 3, No. 1 (1980):8–10.

114. Ibid., pp. 11–12.

115. Philip Hodges, "Pre-Retirement Planning: A Business Perspective," *Generations* (Summer 1982):72.

116. Al Peterson, Public Affairs Coordinator, Action for Independent Maturity, Washington, D.C., personal communication with author, October, 1982.

117. A. Monk, "A Social Policy Framework for Pre-Retirement Planning," *Industrial Gerontology* (Fall 1972):63–70, quoted in Olson, "Status of Retirement Programs," p. 183.

118. Research and Forecasts, "Retirement Preparation," p. 7.

119. Julie Winter, *Internationales Seminar 1980 zur Fragen der Vorbereitung auf das Altern*, ISVA, 1980.

120. Ibid.

10

Formalized Participation in Decision Making

Charlotte Nusberg

In a number of European countries, especially Sweden, Norway, Germany, the Netherlands and France, there appears to be a growing trend toward giving the elderly increased power over decisions affecting their lives. While pressure groups representing the elderly continue to exercise strong influence on political processes in many of these countries, much as they do in the United States, recent efforts have focused more on giving the elderly a *formalized* means of participation in decision making. Examples include the establishment of councils of the elderly, at the municipal, county and national levels, which advise government on concerns of the aging, and councils of residents, in homes for the aged and nursing homes, which advise management on matters that affect the well-being of the residents.

In some countries, such as Sweden, such formalized participation by the elderly in decision-making processes is the result of prolonged efforts by pensioner organizations to increase the say of the elderly in policies that affect their lives.[1] While there is no conscious adherence to anything like a ''Maslovian'' hierarchy of values on the part of Swedish pensioners, the focus of their energies over the past few decades does suggest that once the hard struggles over increased pensions and improved social services are won, the next order of priorities is greater control over or responsibility for policies which have major impact on one's life. Sweden's new Social Welfare Act (1982), in fact, places great emphasis on individual participation and responsibility. Self-determination is considered basic to such a policy.[2]

In countries such as Germany, pressures for extended participation by the elderly have come primarily from policy-makers and professionals serving the aging, rather than from the elderly themselves.[3] The pressures result from a belief that the elderly need to be encouraged to help themselves and that formalized means of participation will help keep the elderly integrated in the community. Undoubtedly the hope also exists that increased self-help on the part of the elderly may reduce the need for projected increases in social welfare costs as the number of old people increases in coming years.

COUNCILS OF THE ELDERLY

An increasingly widespread form of formalized participation is "councils of the elderly" at all levels of government. These councils serve primarily in an advisory capacity for proposed changes in social security policy and regulations and welfare measures primarily affecting the aged. Norway, for example, has established a "negotiation and contact committee" at the national level, on which representatives of pensioners and key government ministries serve.[4] All proposed legislation or changes in regulations impacting on the lives of the elderly must first be referred to this committee for discussion before they are submitted to Parliament.

In Sweden, pensioners' organizations have won the right to have their representatives serve together with government officials on "pensioners' councils" at the municipal and county levels of government, and these organizations are now demanding consultation directly with the National Ministry of Social Affairs, as well.[5]

Residents' councils in Sweden preceded the establishment of pensioners' councils. It was dissatisfaction with only being able to influence the situation in institutional forms of care that led to the formation of the first pensioners' council in Stockholm in 1969. Today, there are pensioners' councils in 252 of the 279 local governments in Sweden.[6] Another dozen are in the process of being established.

Swedish councils serve in an advisory capacity to assure that the wishes of pensioners are considered, and they provide a forum for consultation and information exchange between the local Social Welfare Boards and pensioners. The range of subjects discussed can be quite broad, including town planning, construction, social services, and budgetary matters. The Social Welfare Board is required to inform the local pensioners' council of any planned changes in services to the elderly in order to obtain its input before final decisions are made.

The number of delegates on municipal councils varies from seven to twelve, and usually the members represent pensioners' organizations or political parties.[7] The councils meet at least four times a year.

Pensioners' councils at the county level of government in Sweden operate in a similar fashion to municipal councils. Because county government has control over health care, pensioners' councils at this level become more involved with issues such as long-term care and home health services.

Pensioners' councils are generally viewed as a positive development in Sweden, although their level of effectiveness will vary with the knowledge and experience of council members. Some councils, however, have complained that they are not consulted enough or that they come into the decision-making process too late to really influence policies.[8]

Since 1974–1975, local governments and welfare organizations in the Federal Republic of Germany have encouraged the formation of local councils of the elderly, to be elected by older people themselves. Ther are now about thirty such councils in towns throughout Germany and there are an additional twenty in the rural districts of the state of Baden-Württemberg, the members of which, however, are appointed, not elected.[9]

Where the councils are elected, election procedures vary from one town to another. In some cases, all persons over age sixty are eligible to vote; in others, only residents of nursing homes or homes for the aged and participants in senior and adult day centers may vote.[10] Really democratic elections are usually considered too expensive to implement. On the whole, participation by the elderly in electing their councils has been low, although participation rates can be affected by publicity campaigns.[11] The number of delegates on councils of the elderly ranges from five to fifty-eight and the delegates do not always have to be older people. In Bielefeld, for example, only 50 percent of the council's members must be over 60.[12]

As in the Scandinavian countries, the functions of Germany's councils are mainly advisory in nature, although the council envisaged for the city/state of Hamburg will have the right to submit petitions through the elected deputies of Hamburg's legislative chamber.[13] Council members usually view their role as primarily one of intermediary between the elderly and those governmental and welfare offices in charge of developing policies and programs for pensioners. Some of the councils also consider it their responsibility to reach out to older persons not usually reached by more traditional means, and in some towns they hold regular office hours where such persons can obtain advice of various kinds. A few have organized public forums to discuss the role of the elderly in society or monitor government administration.

While a number of the councils are subsidized by government, they all jealously guard their independence and spurn all efforts to subordinate them to local administrations. Many, however, suffer from lack of material resources; a good number don't even have office space.

Councils of the elderly in Germany are still too new to permit any lasting conclusions about their impact and effectiveness. The relatively small numbers of older persons turning out to elect representatives to the councils has been a subject of some concern. Some point to the non-representative backgrounds of the council members, most of whom were already active in politics or with some other organization prior to their election—a perspective very different from that of the average pensioner.[14]

The general ineffectiveness of a number of the councils is attributed to insufficient financing, incompetent representation, and a lack of legally defined rights and responsibilities vis-à-vis local government.[15] Only one of Germany's senior councils has a seat and vote on the social committee of its municipality.[16] Too often, the effectiveness of the councils depends on the good will of the local administration.

Perhaps one of the most serious charges made is that the existence of senior councils drives older people from other forms of political activity that may have a larger impact on the lives of the elderly.[17] Senior councils, it is contended, perpetuate the segregation of the elderly from the mainstream of life. This has led some critics of senior councils to call for a redirection of energies toward greater representation by the elderly in decision-making bodies together with all other age groups, rather than toward an expansion of age-segregated advisory bodies.[18]

On the other hand, a meeting in 1979 of six councils of the elderly then in existence called for the creation of additional councils, and the experience of the oldest senior council in Germany, described below, suggests that they can be effective in representing the interests of older people in local affairs.[19]

The Hannover Model

Formed in 1974, Hannover's council is composed of nine persons, chosen by 200 delegates elected by the elderly.[20] Every citizen aged 60 or older may vote and may also nominate candidates as delegates, provided at least nineteen other seniors have also signed the petition. The council serves a term of three years and to date has been composed of individuals with many years of experience in working with older people.

When the council was first set up, it was granted a small annual budget but had no defined responsibilities. As a result, the council thus far has interpreted its primary responsibility as that of listening to the views and complaints of older citizens and doing its best to remedy them—whether at the individual or institutional level. Among the council's successes have been fare reductions in public transportation, advocacy for residents in long-term care facilities regarding fee structures and improved staff/patient ratios, inclusion of a course in geriatrics at the local medical college, organization of a seminar by a local adult education association for older people serving on elected residents' councils, and preservation of a favorite indoor bathing facility which had been scheduled to be torn down.

Important factors contributing to the success of Hannover's council are its political neutrality and its independence from government bodies and other interest groups. It also works closely with associations active in the field of aging.

The Hannover model, as it is called in Germany, is considered a successful one by both the elderly and the city administration.

COUNCILS OF RESIDENTS

A second major example of formalized participation by the elderly in decision making is the mandated requirement that homes for the aged and nursing homes in Germany, France and the Netherlands have elected "councils of residents" which participate in an advisory capacity in most decisions affecting the well-being of the residents. (French regulations, however, do not have the force of law, and to date, only a minority of institutions have complied with the requirement.) In Sweden, where residents' councils are not required by law, there is now, nevertheless, a pensioners' council in almost every institution, service house, day center and club for older people.[21] This is also true in the large majority of non-profit homes in the United States and, to a lesser extent, in the proprietary homes.[22]

Residents' councils are thought desirable to overcome alienation and enhance human dignity among the institutionalized. Generally, council representatives make proposals for improvements in daily home activities, participate in discussions concerning administrative decisions, accept suggestions and grievances from residents and facilitate the admission of new residents.

In Sweden, there are usually three to seven members on such councils, elected annually both by the pensioners served by the institution and those living in the surrounding area. The councils meet at least four times a year, and their meetings are attended by a representative from the staff and one from the local social services administration. The minutes of the meeting are sent to the institution's administration and the local pensioners' council.[23]

In order to increase the effectiveness of residents' councils, some of the homes' sponsors in Germany have provided training programs for council members. And the approximately 1,700 "residents' committees" in the Netherlands have banded together in a national organization, the National Consultative Committee for Residents of Homes for the Aged (Landelijk Overleg Bewonercommissies Bejaardentehuizen) to increase their effectiveness, provide training sessions to committee members, promote cooperation among committees, and exert their influence at a national level on matters affecting the homes.[24]

While there is no legal requirement in Canada regarding the establishment of residents' councils, the following case study provides an excellent example of what one council can accomplish.

A Case of Consumer Representation: The Residents' Council of the Sherbrooke Community Centre

The Sherbrooke Community Centre in Saskatoon, Saskatchewan, was the first in the province in 1974 not only to have an elected "council of residents," but also to allocate two seats on its board of directors to residents.[25] Sherbrooke is a 326-bed facility providing two hours of nursing care a day to many of its residents.

The council consists of eight members elected annually by all residents, plus one member elected by participants in Sherbrooke's day care program. The council meets monthly. The executive director of the home and the director of nursing attend as "ex officio members." Its minutes are made widely available to both staff and residents. The council also has responsibility for choosing the two residents who serve on the board of directors.

During the first six to nine months of its existence, the council was used mainly as a voice for residents' complaints, but its members quickly learned that joining together with Sherbrooke's administration in finding solutions to problems would be much more beneficial to the residents. In the six years of its existence, the council has shown that consumer representation can produce some dramatic policy changes. Among the changes that have taken place as a result of the council's recommendations are:

1) Provision of alternative menus to residents, which has virtually eliminated complaints about the food service;

2) Employment of a dietitian;

3) Purchase of more than $75,000 of special equipment for the dietary department;

4) Establishment of 67 part-time paid jobs for residents in Sherbrooke's various departments;

5) Establishment of a $500,000 recreation center for use by residents and others in the community;

6) Sponsorship of a minor league baseball team which has fostered strong intergenerational friendships between the players and residents; and

7) Approval by the city council of residents' request for a crosswalk with lights for paraplegics in front of the home, so the residents can reach the shopping center across the street in safety.

This last achievement really made the residents aware of their political power, a feeling that is reinforced by the regular visits of candidates for political office in federal, provincial and local elections. Consumer representation on the board of directors has also been effective several times in reversing decisions that would have adversely affected the pocketbooks of residents.

While Sherbrooke's administration plays a passive role in relation to the operation of the residents' council, it is always available to assist in problem-solving and to bring the council's ideas to the appropriate individual or department.

The German Experience

The first extensive study done on the effectiveness of mandated residents' councils in Germany, where they have existed since 1975, indicates that, by and large, they have been successful in improving the residents' quality of life, enhancing the homes' social climate, and encouraging more residents to come forth and serve on the councils—all this in spite of the fact that most of the councils were created at the initiative of management, not by the residents themselves.[26] Councils of residents have now been elected in 90 percent of Germany's homes for the aged and nursing homes.

Many of the councils have been successful in helping to better integrate the homes into the neighboring community by, for example, negotiating improvements in transportation connections to the homes, eliminating dangerous street crossings, establishing pedestrian overpasses, and adapting postal facilities to the residents' needs, and by inviting the community to social and cultural events held in the homes. Others, however, have remained inactive, either because of lack of interest on the part of residents or the administration or because of a high degree of incapacity on the part of the residents.

The fear that residents' councils would merely become "rubber stamps" for management's decisions has not materialized. While management has a right to be present at council meetings, the council may ask management to stay away when certain issues are to be discussed. On the other hand, if management is asked to participate, it must do so. Meetings must be called whenever management or the majority of the council members request them. Directors of homes have played an active role in providing materials and technical assistance to the councils and have generally sought their opinion before making administrative decisions. Both management and the homes' sponsoring organizations have appreciated the role played by the councils in adjusting differences between residents and management. On occasion, however, conflicts have arisen, especially where both sides lacked experience in resolving opposing interests. Another difficult area is identifying the dividing line between advising on administrative matters and participating in policy decisions.

Electing councils in homes where a large proportion of the residents are both mentally and physically handicapped is also problematic. Some homes have avoided establishing councils because of the difficulties involved. Others, however, have encouraged the still relatively well residents to run for council seats and to consciously undertake a commitment to represent the more severely disabled. The German government is studying ways to protect the interests of all concerned—the residents, management and the homes' sponsoring organizations—in cases where councils really cannot practically be formed.

Regulations covering the size and term of the councils have, on the whole, worked well. From one to nine residents may be elected to the councils, depending on the size of the home, but every home with more than five residents must establish a council. Any individual who has been a resident for two months may be nominated, provided three other residents have signed a petition for the candidate. (All who have been resident one month may vote.) The two-year term of office has proven to be a reasonable compromise between the need for continuity and the need for change if a council member becomes too disabled to serve but is unwilling to resign.

No study comparable to the breadth of the German one has yet been done in other countries outside the United States. However, a smaller study of residents' committees in seventy-one homes for the aged in the Netherlands revealed that they were operating in somewhat less than an ideal fashion.[27] First, the committees had been established in only forty-four of the homes; these tended to be in homes that had at least seventy-five places. Second, men tended to be over-represented on the committees; in fact, there was a correlation between the number of male residents and the very existence of residents' committees. Third, contrary to recommendations made by a national organization representing homes for the aged, the residents' committees and management agreed that the committees should not participate in policy matters such as the home's budget, staff appointments or building additions or renovations. Committee members felt unqualified to deal with such matters. Committees and management did agree, however, about working together regarding matters of safety, health and hygiene; changes in rates; and rules affecting the residents' freedom. Finally, it appeared that residents not involved directly in the committees were apathetic about their functioning. The researchers concluded that this lack of interest on the part of the residents reflects the lack of opportunity to hold responsible positions that many experienced during their active years.

Despite these problems, legislation has been introduced in Parliament by the Dutch Labor Party to make compulsory the organization of residents' committees which would have the power to participate in the management of institutions.[28] The Labor Party has also organized teams to visit homes and advise residents on their rights and on how they might set up residents' committees.

POLICY ISSUES AND IMPLICATIONS FOR THE FUTURE

Except for the Scandinavian countries, where the impetus to form senior councils to advise governmental bodies came from the elderly themselves, councils of the elderly and residents' councils were formed by policy-makers on behalf of older people in the belief that they could serve to increase their well-being, encourage self-help, and assist decision-makers in making policies based on the expressed needs and desires of the older population.

Some of the problems that have arisen in their operation relate to the fact that they were externally imposed. Many older people simply did not have the interest or the skills to make effective use of the new mechanisms at their disposal. On the other hand, with passing time, older people have learned to value these institutions and participate more fully in them. Furthermore, future cohorts of the elderly, who will be more educated and probably more self-assertive than the existing generation, may well take greater advantage of opportunities to share in decision-making and may even begin to demand a policy-making role.

A trend that augurs less well for the future, at least, of residents' councils in nursing home settings, is the fact that long-term care patients are entering these facilities at greater ages and staying for shorter periods of time. This may play havoc with the continuity of representation on residents' councils. A possible countervailing trend is that residents' councils in some places have also stimulated the creation of family and community councils by homes; these may serve to increase the homes' accountability to their patients.

The experience of residents' councils in the United States suggests that their success may also depend on being given responsibility which is then followed through on by the administration; on encouragement of participation by as many residents as possible in the decision-making process; and on building upon the residents' previous experiences with group decision-making.[29]

Another issue which has not yet been widely addressed is the extent to which councils of seniors established to influence government perpetuate the segregation of the elderly from the rest of society and perhaps invite a possible backlash in the future. While special rights for the elderly in order to encourage their fuller participation in society can probably be justified, will this be possible when a more educated and perhaps more politically astute cohort of elders begins to use the mechanisms that have been put in place for a politically more passive generation?

In any event, pressure for more formalized and meaningful modes of participation by the elderly in decision-making is likely to increase everywhere, because the elderly of tomorrow will be better educated, may share a greater group identity, and will likely be more assertive in insisting on their rights. The popularity of institutions such as "silver-haired legislatures" and the increasing incidence of resident representation on boards of directors of homes for the aged and nursing homes in the United States attests to the potential responsiveness of American elderly to formalized means of participation in decision-making.

NOTES

1. Tullia von Sydow, "Self-Determination by the Elderly in Sweden," in Charlotte Nusberg (ed.), *Self-Determination by the Elderly* (Washington, D.C.: International Federation on Ageing, 1981), p. 13.

2. Ibid., p. 14.

3. Charlotte Nusberg, "Formalized Participation by the Elderly in Decision-making a Growing Trend in Western Countries," *Ageing International* 7, No. 1 (Spring 1980):16.

4. Personal communication from Kaare Salvesen, Deputy Director General, Norwegian Ministry of Social Affairs, June 29, 1979.

5. Von Sydow, "Self-Determination by the Elderly in Sweden," p. 13; Valter Ekberg, "Pensioners' Organizations: An Active Part of Sweden Society," *Current Sweden* (May 1978), p. 5.

6. Von Sydow, "Self-Determination by the Elderly in Sweden," p. 13.

7. Ibid.

8. Ibid., p. 14.

9. Sigrid Lohmann, "Experiences of Elected Councils of Seniors in the Federal Republic of Germany," in Nusberg (ed.), *Self-Determination by the Elderly*, p. 15.

10. Ibid.

11. Ibid.

12. Burckhard Wiebe, "German Federal Republic: How are the Interests of the Elderly Brought Forward?" *EURAG Newsletter* (September 1981):50.

13. *Staatliche Pressestelle*, Hamburg, West Germany, July 13, 1979.

14. Lohmann, "Experiences of Elected Councils," p. 16.

15. Wiebe, "German Federal Republic," p. 51.

16. Ibid., pp. 51–52.

17. Lohmann, "Experiences of Elected Councils," p. 16.

18. Wolfgang Plum and Egon Schleusner, quoted in Wiebe, "German Federal Republic," p. 52.

19. *Presse-und Informationsdienst des KDA* (March 1980):9–10.

20. Ibid., pp. 8–10.

21. Von Sydow, "Self-Determination by the Elderly in Sweden," p. 13.

22. David C. Crowley, "Self-Determination by the Elderly in Homes for the Aging," in Nusberg (ed.), *Self-Determination by the Elderly*, p. 23.

23. Von Sydow, "Self-Determination by the Elderly in Sweden," p. 13.

24. *Leeftijd* (3/1979).

25. Nusberg, "Formalized Participation," p. 18.

26. "Erfahrungsbericht der Bundesregierung ueber die Auswirkungen der Mitwirkungsverordnung des #5 des Heimgestzes," *Nachrichtendienst des Deutschen Vereins fuer offentliche und private Fuersorge* (April 1979).

27. *Nederlands Tijdschrift voor Gerontologie*, No. 3 (1978).

28. *Leeftijd* (1/1981).

29. Crowley, "Self-Determination by the Elderly in Homes," p. 24.

11

Conclusion

Charlotte Nusberg

Some countries with profiles broadly comparable to that of the United States have been more successful in abolishing poverty among their elderly and reducing some of the insecurities that can accompany aging. This has been accomplished through national pension schemes and the provision of a system of accessible services which permit quality long-term care either in the community or in institutions. To be sure, no country is without its problems in dealing with an elderly population, and it would be hard to name an industrialized nation that is not concerned about how it will continue to meet the challenge of an aging society. However, systems of assistance that can be built upon are already in place. This is often not the case in the United States.

How have such successes been achieved elsewhere? One area at which to look is the strong role played by government in setting policies and supporting programs. This can range from the publicly financed and dominated National Health Service in the United Kingdom to the less visible guarantee of private loans for housing renovation in France. In the somewhat less individualistic societies examined in this book, government is not considered an enemy and its activities in support of the "welfare state" have largely been welcomed.

By and large, other countries have favored the creation of public universal systems of service provision rather than ones focused categorically on specific age groups, such as the elderly. Furthermore, wherever possible the trend has been in the direction of providing services according to functional need rather than on the basis of means or income tests.

A number of assumptions underlie such policies. One is the belief that in the long run, universally available services are politically more viable than narrowly focused categorical programs. If everyone thinks that he or she may one day stand to benefit from available services, the willingness to support the level of taxation required to fund such programs is likely to be enhanced. A second assumption is that universally available public services, whether directly provided by government or simply funded through it (and administered by the nonprofit sector), are a more efficient and cost-effective way of running a system than tolerating fragmentation among public and private service providers. A more uniform system of service provision results in fewer persons' needs going unmet. This is achieved in part because the persons searching for assistance have a greater understanding of how the service system works. A third assumption is that the services available to everyone in need are likely to be of higher quality than those reserved for the poor alone. Finally, it is the belief of many that providing quality health and social services is simply not compatible with the profit motive unless it can be rigorously monitored by government.

A strong role for government in the provision of services has, of course, been predicated on much higher tax rates than those to which Americans are accustomed. By and large, such tax burdens have been accepted without much complaint by the public in the realization that almost all benefit in some way from the services purchased with these outlays. Of course, high rates of taxation are much more tolerable when overall income is increasing for everyone and benefits are readily available to those eligible for them. During the current recession, a number of countries have already had to face the protests of benefit recipients whose allowances were threatened by budget retrenchments. Acquired rights do tend to become "sacred" rights, and where benefit levels are relatively high for many groups, any cutbacks will be politically volatile.

Thus far, with some exceptions, benefits for the elderly have largely remained intact. Where economies have been introduced in national pension systems, they have focused mainly on limiting or delaying the expansion of benefits rather than on reducing existing benefits. In some countries older people are being asked to pay something towards their health insurance premiums, which may not have been the case before. In others, higher user fees are being imposed for social services. And almost everywhere, there is increased emphasis on using volunteers and making better use of family and neighbors in the care of the elderly. Cost-effectiveness studies are now being performed with greater frequency, and considerable attention continues to be focused on finding community alternatives to institutional care.

What, however, if the recession deepens and continues for a much longer period of time? Can the welfare state be sustained? Signs of erosion are already apparent in countries such as Canada, the United Kingdom and the Federal Republic of Germany. The evidence to date is inconclusive. In the short run there are a number of alternatives that can be pursued, while keeping intact the systems that have been developed for the return of more affluent times. For example, higher user fees can be charged or services can be limited to those in greatest need. In the long run, of course, greater selectivity in providing services may undermine the political support that has permitted the high taxation rates which fund universal service systems.

Current economic pressures aside, the welfare state has come under other kinds of criticism as well. Some consider it detrimental to personal initiative; in several of the Scandinavian countries, for example, there are few volunteers engaged in providing social services. In the United Kingdom, some critics have described existing service provision as both inadequate and too expensive.

Despite signs of trouble in the welfare states, theirs has still been a remarkable achievement. Most of the industrialized countries discussed in this book already have a larger proportion of older persons than does the United States. In fact, the United States won't share the demographic profile of many European countries, which have 14–15 percent of their population 65 and older, until well into the next century. The welfare states have shown that there are humane and practical ways to meet the challenges posed by aging populations.

How does the United States compare? Certainly it shares similar policy goals with other countries. There is practically a universal consensus among industrialized countries about the desirability of permitting older people to stay on in their own homes for as long as possible, providing them with options in major life decisions, and encouraging their integration into the larger society. Where countries differ from each other is the extent to which these lofty policy goals are translated into programs.

Many of the policies and programs described in this book can, in fact, be found in the United States as well. However, there is greater likelihood that they may be available only in a few states or localities, or on an experimental basis. Few have become the basis for nationally based, universal programs. The result is that, with the exception of Social Security and Medicare, service provision for the elderly is quite uneven across the country and from locality to locality. Even in the areas of income security and health care coverage, the U.S. experience differs considerably from that of other countries. The United States is unique among industrialized nations in the extent to which it limits its revenue sources for Social Security to employer/employee contributions, and it is one of the few industrialized countries which has neither a national health service nor a national health insurance program for the general population. Americans remain very poorly protected against the costs of chronic illness.

Many factors account for the slower development of the welfare state in the United States, including this country's complex federal structure; the difficulties involved in political decision-making resulting from a very heterogeneous population; poorly disciplined political parties and the separation of powers; a distrust of governmental power; confidence in the ability of the private sector, both for-profit and non-profit, to meet many social welfare needs; a tradition of relatively low taxes; and a strong sense of responsibility on the part of individuals for their own circumstances.

At the same time, there are areas in which other countries have looked to the United States for leadership in the field of aging. For example, it is the United States which took the lead among western nations in raising the age at which mandatory retirement could be imposed for the majority of employees, and in promoting both pre-retirement education and higher educational opportunities for the elderly. And in both basic and applied research in gerontology, the United States remains at the forefront.

The United States probably also has the most extensive network of organizational representation of the elderly, through pensioners' groups or more broadly based organizations such as the AARP or the National Council of Senior Citizens. A high proportion of older persons continues to be active as volunteers in service both to each other and to the larger community. Thus, to some extent, opportunities to remain active in retirement are richer and more varied in the United States than in other societies.

Despite these strengths, the likelihood of finding older persons living in squalid or life-threatening conditions is still too common in the United States. This is true for older persons living in both the community and in institutional forms of care. While our rhetoric regarding the importance of family care for the elderly has become pretty sophisticated, follow-up action to assist families and others in this task has not been forthcoming. And for too many older individuals with no family carers available, a range of community services to enable them to continue living independently at home simply does not exist. For older persons who must live under institutional forms of care, incidents of abuse seem to be reported more frequently where the for-profit sector plays a dominant role in nursing home provision and is subject to relatively weak public control.

While these matters are already of considerable concern to many today, they are likely to become even more pressing in the years ahead. The U.S. population is continuing to age, and the population most in need of services—those over age 80—is the most rapidly growing age group. At the same time, the number of adult daughters available to take care of older parents will be fewer because of both lower fertility among some cohorts of future older persons and increased labor force participation by women. Thus, unless the pattern of chronic illness in old age changes dramatically for the better, the need for public service provision is likely to increase. And older persons of the future, many of whom will have been acculturated to expect greater service provision from the public sector, are likely to be more demanding of quality care than was the case with earlier generations, who were politically more passive.

At present, the United States does not have a coherent national policy towards its elderly. Pressures to develop one can only increase. In many ways, the United States is in a fortunate position to develop such a policy. It remains one of the richest countries in the world, richer than many of the countries discussed in this book. And its public retains much good will towards the elderly. This is reflected in public opinion polls, which have shown the public as believing that the government should do more for the elderly and as having a concomitant willingness to pay higher taxes in order to make needed benefits available to them. The United States also still has some time before it in which to plan policy before the number of older persons reaches the same proportion as now exists elsewhere. And finally, the United States can learn from the experiences of other countries where, in many ways our future may presently be reflected.

While the United States may not wish to go as far as other countries have in the degree of government involvement in social welfare matters or the level of taxation that is imposed, some move in this direction seems to be necessary in developing a national policy for the elderly. Our lack of action thus far can be explained more easily by failure of political will than by lack of economic resources.

A range of programs and policy options have been described in the preceding chapters which, even with today's economic constraints, could help to improve the lives of many older persons, yet do not carry high costs. But a few are

1) Consideration of earnings splitting and voluntary contributions for Social Security;

2) Encouragement of grass-roots-based "adjustment" groups in large firms to improve conditions of older worker employment;

3) Dissemination of information on successful models for a phased retirement;

4) Facilitating the construction of "granny annexes" and providing loan guarantees to stimulate housing for the elderly;

5) Dissemination of information about the aging process and care of the elderly to family members and other informal care providers;

6) Consideration of a specialty of geriatric medicine and short-term geriatric treatment and rehabilitation centers;

7) Encouragement of the formation of interdisciplinary assessment teams to diagnose the health conditions and social situations of older persons;

8) Promotion of one-stop service centers where older persons and their families can seek and obtain assistance;

9) Mobilization of non-traditional personnel, such as postmen and others in helping to watch over vulnerable older persons; and

10) Encouragement for broader use of the media for pre-retirement education and education directed at improved self-care, as well as self-actualization.

The opportunities are great and so are the costs of not acting.

Bibliography

Ageing in Australia. Report prepared for the World Assembly on Aging (Canberra: Australian Department of Social Security, 1982).

Ageing in the United Kingdom. Report prepared for the World Assembly on Aging (London: Department of Health and Social Security, 1982).

Ageing New Zealanders. Report prepared for the World Assembly on Aging, 1982.

Aging in the Eighties: America in Transition (Washington, D.C.: National Council on the Aging, 1981).

Aging in Finland. Report prepared for the World Assembly on Aging (Helsinki: Ministry of Social Affairs and Health, 1982).

Aging in France. Report prepared for the World Assembly on Aging (Paris: Ministère des Affaires Sociales et de la Solidarité Nationale, 1982).

Aging in Norway. Report prepared for the World Assembly on Aging (Oslo: Ministry of Health and Social Affairs, 1982).

Amann, Anton. *The Status and Prospects of the Aging in Western Europe*, Eurosocial Occasional Paper No. 8 (Vienna, 1981).

Ammundsen, Esther. "The Future of Health-related Care for the Elderly in Europe," in B. Herzog (ed.), *Aging and Income: Programs and Prospects for the Elderly* (New York: Human Sciences Press, 1978).

———. "The Transition from Private to Public Provision of Nursing Homes in Denmark," *Danish Medical Bulletin* 29, No. 3 (March 1982).

Andersen, Bent Rold. "Commentary on the Basic Document," *New Directions in Social Policy—A Critical Examination of the Scandinavian Experience and Its Lessons for the Region* (Paris: Regional Office for Europe, International Council on Social Welfare, 1979).

"Australia's 'Granny Flats' Capture U.S. Interest," *Ageing International* 8, No. 4 (Winter 1981).

Bergmann, K., et al. "Management of the Demented Elderly Patient in the Community," *British Journal of Psychiatry* 132 (1978).

Brocklehurst, John C. "A Different Dimension," *Health and Social Service Journal* (May 9, 1980).

Butler, Robert N., and Lewis, Myrna I. *Aging and Mental Health*, 3rd ed. (St. Louis, Mo.: C. V. Mosby Co., 1982).

Callahan, James J., et al. "Responsibility of Families for Their Severely Disabled Elders," *Health Care Financing Review* (Winter 1980).

Catalogue of Developments in the Care of Old People. Report prepared for the group on Ageing and Later Life of the Personal Social Services Council (London: Personal Social Services Council, March 1980).

Chebotarev, Dmitri F., and Sachuk, Nina N. "A Social Policy Directed Toward the Health and Welfare of the Aged in the Soviet Union," *Journal of the American Geriatrics Society* 27, No. 2 (February 1979).

————; ————; and Verzhikovskaya, N.V. "Status and Condition of the Elderly in Socialist Countries of Eastern Europe" (report prepared for the World Assembly on Aging, Kiev: Institute of Gerontology, 1982).

Ciuca, A. "The Elderly and the Family," in G. Dooghe and J. Helander (eds.), *Family Life in Old Age* (The Hague: Martinus Nijhoff, 1979).

"Community Guidelines on Flexible Retirement" (Brussels: Commission of the European Communities, July 14, 1980).

Cooper, Brian, and Sosna, Ute. "The Epidemiology of Mental Disorders in Late Life: Report of a Psychogeriatric Field-Study" (paper presented at the 12th International Congress of Gerontology, Hamburg, West Germany, July 12–17, 1981).

Crona, Göran. "Partial Retirement in Sweden—Developments and Experiences" (paper presented at the 9th World Congress of Sociology, Uppsala, Sweden, August 1978).

————. "Partial Retirement in Sweden" (paper presented at the 12th International Congress of Gerontology, Hamburg, West Germany, July 1981).

Crowley, David C. "Self-Determination by the Elderly in Homes for the Aging," in Charlotte Nusberg (ed.), *Self-Determination by the Elderly* (Washington, D.C.: International Federation on Ageing, 1981).

Daatland, Svein Olav. "Flexible Retirement in Industrial Companies," *Aging and Work* (Summer 1980).

Dalgaard, Ole Zeuthen. "Care of the Elderly in Denmark: Special Aspects Including Geriatrics and Long-Term Medicine," *Danish Medical Bulletin* 29, No. 3 (March 1982).

Dieck, Margret. "Residential and Community Provisions for the Frail Elderly in Germany—Current Issues and Their History," *Gerontologist* 20 (June 1980).

Doron, Abraham. *Social Services for the Aged in Eight Countries* (Jerusalem: Brookdale Institute of Gerontology and Adult Human Development, 1979).

Eliasson, I. "How to Provide Work for the Disabled During a Recession" (paper presented at the ILO European Symposium on Work for the Disabled, Stockholm, 1980).

Erdal, Inger. "Social Services for the Elderly," *Danish Medical Bulletin* 29, No. 3 (March 1982).

"Erfahrungsbericht der Bundesregierung ueber die Auswirkungen der Mitwirkungsverordnung des #5 des Heimgesetzes." *Nachrichtendiest des Deutschen Vereins fuer offentliche und private Fuersorge* (April 1979).

Evans, G., et al. "The Management of Mental and Physical Impairment in Non-Specialist Residential Homes for the Elderly," Research Report No. 4 (Manchester, England: University Hospital of South Manchester, Research Section, Psycho-geriatric Unit, January 1981).

Foreign Programs for the Elderly. HUD International Special Supplement No. 10 (Washington, D.C.: U.S. Department of Housing and Urban Development, December 1973).

Frankfather, Dwight L.; Smith, Michael J.; and Caro, Francis G. *Family Care of the Elderly* (Lexington, Mass.: Lexington Books, 1981).

Friis, Henning. "The Aged in Denmark: Social Programmes," in Morton Teicher et al. (eds.), *Reaching the Aged: Social Services in Forty-four Countries* (Beverly Hills, Calif.: Sage Publications, 1979).

————. "Social Programmes for the Aged in Denmark," *EURAG Newsletter* (June 1980).

Gautrat, M., and Tugendhaft, M. "Recherche sur l'Acquisition des Connaissance du Troisième Age," *Gérontologie* (July 1980).

Gilhooly, Mary. "Social Aspects of Senile Dementia," in Rex Taylor and Anne Gilmore (eds.), *Recent Trends in British Gerontology* (Hampshire, England: Gower Publishing Co., 1982).

Glasscote, Raymond; Gudeman, Jon E.; and Miles, Donald. *Creative Mental Health Services for the Elderly* (Washington, D.C.: Joint Information Service of the American Psychiatric Association and the Mental Health Association, 1977).

Glendenning, Frank (ed.). *Care in the Community: Recent Research and Current Projects* (Stoke-on-Trent, England: Beth Johnson Foundation Publications, 1982).

Gommers, A.; Hankenne, B.; and Rogowski, B. "Help Structures for the Aged Sick: Experiences in Seven Countries," in Teicher et al. (eds.), *Reaching the Aged.*

Greengross, Sally. "Caring for the Carers," in Glendenning, (ed.), *Care in the Community.*

Grunow, Dieter. "Sozialstationen: A New Model for Home Delivery of Care and Service," *Gerontologist* 20 (June 1980).

Heumann, Leonard F. "Sheltered Housing for the Elderly: The Role of the British Warden," *Gerontologist* 20 (June 1980).

Hörl, Josef, and Rosenmayr, Leopold. "Assistance to the Elderly as a Common Task of the Family and Social Service Organizations," *Arch. Gerontol. Geriatr.* 1 (1982).

Horlick, Max, and Skolnick, Alfred M. *Mandating Private Pensions: A Study of European Experience* (Washington, D.C.: U.S. Department of Health, Education, and Welfare, Social Security Administration, Office of Policy, 1979).

Hoskins, Dalmer, and Bixby, Lenore H. *Women and Social Security: Law and Policy in Five Countries* (Washington, D.C.: U.S. Department of Health, Education, and Welfare, 1973).

Howenstine, E. Jay. *Foreign Experience in the Financing of Housing for the Elderly* (Washington, D.C.: Department of Housing and Urban Development, 1973).

International Labour Organisation (ILO). *Older Workers: Work and Retirement* (Geneva, 1979).

Just Another Age. Report prepared for the World Assembly on Aging (Stockholm: Ministry of Health and Social Affairs, 1982).

Kahn, Alfred J., and Kamerman, Sheila B. *Social Services in International Perspective* (Washington, D.C.: U.S. Department of Health, Education, and Welfare, Social and Rehabilitation Service, Office of Planning, Research and Evaluation, 1976).

Kamerman, Sheila B. "Community Services for the Aged," *Gerontologist* 16, No. 6 (December 1976).

Kane, Robert L., and Kane, Rosalie. *Long-Term Care in Six Countries: Implications for the U.S.* (Bethesda, Md.: U.S. Department of Health, Education, and Welfare, Public Health Service, National Institutes of Health, 1976).

Kemp, Fred. "The Need for Preparation for Retirement," in *Preparation for Retirement: Its Significance and Present Status in Europe* (symposium sponsored by the Norwegian Institute of Gerontology, November 1977).

Kirkpatrick, Elizabeth K. "The Retirement Test: An International Study," *Social Security Bulletin* (July 1974).

————. "Social Security Benefits for Women in the Federal Republic of Germany, Switzerland, and the United Kingdom," in *Social Security in a Changing World* (Washington, D.C.: U.S. Department of Health, Education, and Welfare, 1979).

Lawton, M. Powell. "Environments and Living Arrangements," in *International Perspectives on Aging: Population and Policy Challenges* (New York: U.N. Fund for Population Activities, 1982).

Lohmann, Sigrid. "Experiences of Elected Councils of Seniors in the Federal Republic of Germany," in Nusberg (ed.), *Self-Determination by the Elderly.*

Maeda, Daisaku. "The Cultural Forces Encouraging and Supporting Caregivers in Japan," (paper presented at the 12th International Congress of Gerontology, Hamburg, West Germany, July 12–17, 1981).

———— and S. Sussman, Marvin B. "Japan-U.S. Cross-Cultural Study on the Knowledge of Aging, the Attitude Toward Old People, and the Sense of Responsibility for Aged Parents," *Japanese Journal of Gerontology* (March 1980).

McArdle, Frank B. "Sources of Revenue of Social Security Systems in Ten Industrialized Countries," in *Social Security in a Changing World* (Washington, D.C.: U.S. Department of Health, Education, and Welfare, 1979).

McRae, John. "Elderly Housing in Northern Europe" (paper presented at the annual meeting of the Western Gerontological Society, Tucson, Ariz., April 1978).

Moroney, Robert M. *The Family and the State: Considerations for Social Policy* (London and New York: Longman Group, 1976).

Netherlands National Report on Aging Policy. Report prepared for the World Assembly on Aging (Rijswijk: Ministry of Cultural Affairs, Recreation and Social Welfare, 1982).

Nusberg, Charlotte. "Educational Opportunities for the Elderly in Industrialized Countries Outside the United States," *Educational Gerontology* 8 (July/August 1982).

————. "Formalized Participation by the Elderly in Decision-making a Growing Trend in Western Countries," *Ageing International* 7, No. 1 (Spring 1980).

————. "Report on an International Conference on Mobility for the Elderly and Handicapped," *Ageing International* 6, No. 1 (Spring 1979).

Olson, Sandra K. "Current Status of Retirement Preparation Programs," *Aging and Work* 4, No. 3 (Summer 1981).

Organisation for Economic Co-Operation and Development (OECD) *Old Age Pension Schemes* (Paris, 1977).

Osako, Masako. "How Japanese Firms Are Coping with the Effects of an Aging Labor Force on Industrial Productivity," *Aging and Work* 5, No. 1 (1982).

Peace, Sheila. "Review of Day Hospital Provision in Psychogeriatrics," *Health Trends*, No. 4 (November 1982).

————. " 'Small Group' Housing in the Community, Part II: Variations on Sheltered Housing," *Ageing International* 8, No. 2 (Summer 1981).

Pedersen, Don Ove. "Housing Problems of the Elderly," *Danish Medical Bulletin* 29, No. 3 (March 1982).

Peterson, Richard, et al. "Adult Education in Nine Industrialized Countries," Vol. 2, report prepared for the National Center for Education Statistics (mimeographed, Princeton, N.J.: Educational Testing Service, 1980).

President's Commission on Pension Policy. *Coming of Age: Toward a National Retirement Income Policy* (Washington, D.C., February 26, 1981).

Report on the Situation of the Elderly in the Federal Republic of Germany. Report prepared for the World Assembly on Aging (Berlin: German Center of Gerontology, May 1982).

Revutskaya, R. G. "The Union of the Soviet Socialist Republics," in John C. Brocklehurst (ed.), *Geriatric Care in Advanced Societies* (Baltimore: University Park Press, 1975).

Rix, Sara, and Fisher, Paul. *Retirement Age Policy: An International Perspective* (Elmsford, N.Y.: Pergamon Press, 1982).

Rosenmayr, Leopold. "The Family—A Source of Hope for the Elderly," in Ethel Shanas and Marvin B. Sussman (eds.), *Family, Bureaucracy, and the Elderly* (Durham, N.C.: Duke University Press, 1977).

Ross, Stanford G. "Social Security: A Worldwide Issue," in *Social Security in a Changing World.*

Rubenstein, James M. "Housing the Elderly in France and the Netherlands" (paper presented at the annual meeting of the Gerontological Society of America, Dallas, Tex., November 1978).

————. "Housing Policy Issues in Three European Countries" (paper presented at the annual meeting of the Gerontological Society of America, Washington, D.C., November 1979).

Schorr, Alvin. *Thy Father and Thy Mother: A Second Look at Filial Responsibility and Family Policy* (Washington, D.C.: U.S. Social Security Administration, July 1980).

Schulz, James H. "Pension Policy at a Crossroads: What Should Be the Pension Mix?" *Gerontologist* 21 (February 1981).

————, et al., *Providing Adequate Retirement Income* (Hanover, N.H.: University Press of New England, 1974).

Senior Citizens' Provincial Council. *Regina Social Support Study* (Saskatchewan, Canada, 1981).

Shanas, Ethel. "Health Status of Older People," *American Journal of Public Health* 64, No. 3 (March 1974).

Shchirina, M. G. "Services in the U.S.S.R.," in J.G. Howell, (ed.), *Modern Perspectives in the Psychiatry of Old Age* (New York: Brunner/Mazel, 1975).

Sekiguchi, Shiro. "How Japanese Business Treats Its Older Workers," *Management Review* (October 1980).

————."The Problems Faced in the Japanese Industrial Workplace" (paper presented at a seminar sponsored by the Japan Society, The Aging Labor Force: Implications for Japan and the U.S., New York, June 6, 1980).

Sidel, Victor W., and Sidel, Ruth. *A Healthy State* (New York: Pantheon Books, 1977).

Smirnov, S. "The Employment of Old-Age Pensioners in the U.S.S.R.," *International Labour Review* (July/August 1977).

"Socio-Economic Policies for the Elderly: Questionnaire and Analytical Synthesis Report" (unpublished report, OECD, Paris, May 19, 1980).

Soloviev, A. G. "The Employment of Pensioners in the National Economy of the U.S.S.R.," *International Social Security Review* No. 2 (1980).

Sternheimer, Stephen. "Retirement and Aging in the Soviet Union: Who Works, Who Doesn't and What Can Be Done About It" (paper presented at the American Association for the Advancement of Slavic Studies, New Haven, Conn., October 11, 1979).

Swank, Constance. *Phased Retirement: The European Experience* (Washington, D.C.: National Council for Alternative Work Patterns, 1982).

Thompson, E., and Motuz, C. "The Manitoba/Canada Home Care Study: Some Preliminary Findings" (paper presented at the annual meeting of the Canadian Association on Gerontology, Halifax, Nova Scotia, November 1979).

Thornton, Patricia, and Moore, Jeanette. "The Placement of Elderly People in Private Households" (research monograph, Leeds, England: Department of Social Policy and Administration, 1980).

Tinker, Anthea. "Housing the Elderly: How Successful Are Granny Annexes?" HDD occasional paper (London: Department of the Environment, January 1976).

Tracy, Martin. "Constant-Attendance Allowances for Non-Work Related Disability," *Social Security Bulletin* (November 1974).

———. "Flexible Retirement Features Abroad," *Social Security Bulletin* (May 1978).

———. "Maintaining Value of Social Security Benefits During Inflation: The Foreign Experience," *Social Security Bulletin* (November 1976).

———. *Retirement Age Practice in Ten Industrialized Countries, 1960–1976* (Geneva: International Social Security Association, 1979).

U.K., Department of Health and Social Security. *Growing Older* (London: Her Majesty's Stationery Office, Cmnd. 8173, March 1981).

———. *Priorities for Health and Personal Social Services in England* (London: Her Majesty's Stationery Office, 1976).

United Nations. *Aging in the Context of the Family*. Report of the Secretary General for the World Assembly on Aging (A/Conf. 113/110, April 29, 1982).

———. "Demographic Considerations." Introductory paper prepared for the World Assembly on Aging (A/AC. 208/8, January 15, 1982).

———. *"Health Policy Aspects of Aging."* Report of the World Health Organization (A/Conf. 113/19, March 26, 1982).

———. *"Housing, Environment and Aging."* Report of the Secretary General for the World Assembly on Aging (A/Conf. 113/13, April 28, 1982).

———. *Human Settlements and the Aging*. Report of the U.N. Centre for Human Settlements (Habitat) for the World Assembly on Aging (A/Conf. 113/25, May 26, 1982).

———. *Income Maintenance and Social Protection of the Older Person: Income Security for the Elderly*. Report of the ILO for the World Assembly on Aging (A/Conf. 113/17, March 3, 1982).

———. "International Plan of Action for the World Assembly on Aging" (A/Conf. 113/mc/L.27, August 4, 1982).

———. *Problems of Employment and Occupation of Older Workers*. Report of the International Labour Organisation for the World Assembly on Aging (A/Conf. 113/15, February 17, 1982).

————. *Report of the World Assembly on Aging* (A/Conf. 113/31, 1982).

————. *Transitions Between Professional Life and Retirement*. Report of the ILO for the World Assembly on Aging (A/Conf. 113/16, February 1982).

United Nations Educational, Scientific, and Cultural Organization. *Education and Aging*. Report for the World Assembly on Aging (A/Conf. 113/20, March 10, 1982).

U.S., Department of Health, Education, and Welfare, The Federal Council on Aging. *Mental Health and the Elderly: Recommendations for Action*. Reports of the President's Commission on Mental Health, Task Panel on the Elderly, and the Secretary's Commission on the Mental Health and Illness of the Elderly (Washington, D.C.: Government Printing Office, 1979).

U.S., Department of Health and Human Services, Social Security Administration. *Social Security Programs Throughout the World, 1979*, Research Report No. 54 (Washington, D.C.: Government Printing Office, 1980).

U.S., House of Representatives, 96th Congress, Select Committee on Aging. *National Conference on Mental Health and the Elderly* (Washington, D.C.: Government Printing Office, 1979).

U.S., Senate, Special Committee on Aging. *Social Security in Europe: The Impact of an Aging Population* (Washington, D.C.: Government Printing Office, 1981).

Vanbremeersch, M. C., and Margarido, A. "Les Etudiants de l'université du 3° âge de l'université de Picardie," *Gérontologie et Société* 13 (June, 1980).

Van Zonneveld, R. J. "Long-term Care for the Elderly in the Netherlands," *Z. Gerontologie*, No. 11, (1978).

————. "The Netherlands," in Brocklehurst (ed.), *Geriatric Care in Advanced Societies*.

Von Sydow, Tullia. "Self-Determination by the Elderly in Sweden," in Nusberg (ed.), *Self-Determination by the Elderly*.

Wiebe, Burckhard. "German Federal Republic: How Are the Interests of the Elderly Brought Forward?" *EURAG Newsletter* (September 1981).

Willcocks, D.; Peace, Sheila; and Kellaher, L. *The Residential Life of Old People: A Study in 100 Local Authority Old People's Homes*. Vols. 1 and 2, Research Reports 12 and 13 (London: Polytechnic of North London, Survey Research Unit, 1982).

World Health Organization. *Psychogeriatric Care in the Community* (Copenhagen: WHO Regional Office for Europe, 1979).

————. *The Well-Being of the World's Aging Citizens: A Status Report*. Background paper prepared for the WHO preparatory conference for the U.N. World Assembly on Aging, Mexico City, December 8–11, 1980 (IRP/ADR/ 101/10, October 24, 1980).

Index

About the Authors

CHARLOTTE NUSBERG is Director of the Publications Division for the International Federation on Ageing and International Activities Coordinator for the American Association of Retired Persons. She is editor of the journal *Ageing International*. Her articles have appeared in *Aging* and *Educational Gerontology* as well as in the publications of the Federation.

MARY JO GIBSON is Associate Editor for the International Federation on Ageing and a Program Specialist for the American Association of Retired Persons. She is the editor (with Charlotte Nusberg and John W. Riley) of the forthcoming *International Glossary of Social Gerontology*.

SHEILA M. PEACE is a Research Fellow in the Department of Applied Social Studies, Polytechnic of North London, England. During 1980–81 she worked as an international intern with the International Foundation on Ageing in Washington, D.C. She is the author of *An International Perspective on the Status of Older Women,* as well as reports and articles on residential care, housing provision, mental health, and the activity patterns of old people.